Systems Reliability, Maintainability and Management

Systems Reliability, Maintainability and Management

BALBIR S. DHILLON
Department of Mechanical Engineering
University of Ottawa

PBI
a petrocelli book
new york/princeton

Designed by Diane L. Backes
Typesetting by Backes Graphics

Printed in the U.S.A.
1 2 3 4 5 6 7 8 9 10

Library of Congress Cataloging in Publication Data

Dhillon, B.S.
Systems reliability, maintainability, and management.

Includes index.
1. Reliability (Engineering) 2. Maintainability (Engineering) I. Title.
TA169.D474 1983 658.5'62 83-13354
ISBN 0-89433-195-7

To my beautiful daughter Jasmine.

Table of Contents

PREFACE xi

1 INTRODUCTION 1

System reliability, maintainability and management 1/ Hazard rate curves 2/ Maintainability 2/ Scope of the book 4/ Exercises 5/ Notes 5

2 RELIABILITY AND MAINTAINABILITY MATHEMATICS 7

Laplace transforms 7/ Binomial theorem 10/ Selective series 11/ Maxima and minima 12/ Differentiation 13/ Integration 14/ Mean value theorem for integrals 15/ Basic probability 15/ Probability distributions 17/ Summary 24/ Exercises 24/ Notes 26

3 HAZARD RATE MODELS 27

General hazard rate models 27/ Conventional hazard rate models 28/ Complex hazard rate models 32/ Bathtub hazard rate models 32/ Non-conventional hazard rates 40/ Summary 42/ Exercises 42/ Notes 43

4 INTRODUCTION TO SYSTEMS ENGINEERING AND QUALITY CONTROL 45

Systems engineering 46/ Quality control 48/ Summary 50/ Exercises 51/ Notes 51

5 BASIC RELIABILITY THEORY 53

Basic functions 53/ Nonrepairable single component reliability evaluation models 58/ Repairable single component reliability evaluation models 64/ Summary 69/ Exercises 69/ Notes 70

6 RELIABILITY EVALUATION OF SYSTEMS USING STATIC MODELS 71

Reliability evaluation of simple systems 71/ Reliability evaluation of complex systems 82/ Summary 88/ Exercises 89/ Notes 90

7 RELIABILITY TOOLS 91

Time dependent analysis of reliability networks 91/ System reliability evaluation by using the joint-density-function approach 107/ Confidence limits for mean time between failures 108/ Reliability growth modeling 112/ Software reliability 113/ Summary 114/ Exercises 115/ Notes 117

8 MANAGEMENT AND VALUE ENGINEERING 119

Management 120/ Value engineering 126/ Summary 128/ Exercises 128/ Notes 128

9 MANAGERIAL RELIABILITY AND MAINTAINABILITY 131

Product assurance group 131/ Product reliability prediction 133/ Selection of parts suppliers 133/ Mathematical models for reliability and maintainability managers 134/ Reliability Manual 138/ Summary 139/ Exercises 139/ Notes 139

10 ENGINEERING SYSTEM ECONOMICS 141

Formulas to calculate time value of money 141/ Depreciation methods 143/ Procedure for cost-effectiveness analysis 146/ Operation cost estimation technique 146/ Corrective maintenance cost estimation model 148/ A model to optimize repair effort 149/ Equipment replacement model I 150/ Equipment replacement model II 150/ Life cycle costing 152/ Summary 153/ Exercises 153/ Notes 154

11 RELIABILITY AND MAINTAINABILITY CONTRACTING 155

Types of contracts 156/ Factors to determine types of contracts 156/ Attributes of the contract negotiator 158/ Managing and monitoring a reliability program 158/ Reliability documents 159/ Warranties 160/ Summary 163/ Exercises 163/ Notes 163

12 CONFIGURATION MANAGEMENT 165

Configuration management history 165/ Changes to product 166/ Goals of configuration management 167/ Life cycle phases of a product 168/ Techniques of configuration management 169/ Important characteristics of configuration management 169/ Attributes of a configuration manager 170/ Summary 171/ Exercises 171/ Notes 171

13 MAINTAINABILITY PRINCIPLES 173

Definitions used in maintainability engineering 174/ Maintainability management 174/ System effectiveness model 177/ System operational readiness models 177/ System availability models 180/ Maintainability functions 182/ Summary 185/ Exercises 185/ Notes 187

14 EQUIPMENT MAINTENANCE AND REPLACEMENT POLICIES 189

Formulas to calculate maintenance parameters 190/ Availability formulas 191/ Equipment maintenance and replacement decision models 193/ Summary 200/ Exercises 200/ Notes 201

15 QUEUING THEORY APPLICATIONS IN MAINTAINABILITY ENGINEERING 203

Examples of waiting lines 203/ Poisson model 206/ Mathematical models of waiting lines 208/ Summary 220/ Exercises 220/ Notes 221

16 FAILURE MODES AND EFFECTS ANALYSIS 223

Failure modes and effects analysis steps 224/ Failure modes, effects and criticality analysis 228/ Fault trees 229/ FMEA and fault tree analysis 234/ Summary 235/ Exercises 235/ Notes 236

17 RELIABILITY AND MAINTAINABILITY ALLOCATION 239

Reliability allocation technique I 239/ Reliability allocation technique II 243/ Reliability allocation technique III 244/ Reliability allocation technique IV 247/ Reliability allocation technique V 247/ Reliability allocation technique VI 248/ Maintainability allocation method 248/ Summary 252/ Exercises 252/ Notes 253

18 RELIABILITY AND MAINTAINABILITY DATA COLLECTION AND ANALYSIS 255

Reliability data collection 255/ Failure data analysis 260/ Summary 264/ Exercises 265/ Notes 265

INDEX 267

Preface

From the last number of decades the reliability and maintainability techniques and procedures have been applied to design reliable and maintainable systems, especially in the aerospace and defense industries. Today, due to the success in these areas, the reliability and maintainability theories and models are being applied to produce various types of engineering products. This leads us to believe that the applications of reliabiity and maintainability are on the increase. Furthermore, from the last number of years there have been a considerable growth in the published literature on reliability and maintainability.

Because of growth in reliability and maintainability applications and literature have inspired an interest in the management area too. In addition, because of tight economic environments, the reliability and maintainability engineers and other specialists have to look at the reliability and maintainability fields from the various management aspects to produce reliable and maintainable products at a minimum cost. Therefore, sometimes they get involved in diverse areas such as configuration management, contracting, economics, value analysis, quality control, developing equipment replacement policies and optimizing equipment repair facilities. Now, it may be said that to improve system reliability and maintainability effectively, the reliability, maintainability and management are inseparable.

For the first time to the author's knowledge this book is written to integrate reliability, maintainability and management into a single volume. In this book generally the author has emphasized more on the structure of concepts than going into the minute details. However the book is written in such a manner that it requires no prior knowledge on any of the topics of the book to understand its contents.

Chapter 1 briefly introduces the contents of the book by defining reliability, maintainability and management. In addition the chapter contains discussion on hazard rate curves and maintainability, and definitions of the maintainability associated parameters. The scope of the book is outlined briefly at the end. Essential topics of the mathematics and probability related to reliability and maintainability are discussed in chapter 2. As the basic concept of the reliability theory is the bathtub curve, therefore, chapter 3 presents various functions to represent that curve. The conventional and other hazard rate models are also presented in this chapter. The reliability equations of the commonly used reliability networks are developed for the condition when components hazard rates are described by the bathtub hazard rate curve. Chapter 4 introduces the reliability engineering associated disciplines of system engineering and quality control. In chapter 5 various mathematical models are presented to evaluate reliability and availability of a single component system.

Chapters 6 and 7 are concerned with the reliability evaluation of configurations when components reliabilities are constant and time dependent, respectively.

Chapters 8 through 12 are concerned with management associated topics. Value engineering and basics of management are discussed in chapter 8. In chapter 9 the important items of reliability and maintainability management are described. Chapter 10 presents selective formulas of system economics, and various equipment replacement and associated models. Reliability and maintainability are discussed in chapter 11, which describes various aspects of contracting and two warranty cost models. In chapter 12 the configuration management is discussed in detail.

Chapters 13 through 15 are directly or indirectly associated with the system maintainability. Therefore chapter 13 presents the basics of maintainability and several mathematical models used in the maintainability field. In chapter 14 various mathematical models are presented to make sound equipment maintenance and replacement decisions. The basic queueing theory and related models are the theme of chapter 15.

In chapter 16 the failure modes and effects analysis, and fault tree techniques are described. Chapter 17 is comprised of several reliability and maintainability allocation techniques. Failure data collection and analysis are briefly discussed in chapter 18.

This book is intended for people such as engineers, administrators, senior under-graduate and graduate students and other professionals concerned with system reliability, maintainability and management. The book contains several examples with their solutions. In addition, each chapter is composed of a list of exercises. Therefore the book will be useful for long and short courses on system reliability, maintainability and management.

The author acknowledges the contributions of all friends, colleagues and leading professionals who have provided invisible inputs, through various fruitful discussions, to shape my thinking on several areas of the book. I am deeply indebted to my parents, brother, relatives and many friends for their interest and encouragement throughout. Last but not least, I thank my wife Rosy for typing the entire manuscript, proofreading and so on. Her patience, tolerance and encouragement were also appreciated throughout.

Balbir S. Dhillon
Ottawa, Ontario

1

Introduction

In recent years the importance of systems reliability and maintainability has been given considerable attention, especially when designing systems for use in aerospace, defense, power generation, and so on. The field of reliability, to people who are less familiar with the subject, may appear to be relatively new, however it is not. Its history goes back to the Second World War when the Germans introduced the concept to improve reliability of their VI and V2 rockets.

The modern reliability discipline had its origins in the development of defense and aerospace systems. Because of competition in the market, economic reasons, and sophistication in systems and technology, today the application of reliability and maintainability techniques is steadily growing into various other areas.

SYSTEM RELIABILITY, MAINTAINABILITY, AND MANAGEMENT

Today's competitive environments, tight economic situation, complex technology, and so on, demand reliable and maintainable systems produced at a minimum cost. Therefore, a reliability and maintainability manager or engineer must look into various management and economics aspects associated with the system development and its operation. For example, he or she may get involved directly or indirectly with such diverse areas as configuration management, life cycle costing, reliability and maintainability contracting, value engineering, optimizing equipment repair facilities, and so on. This means that a reliability and maintainability engineer not only has to be a specialist in that area but also is required to know various management-associated disciplines.

The following three definitions are concerned with the topics of this book:

Reliability: the probability that an item (system) will function satisfactorily when used according to specified conditions for at least a specified time interval.[1]

Maintainability: the probability that a failed system within a specified time interval will be restored to operable condition.[2]

Management: There are various definitions, however the one relevant here is as follows: "Management is a distinct process composed of controlling, organizing, planning and actuating carried out by using manpower and other resources to evaluate and fulfill specified objectives."[3]

HAZARD RATE CURVES

The definition of hazard rate (or the instantaneous failure rate) of an item is as follows:

$$\lambda(t) = \lim_{\Delta t \to 0} \left\{ \frac{R(t) - R(t+\Delta t)}{\Delta t \cdot R(t)} \right\} \tag{1.1}$$

where

$\lambda(t)$ is the item hazard rate

$R(t)$ is the item reliability at time t

Δt is the time interval

Four typical hazard rate curves are shown in Figure 1.1: bathtub curve, mechanical component hazard rate curve, linearly, and nonlinearly increasing hazard rates. The objective of the figure is to show that an item hazard rate may follow any one of these curves or any other hazard rate curves. However, in the field of reliability it is believed that many components follow the bathtub hazard rate concept, especially electronic components. This curve is discussed further in chapter 3.

MAINTAINABILITY

The history of maintainability goes back to the early 1950s.[4] In the late 1950s attention to maintainability features was given when designing new equipment.

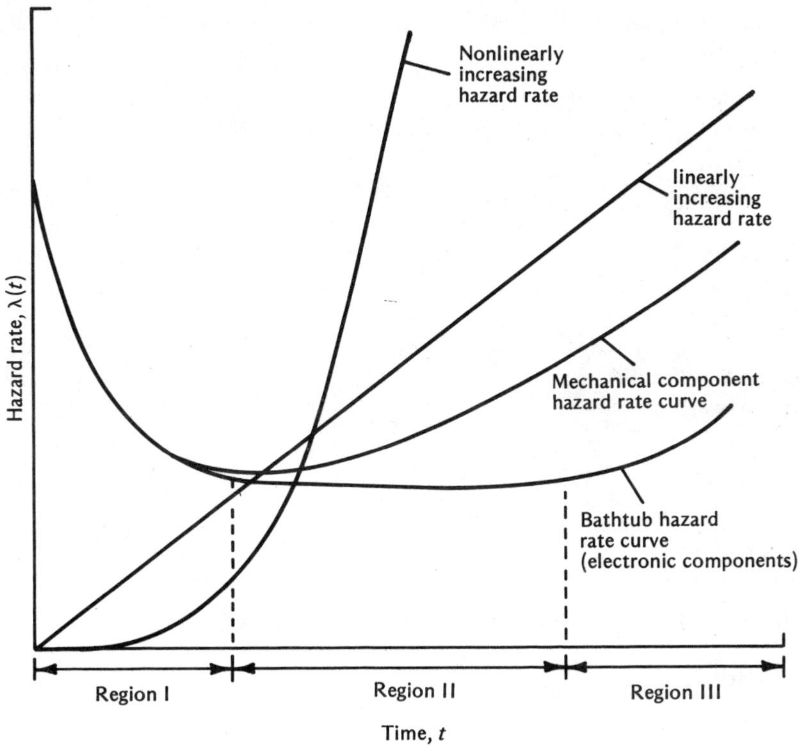

Figure 1.1 Typical hazard rate curves

During this period the MIL-M-26512 document concerning maintainability was published by the United States Air Force. Since then other military documents have appeared concerning maintainability; examples include MIL-STD-470, MIL-STD-778, MIL-STD-471, MIL-STD-721B, MIL-HDBK-472, AMCP 706-134, and so on. In addition, several books and articles have been written on the subject.

In the maintainability field the terms mean time between failures (MTBF) and mean time to repair (MTTR) are frequently used.[2]

MTBF: the total working age of a population of a product over (divide) the total failures that occurred within the population during the measurement period.

MTTR: the total corrective maintenance performing time over (divide) the total corrective maintenance actions performed within the specified time interval.

To compute steady-state unavailability, *UA*, of an item, the above two measures are utilized as follows:

$$UA = \frac{\text{mean time to repair}}{\text{mean time to repair} + \text{mean time between failures}}$$

$$= \frac{\text{MTTR}}{\text{MTTR} + \text{MTBF}} \tag{1.2}$$

Example 1.1

A system's constant failure and constant repair rates are $\lambda = 0.002$ failures/hour and $\mu = 0.004$ repairs/hour, respectively. Calculate the system steady-state unavailability.

$$\text{system MTBF} = \frac{1}{0.002} = 500 \text{ hours}$$

$$\text{system MTTR} = \frac{1}{0.004} = 250 \text{ hours}$$

Substituting the above calculated hours in equation (1.2) yields:

$$UA = \frac{250}{250 + 500} = 0.3333$$

The system's unavailability is 33.33%.

SCOPE OF THE BOOK

To produce reliable and maintainable systems at a minimum cost, a manager or an engineer not only has to know reliability and maintainability theory but must also know various management-oriented areas.

At present an engineer or a manager needing information on system reliability, maintainability and management (RMM) will have difficulty finding this information within the framework of a single book. To the author's knowledge no other textbook treats the topic of RMM within a single volume. Therefore, this text is an attempt to fulfill this vital need.

To understand this book no prior knowledge of RMM is necessary. The mathematics essential to understand certain material is given in chapter 2. Other necessary mathematics is presented within each chapter before its utilization. A large number of examples with solutions help to make the book more self-explanatory. Several exercises are presented at the end of each chapter.

This book will be useful to reliability and maintainability analysts, system engineers, design engineers, managers, project engineers, and students of reliability, maintainability and management.

EXERCISES

1.1. Explain the bathtub hazard rate curve shown in Figure 1.1.

1.2. Define the term system steady-state availability.

1.3. Explain the terms hazard rate and failure rate.

NOTES

1. W.H. Von Alven, ed., *Reliability Engineering* (Englewood Cliffs, N.J.: Prentice-Hall, 1964), pp. 6-9.
2. *Definitions of Effectiveness Terms for Reliability, Maintainability, Human Factors and Safety,* MIL-STD-721B, 22 August 1966, pp. 5-7.
3. G.R. Terry, *Principles of Management* (Homewood, Ill: Richard D. Irwin, 1972), pp. 4.
4. "Maintainability Engineering Theory and Practice," in *Engineering Design Handbook,* AMCP 706-133 (Alexandria, Va: Headquarter of U.S. Army Material Command, 1976), pp. 13-14.

2

Reliability and Maintainability Mathematics

Mathematics is an indispensable tool in the field of reliability and maintainability. Therefore, this chapter briefly presents mathematical concepts essential to perform reliability and maintainability analysis.

LAPLACE TRANSFORMS

The Laplace transform, $P(s)$, of a function $p(t)$ is given by

$$P(s) = \int_0^\infty e^{-st} \cdot p(t) \cdot dt \tag{2.1}$$

where

t is time

s is the Laplace transform variable

Example 2.1

A component's failure times are represented by

$$p(t) = \lambda e^{-\lambda t} \tag{2.2}$$

where λ is the constant failure rate of the component. Find the Laplace transform of equation (2.2).

Substituting equation (2.2) in equation (2.1) results in:

$$P(s) = \int_0^\infty e^{-st} \cdot (\lambda e^{-\lambda t})\, dt$$

$$= \lambda \int_0^\infty e^{-(s+\lambda)t}\, dt \qquad (2.3)$$

Integrating equation (2.3) leads to:

$$P(s) = \lambda \left[\frac{e^{-(s+\lambda)t}}{-(s+\lambda)} \right]_0^\infty$$

$$P(s) = \frac{\lambda}{s+\lambda} \qquad (2.4)$$

Example 2.2

Find the Laplace transforms of the following two functions:

$p(t)$

$p(t) = \lambda$, where λ is a constant

Thus, utilizing the above functions in equation (2.1) yields the following Laplace transform equations, respectively:

$$P(s) \qquad (2.5)$$

$$P(s) = \int_0^\infty e^{-st} \cdot \lambda\, dt = \frac{\lambda}{s} \qquad (2.6)$$

Example 2.3

Find the Laplace transforms of the following items:

$p(t) = t^\alpha$ for $\alpha = 0, 1, 2, 3, \ldots$

$$\frac{d\,p(t)}{dt}$$

$$\frac{dP(t)}{dt} + \lambda p(t) = 0$$

at $t = 0, p(0) = 1$.

With the aid of equation (2.1), the Laplace transforms are, respectively:

$$P(s) = \int_0^\infty e^{-st}\, t^\alpha dt = \frac{\alpha!}{s^{\alpha+1}} \tag{2.7}$$

$$sP(s) - p(0) \tag{2.8}$$

$$sP(s) - p(0) + \lambda P(s) = 0 \tag{2.9}$$

Substituting the initial condition in equation (2.9) yields:

$$(s+\lambda)P(s) = 1$$

$$P(s) = \frac{1}{s+\lambda} \tag{2.10}$$

The inverse Laplace transforms of selected functions are given in Table 2.1. Laplace transforms of other functions may be found in the literature.[2,4]

Table 2.1. Inverse Laplace Transforms

Laplace transform $P(s)$	*Inverse Laplace transform* $p(t)$
$\int_s^\infty f(x) \cdot dx$	$\{p(t)\}/t$
$\frac{1}{s+\lambda}$	$e^{-\lambda t}$
λ/s	λ
$s^{-m}, m>0$	$(t^{m-1})/\Gamma(m)$
$\{(s-\lambda)(s-\beta)\}^{-1}; \lambda \neq \beta$	$\{e^{\beta t} - e^{\lambda t}\}/(\beta-\lambda)$
$(s-\lambda)^{-m}, m>0$	$\{t^{m-1} \cdot e^{\lambda t}\}/\Gamma(m)$
$P(s)/s$	$\int_0^t p(x) \cdot dx$
$\frac{dP(s)}{ds}$	$-t\,p(t)$

BINOMIAL THEOREM

For positive k this is

$$(\alpha+\beta)^k=\alpha^k+\binom{k}{1}\alpha^{k-1}\cdot\beta+\binom{k}{2}\alpha^{k-2}\cdot\beta^2+\binom{k}{3}\alpha^{k-3}\beta^3+\ldots+\beta^k$$

$$=\sum_{r=0}^{k}\binom{k}{r}\beta^r\alpha^{k-r} \tag{2.11}$$

where

$$\binom{k}{i}={}_kC_i=(k!)/(k-i)!\,i! \tag{2.12}$$

We should note here that

$0\,!=1\,!=1$

Example 2.4

Find the value of $\binom{5}{3}$ by utilizing equation (2.12). Thus:

$$\binom{5}{3}=\frac{5\,!}{(5-3)\,!\;3\,!}=\frac{(5)\cdot(4)\cdot(3)\cdot(2)}{(2)\cdot(3)\cdot(2)}$$

$$=10$$

The following are some of the properties of binomial coefficients:

$$\binom{k}{i}+\binom{k}{i+1}=\binom{k+1}{i+1} \tag{2.13}$$

$$\binom{k}{0}+\binom{k}{1}+\binom{k}{2}+\binom{k}{3}+\ldots+\binom{k}{k}=2^k \tag{2.14}$$

$$\binom{k}{0}^2+\binom{k}{1}^2+\binom{k}{2}^2+\ldots+\binom{k}{k}^2=\binom{2k}{k} \tag{2.15}$$

$$\binom{k}{1}+\binom{k}{3}+\binom{k}{5}+\ldots=2^{k-1} \tag{2.16}$$

Pascal's Triangle

To obtain coefficients of the binomial expansion, Pascal's triangle is utilized. In other words, the coefficients of $(\alpha+\beta)^k$ are written in the following form:

Pascal's Triangle

$(\alpha+\beta)^0$					1				
$(\alpha+\beta)^1$				1		1			
$(\alpha+\beta)^2$			1		2		1		
$(\alpha+\beta)^3$		1		3		3		1	
$(\alpha+\beta)^4$	1		4		6		4		1
.									
.									
.									

In the array of numbers called Pascal's triangle, note that the first and the last digits in each row of the triangle are equal to unity. Any other number in the triangle was obtained by adding two numbers from the preceding row which were on the left-hand side and the right-hand side of the number in question.

Example 2.5

Expand $(\alpha+\beta)^3$ with the aid of Pascal's triangle. Thus:

$(\alpha+\beta)^0$				1			
$(\alpha+\beta)^1$			1		1		
$(\alpha+\beta)^2$		1		2		1	
$(\alpha+\beta)^3$	1		3		3		1

In the last row of the triangle are the coefficients of $(\alpha+\beta)^3$. By utilizing these coefficients we can write the expanded form of $(\alpha+\beta)^3$ as follows:

$$\alpha^3+3\alpha^2\beta+3\alpha\beta^2+\beta^3$$

SELECTIVE SERIES

This section presents the following selective series:

Exponential

$$1+t+\frac{t^2}{2!}+\frac{t^3}{3!}+\frac{t^4}{4!}+\ldots=e^t \tag{2.17}$$

for $-\infty<t<\infty$ where t is the variable.

Logarithmic

$$t - \frac{t^2}{2} + \frac{t^3}{3} - \frac{t^4}{4} + \ldots = \ell n\,(1+t) \tag{2.18}$$

for $-1 < t \leqslant 1$.

Geometric

$$\theta + \theta t + \theta t^2 + \theta t^3 + \ldots + \theta t^{m-1} = \frac{\theta\,(1 - t^m)}{(1-t)} \tag{2.19}$$

where θ is a constant.

MAXIMA AND MINIMA

In many cases to make rational reliability or management decisions we may have to find the maxima or the minima of a function. This section presents the commonly known procedure to find the maxima or the minima of a single variable function. At $t = t_1$, the function $f(t)$ has either a maximum or a minimum if the following conditions are satisfied:

1. maximum–if $f'(t_1) = 0$ and $f''(t_1) < 0$. The single prime denotes differentiation with respect to variable t and the double prime denotes the second derivative with respect to t.
2. minimum–if $f'(t_1) = 0$ and $f''(t_1) > 0$.

Example 2.6

Find the maximum of the following function:

$$f(t) = 80t - 4t^2 \tag{2.20}$$

Differentiating function (2.20) with respect to t yields:

$$\frac{df(t)}{dt} = f'(t) = 80 - 8t = 0 \tag{2.21}$$

Solving the above equation for t results in:

$$t_1 = 10$$

Differentiating equation (2.20) twice with respect to t leads to:

$$\frac{d^2f(t)}{dt^2} = f''(t) = -8$$

Thus at $t_1 = 10$ the maximum value of equation (2.20) is 400.

DIFFERENTIATION

The derivative of function $f(t)$, with respect to variable t, is given by:

$$\frac{df(t)}{dt} = \lim_{\Delta t \to 0} \frac{f(t+\Delta t)-f(t)}{\Delta t} \tag{2.22}$$

Some of the rules of differentiation are as follows:

1) $$\frac{d\,(m\,t^k)}{dt} = m\,k\,t^{k-1} \tag{2.23}$$

where m and k are the constants.

2) $$\frac{dm}{dt} = 0 \tag{2.24}$$

3) $$\frac{d\,(xy)}{dt} = x\frac{dy}{dt} + y\frac{dx}{dt} \tag{2.25}$$

where x and y are functions (of t).

4) $$\frac{d}{dt}(x^k) = k\,x^{k-1} \cdot \frac{dx}{dt} \tag{2.26}$$

5) $$\frac{d}{dt}\left(\frac{x}{y}\right) = \left\{y\frac{dx}{dt} - x\frac{dy}{dt}\right\} / y^2 \tag{2.27}$$

6) $$\frac{d}{dt}(\ln x) = \frac{1}{x} \cdot \frac{dx}{dt} \tag{2.28}$$

7) $$\frac{d}{dt}(e^x) = e^x \frac{dx}{dt} \tag{2.29}$$

Example 2.7

Find the derivative of the following function:

$$R(t) = e^{-\left(\sum_{i=1}^{n} \lambda_i\right)t} \tag{2.30}$$

where

λ_i is the constant failure rate of the ith component

n is the number of components forming a series configuration

t is time

Differentiating equation (2.30) with respect to t results in:

$$\frac{dR(t)}{dt} = -\left(\sum_{i=1}^{n} \lambda_i\right) \cdot e^{-\left(\sum_{i=1}^{n} \lambda_i\right)t} \tag{2.31}$$

INTEGRATION

In order to present a definition of a definite integral, let a function, $f(t)$, be defined in an interval, $\alpha \leqslant t \leqslant \beta$. Thus, the definite integral of function $f(t)$ between $t=\alpha$ and $t=\beta$ is given by

$$\int_\alpha^\beta f(t) \cdot dt = F(t)\,|_\alpha^\beta = F(\beta) - F(\alpha) \tag{2.32}$$

where $F(t)$ denotes a function whose $dF(t)/dt = f(t)$.

The following are some of the properties of definite integrals:

$$\int_\alpha^\alpha f(t) \cdot dt = 0 \tag{2.33}$$

$$\int_\alpha^\beta f(t) \cdot dt = - \int_\alpha^\beta f(t) \cdot dt \tag{2.34}$$

$$\int_\alpha^\beta f(t) \cdot dt = \int_\alpha^\theta f(t) \cdot dt + \int_\theta^\beta f(t) \cdot dt \tag{2.35}$$

$$\int_\alpha^\beta \{f(t) \pm g(t)\}\, dt = \int_\alpha^\beta f(t) dt \pm \int_\alpha^\beta g(t) \cdot dt \tag{2.36}$$

where $g(t)$ is an integrable function in interval $[\alpha, \beta]$.

$$\int_\alpha^\beta x^k\, dx = \frac{x^{k+1}}{k+1}\,\Big|_\alpha^\beta \tag{2.37}$$

for $k \neq 1$ where k is a constant.

Example 2.8

Evaluate

$$\int_0^\infty e^{-\lambda t} dt \tag{2.38}$$

where λ is a constant.

$$\int_0^\infty e^{-\lambda t^k}\, dt \tag{2.39}$$

From equation (2.38) we get

$$\int_0^\infty e^{-\lambda t}\, dt = \left[- \frac{e^{-\lambda t}}{\lambda} \right]_0^\infty = \frac{1}{\lambda} \tag{2.40}$$

and similarly

$$\int_0^\infty e^{-\lambda t^k}\, dt = \frac{\Gamma(1/k)}{k\lambda^{1/k}} \tag{2.41}$$

where $\Gamma(1/k)$ is the gamma function.

The definition of the gamma function is:

$$\Gamma(k) = \int_0^\infty t^{k-1}\, e^{-t}\, dt \quad \text{for } k>0 \tag{2.42}$$

MEAN VALUE THEOREM FOR INTEGRALS

The mean value, m, of a continuous function $f(t)$ defined in interval $[\alpha, \beta]$ is given by:

$$m = \frac{1}{(\alpha - \beta)} \cdot \int_{\alpha}^{\beta} f(t) \cdot dt \tag{2.43}$$

Example 2.9

Find the mean value of function

$$f(t) = c - t \tag{2.44}$$

for $0 \leqslant t \leqslant c$ where c is a constant.

By substituting equation (2.44) in equation (2.43) and integrating, the mean value is:

$$m = \frac{1}{c-0} \int_0^c (c - t)\, dt$$

$$= \frac{1}{c} \left[ct - \frac{t^2}{2} \right]_0^c$$

$$= \frac{c}{2} \tag{2.45}$$

BASIC PROBABILITY

In order to give the basic definition of probability, we assume that an event can occur in m ways and that in n ways it fails to occur. The total number of ways, $(m+n)$, are considered equally likely. Thus the probability, P, of the event occurrence is given by:

$$P = \frac{m}{n+m} \tag{2.46}$$

Similarly, the probability of the event's non-occurrence, Q, is given by:

$$Q = \frac{n}{n+m} \tag{2.47}$$

The probability of the event's occurrence plus the probability of its non-occurrence is always equal to unity, that is:

$$P + Q = \frac{m}{n+m} + \frac{n}{n+m} = 1 \tag{2.48}$$

Mutually Exclusive Events

The mutual exclusiveness of two or more events results if the happening of any one of these events does not include the happening of the remaining events. Thus the union of, say, n events, $X_1, X_2, X_3, \ldots, X_n$, is given by

$$P(X_1 + X_2 + X_3 + \ldots + X_n) = P(X_1) + P(X_2) + P(X_3) + \ldots + P(X_n) \qquad (2.49)$$

where P denotes probability.

Example 2.10

A fluid flow valve can fail in either open mode or closed mode. The device's open mode failure probability is 0.05, and the closed mode failure probability is 0.07. Calculate the probability, Q_t, of the fluid flow valve failure.

Thus for two events (open and closed modes), utilizing equation (2.49) results in

$$Q_t = P(X_1) + P(X_2) = 0.05 + 0.07 = 0.12$$

where

$P(X_1)$ is the valve's open mode failure probability

$P(X_2)$ is the valve's closed mode failure probability

Independent Events

If the happening or non-happening of any one of the n events does not affect the occurrence probabilities of any of the other $(n - 1)$ events, then all these n events are said to be independent.

Example 2.11

Two independent components, A and B, are forming a series configuration. In other words, if any one of the components fails then the series system (configuration) fails. The probabilities of success of components A and B are 0.9 and 0.95, respectively. Compute the configuration reliability, R_s.

The configuration reliability is simply given by:

$$R_s = P(A) \cdot P(B) = (0.9) \cdot (0.95) = 0.855$$

Dependent Events

If the happening or non-happening of any one of the n events affects the occurrence probabilities of any of the other $(n - 1)$ events, then all these n events are said to be dependent. Thus the conditional probability of event X, given that event Y has occurred, is given by:

$$P(X/Y)=\frac{P(X \cdot Y)}{P(Y)} \tag{2.50}$$

Example 2.12

On a 150-mile long highway the occurrence of accidents is equally likely. An accident between zero and 50 miles is denoted by X (event), and an accident between 35 and 110 miles is denoted by Y (event). If an accident occurs between 35 and 110 miles of the highway, calculate the probability of occurrence of event X. In a given interval of the highway, the probability of an accident occurring is proportional to the distance of the interval.[6]

The probability of occurrence of event Y is:

$$P(Y)=\frac{110-35}{150}=\frac{75}{150}=0.5$$

And similarly:

$$P(XY)=\frac{50-35}{150}=\frac{15}{150}$$

Therefore:

$$P(X/Y)=(15/150)/(75/100)=\frac{15}{75}=0.2$$

PROBABILITY DISTRIBUTIONS

This section presents selected probability distributions. The total area under the continuous probability density function is

$$\int_{-\infty}^{\infty} f(t)\,dt=1 \tag{2.51}$$

where

$f(t)$ is the probability density function

t is time

Similarly, the cumulative distribution function, $F(t)$, is defined by:

$$F(t)=\int_{-\infty}^{t} f(x)\cdot dx \tag{2.52}$$

The mean, μ, of a continuous probability distribution is given by:

$$\mu = \int_{-\infty}^{\infty} t\, f(t) \cdot dt \tag{2.53}$$

Similarly, a continuous probability distribution variance, θ^2, is defined by:

$$\theta^2 = \int_{-\infty}^{\infty} (t-\mu)^2 f(t)\, dt \tag{2.54}$$

Example 2.13

The failure times of a certain component are defined by

$$f(t) = \lambda\, e^{-\lambda t} \tag{2.55}$$

for $t \geqslant 0$ where λ is the component constant failure rate.

Prove that the total area under the probability function is equal to unity. Thus, by substituting function (2.55) in the left-hand side of equation (2.51), we get:

$$\text{Total area} = \int_0^\infty \lambda e^{-\lambda t}\, dt = \left[-\frac{\lambda e^{-\lambda t}}{\lambda}\right]_0^\infty = 1$$

Example 2.14

For given probability density function (2.55), obtain the cumulative distribution function. Thus, substituting equation (2.55) in equation (2.52) results in:

$$F(t) = \int_0^t \lambda\, e^{-\lambda t}\, dt = \left[-e^{-\lambda t}\right]_0^t$$

$$= 1 - e^{-\lambda t} \tag{2.56}$$

Example 2.15

For probability density function (2.55), obtain mean and variance formulas. By utilizing equation (2.55) in equation (2.53), we get:

$$\mu = \lambda \int_0^\infty t\, e^{-\lambda t}\, dt = \frac{1}{\lambda} \tag{2.57}$$

Similarly, substituting equation (2.55) in equation (2.54) yields the following variance formula:

$$\theta^2 = \lambda \int_0^\infty (t-\mu)^2\, e^{-\lambda t}\, dt$$

$$= \frac{1}{\lambda^2} \tag{2.58}$$

Exponential Distribution

From equations (2.55) through (2.58), the distribution probability density function, cumulative distribution function, mean and variance formulas, respectively, are as follows:

$$f(t) = \lambda e^{-\lambda t} \tag{2.59}$$

$$F(t) = 1 - e^{-\lambda t} \tag{2.60}$$

$$\mu = \frac{1}{\lambda} \tag{2.61}$$

$$\theta^2 = \frac{1}{\lambda^2} \tag{2.62}$$

The distribution reliability function is given by:

$$R(t) = 1 - F(t) = e^{-\lambda t} \tag{2.63}$$

The plot of equation (2.59) is given in Figure 2.1.

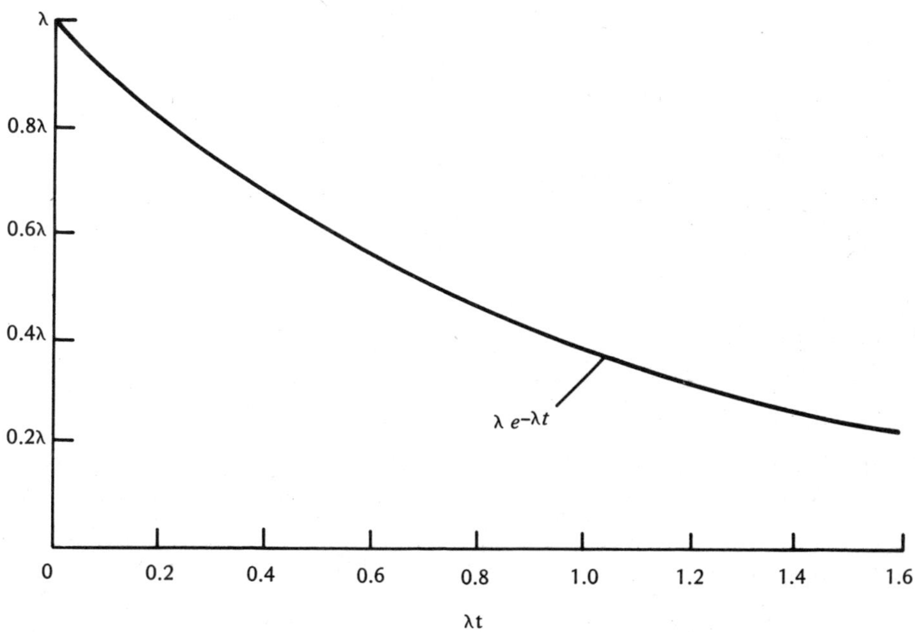

Figure 2.1 Plots of equations (2.59), (2.60), and (2.63)

Example 2.16

A component's failure times are described by function (2.55). The value of $\lambda = 0.002$ failures/hour. If the component starts operating at time $t = 0$, calculate its reliability for a 200-hour mission. In addition, compute the component mean time to failure, μ, and the variance of the times-to-failure, θ^2.

Substituting the given data in equation (2.63) yields the component's reliability for a 200-hour mission as follows:

$$R(100) = e^{-(0.002)(200)} = 0.6703$$

Similarly, utilizing the given data for λ in equations (2.57) and (2.58) yields

$$\mu = \frac{1}{\lambda} = \frac{1}{0.002} = 500 \text{ hours}$$

and

$$\theta^2 = \frac{1}{\lambda^2} = \frac{1}{(0.002)^2} = 250{,}000 \text{ hours}$$

Weibull Distribution

This distribution is frequently used in the field of reliability engineering. The probability density function of the distribution is defined by

$$f(t) = \lambda\, k\, t^{k-1}\, e^{-\lambda t^k} \tag{2.64}$$

for $t > 0$, $k > 0$, $\lambda > 0$, where

k is the shape parameter

λ is the reciprocal of the scale parameter

t is time

Utilizing equation (2.64) in equations (2.52) through (2.54) yields the equations for the cumulative distribution function, mean (mean time to failure), and variance, respectively, as follows:

$$F(t) = \int_0^t \lambda\, k\, t^{k-1} \cdot e^{-\lambda t^k}\, dt$$

$$= 1 - e^{-\lambda t^k} \tag{2.65}$$

$$\mu = \lambda k \int_0^t \{t \cdot t^{k-1} \cdot e^{-\lambda t^k}\}\, dt$$

$$= \lambda^{-1/k}\, \Gamma\left(\frac{1+k}{k}\right) \tag{2.66}$$

$$\theta^2 = \lambda k \int_0^\infty (t-\mu)^2 \cdot \{t^{k-1} \cdot e^{-\lambda t^k}\}\, dt$$

$$= \lambda^{-2/k} \left\{ \Gamma\left(\frac{2+k}{k}\right) - \left\{ \Gamma\left(\frac{1+k}{k}\right) \right\}^2 \right\} \tag{2.67}$$

The following function, $R(t)$, results by subtracting equation (2.65) from unity:

$$R(t) = e^{-\lambda t^k} \tag{2.68}$$

At $k = 1$, equations (2.64) through (2.68) are same as for the exponential distribution [corresponding to equations (2.59)through (2.63)]. At $k = 2$, equations (2.64) through (2.68) are for the Raleigh distribution.

Example 2.17

An electronic device's failure times follow the Weibull distribution with $\lambda = 0.05$ failures/hour and $k = 2$. Calculate the device's mean (mean time to failure) and reliability for a 10-hour mission. Assume that the device starts operating at $t = 0$.

Substituting the given data in equation (2.66) yields the component's mean time to failure:

$$\mu = (0.05)^{-1/2} \left(1 + \frac{1}{2}\right)$$

$$= (0.05)^{-1/2}\, (0.8863)$$

$$= 3.964 \text{ hours}$$

Similarly, utilizing the specified data in equation (2.68) yields:

$$R(50) = \mathrm{e}^{-(0.05)\,(10)^2}$$
$$= 0.0067$$

Binomial Distribution

This is a discrete distribution whose probability density function is defined by

$$f(y:m,p) = \frac{m!}{y!\,(m-y)!}\; p^y\, (1-p)^{m-y} \tag{2.69}$$

for $y = 0, 1, 2, 3, \ldots, m$, where

m is the number of trials

y is successes out of m trials

p is the probability of success

The mean of the distribution is given by:

$$\mu = mp \tag{2.70}$$

Similarly, the distribution variance is:

$$\theta^2 = m(p - p^2) \tag{2.71}$$

Example 2.18

A system consists of three independent and identical units. The probability of each unit operating successfully is 0.8. Calculate the probability of exactly two out of three units operating successfully.

Substituting the specified data in equation (2.69) results in:

$$f(2{:}3, 0.8) = \frac{3!}{2!\,(3-2)!} (0.8)^2 (0.2)^{3-2}$$

$$= 0.384$$

Thus, the probability of exactly two out of three units operating is 0.384.

Poisson Distribution

The assumptions associated with the Poisson process are as follows:

1. An event's occurrence or occurrences are independent.
2. At any instant of time an event occurs randomly.
3. The probability of more than one occurrence in a time interval of Δt is very small (negligible).
4. The probability of an occurrence during a time interval of Δt is given by $\lambda \Delta t$, where λ is the average rate of event occurrence (e.g., λ may denote the constant failure rate of an item).

Thus, the probability of y occurrences (failures) in time interval t is given by:

$$P(y) = \frac{(\lambda t)^y}{y!} e^{-\lambda t} \tag{2.72}$$

The above formula was developed from equation (2.69) as follows:

$$f(y{:}m,p) = P_y = \frac{m!}{y!\,(m-y)!} p^y (1-p)^{m-y} \tag{2.73}$$

If in comparison to y the value of m is large, then we may write:

$$\frac{m!}{(m-y)!} \simeq m^y \tag{2.74}$$

Similarly, if in comparison to m the value of y is small, and the value of p is very small, the term $(1-p)^{m-y}$ is approximated by:

$$(1-p)^m$$

That is

$$(1-p)^{m-y} \simeq (1-p)^m \tag{2.75}$$

Thus, utilizing equations (2.74) through (2.75) in equation (2.73) yields the following:

$$\begin{aligned} P_y &= \frac{m^y}{y!} p^y (1-p)^m \\ &= \frac{(pm)^y}{y!} \cdot (1-p)^m \end{aligned} \tag{2.76}$$

Utilizing equation (2.11) to expand the last right-hand term of equation (2.76) results in:

$$\begin{aligned} (1-p)^m &= \sum_{r=0}^{m} \binom{m}{r} (-p)^r \\ &= \binom{m}{0} + \binom{m}{1}(-p) + \binom{m}{2}(-p)^2 + \binom{m}{3}(-p)^3 + \dots \\ &= 1 - pm + \frac{m(m-1)}{2!} p^2 - \frac{m(m-1)(m-2)}{3!} p^3 + \dots \end{aligned} \tag{2.77}$$

For the large value of m, the terms of equation (2.77) become:

$$m(m-1) \simeq m^2 \tag{2.78}$$

$$m(m-1)(m-2) \simeq m^3 \tag{2.79}$$

Thus, substituting the results of equations (2.78) and (2.79) in equation (2.77) leads to:

$$(1-p)^m \simeq 1 - pm + \frac{(pm)^2}{2!} - \frac{(pm)^3}{3!} + \dots \tag{2.80}$$

The right-hand term of equation (2.80) is same as equation (2.17) if we let $t = -pm$; thus

$$(1-p)^m \simeq e^{-pm} \tag{2.81}$$

Finally, substituting equation (2.81) in equation (2.76) yields:

$$P_y = \frac{(pm)^y}{y!} e^{-pm} \tag{2.82}$$

For $pm = \lambda t$, the above equation is the same as equation (2.72). The mean and variance formulas of the distribution are as follows, respectively:

$$\mu = pm \tag{2.83}$$

$$\theta^2 = pm \tag{2.84}$$

Example 2.19

A system's constant failure rate is $\lambda = 0.005$ failures/hour. Calculate the probability that there will be exactly three failures during a 500-hour interval. Thus substituting the given data in equation (2.72) results in:

$$P(3) = \frac{\{(0.005)(500)\}^3}{3!} e^{-(0.005)(500)}$$

$$= 0.2138$$

The probability of having exactly three failures during the period of 500 hours is 0.2138.

SUMMARY

This chapter briefly summarizes the essential mathematics required to understand subsequent chapters of this book. The following topics are covered: Laplace transforms, binomial theorem, series, maxima and minima, differentiation, integration, mean value theorem for integrals, basic probability, and probability distributions.

EXERCISES

2.1. Find the Laplace transforms of the following functions:

a) $f(t) = e^{\lambda^3 t}$

b) $f(t) = \sum_{i=1}^{n} \lambda_i e^{-\sum_{i=1}^{n} \lambda_i t}$

c) $f(t) = \frac{1}{\Gamma(3)} \cdot t^2$

where

t is the variable

λ is the constant

λ_i is the ith constant

2.2. Calculate the value of each of the following:

a) $\binom{5}{2}$ b) $\binom{7}{3}$ c) $\binom{10}{9}$

2.3. Expand the following factors:

a) $(p+q)^5$, where p denotes the probability of success and q denotes the probability of failure

b) $(p+q)^{7-4}$

2.4. Find the sum of the series

$$\frac{P}{t}+\frac{P}{t^2}+\frac{P}{t^3}+\ldots+\frac{P}{t^m}$$

where P and m are constants.

2.5. Find an expression for the optimum number of units k to maximize the reliability R. The system's reliability, R, is given by

$$R=(1-q_1)^k-q_2^k$$

where

q_1 and q_2 are the device open mode and closed mode failure probabilities, respectively

k is the number of identical and independent units in parallel

2.6. Differentiate the following function with respect to time t:

$$R(t)=-e^{-\lambda t^k}$$

where λ and k are the constants.

2.7. Evaluate

$$\int_0^\infty e^{-\theta^2 t^3}\,dt$$

where θ is a constant.

2.8. Prove that the total area under the probability density function $f(t)$ is equal to unity

$$f(t)=ba\,(bt)^{a-1}\,e^{-\left\{e^{(bt)^a}-(bt)^a-1\right\}}$$

for $b, a>0$ and $t\geqslant 0$, where

a and b are distribution parameters

t is time

2.9. Develop expressions for mean and variance formulas associated with the following probability density function:

$$f(t) = \frac{2t}{\alpha} e^{-\frac{1}{\alpha} t^2}$$

where

t is time

α is the scale parameter

2.10. An electronic device's failure times are Weibull distributed with the shape parameter value equal to 3. The value of the scale parameter is $\lambda^{-1} = 500$ hours. Calculate the device's reliability for a 10-hour mission. Assume that the device starts operating at time $t = 0$.

2.11. Compare briefly the exponential distribution with the Weibull distribution.

2.12. Compare the hazard rates of distributions of exercise 2.11 with the following bathtub hazard rate function

$$\lambda(t) = ab(bt)^{a-1} \cdot e^{(bt)^a}$$

where

a is the shape parameter

b is the reciprocal of the scale parameter

t is the time

2.13. Compare, by plotting, the reliability functions of the exponential and the Weibull distributions.

NOTES

1. A. Drake, *Fundamentals of Applied Probability Theory* (New York: McGraw-Hill, 1967).
2. F. Oberhettinger, L. Badii, *Tables of Laplace Transforms* (New York: Springer-Verlag, 1973, pp. 3-200.
3. J.S. Grandshteyn, I.M. Ryzhik, *Table of Integrals, Series, and Products* (New York: Academic Press, 1980), pp. 211.
4. *Handbook of Mathematical Functions* (Washington, D.C.: National Bureau of Standards, U.S. Government Printing Office, 1964), pp. 1019–1030.
5. W.G. Ireson, ed., *Reliability Handbook* (New York: McGraw-Hill, 1966), pp. 4.1–4.66.
6. A.H.S. Ang and W.H. Tang, *Probability Concepts in Engineering Planning and Design,* vol. 1 (New York: John Wiley & Sons, 1975), pp. 43–44.

3

Hazard Rate Models

In the field of reliability sometimes it is more convenient to fit the hazard rate function of the distribution to the failure data rather than utilizing the other means.[1,2] Furthermore, many reliability analysts and others think more in terms of component failure rate (hazard rate) than in other reliability measures. Once the hazard rate function of a component or a system is known, the mean time to failure, the failure probability density, cumulative distribution, and reliability functions can all be obtained quite easily. Therefore, this chapter presents various hazard rate models. The hazard rate functions here are divided into the following four categories:

1. Conventional hazard rates
2. Complex hazard rates
3. Bathtub hazard rates
4. Nonconventional hazard rates

GENERAL HAZARD RATE MODEL

By definition, the hazard rate function, $\lambda(t)$, of a statistical distribution is given by

$$\lambda(t) = \frac{f(t)}{R(t)} = \frac{\lambda(t) e^{-\int_0^t \lambda(\mathrm{T}) \cdot d\mathrm{T}}}{e^{-\int_0^t \lambda(\mathrm{T}) \cdot d\mathrm{T}}} \tag{3.1}$$

where

t is time

$f(t)$ is the failure probability density function

$R(t)$ is the reliability function

One should note from relationship (3.1) that

$$f(t)=\lambda(t)\cdot e^{-\int_0^t \lambda(T)\cdot dT} \tag{3.2}$$

and

$$R(t)=e^{-\int_0^t \lambda(T)\cdot dT} \tag{3.3}$$

CONVENTIONAL HAZARD RATE MODELS

This section presents hazard rate functions of well-known probability distributions such as Weibull, exponential, gamma, beta, Rayleigh, and so on. The procedures to estimate parameters of all these models are given in Ireson.[3]

Weibull Hazard Rate

This function has wide application in the reliability field. The hazard rate function, $\lambda(t)$, is defined as

$$\lambda(t)=\frac{b}{a}t^{b-1} \tag{3.4}$$

where

b is the shape parameter

a is the scale parameter

t is time

At $b=1$, equation (3.4) reduces to:

$$\lambda=1/a \tag{3.5}$$

Equation (3.5) is known as the constant failure rate, λ, of a component, where a denotes the component mean time to failure. Because of its simplicity the constant failure rate function is used more frequently in reliability analysis than any other hazard rate function. However, many components actually exhibit constant failure rate characteristics, especially in the case of electronic components.

Similarly, at $b=2$, function (3.4) reduces to:

$$\lambda(t)=\frac{2}{a}t \tag{3.6}$$

This function is known as the Rayleigh hazard rate function or the linearly increasing hazard rate function. As can easily be seen from equation (3.6), as time t increases, the value of hazard rate $\lambda(t)$ increases linearly.

At $a=1$, the plots of equation (3.4) for the various fixed values of b are shown in Figure 3.1.

Substituting equation (3.4) in equation (3.2) and integrating yields the component failure probability density function

$$f(t)=\frac{b}{a}t^{b-1}\cdot e^{-\frac{1}{a}t^{b}} \tag{3.7}$$

Example 3.1

A mechanical component's failure times are represented by the Weibull hazard rate function. The values of the distribution shape and scale parameters are $b=2$ and $a=2{,}500$ hours, respectively. Calculate the value of the hazard rate at $t=100$ hours.

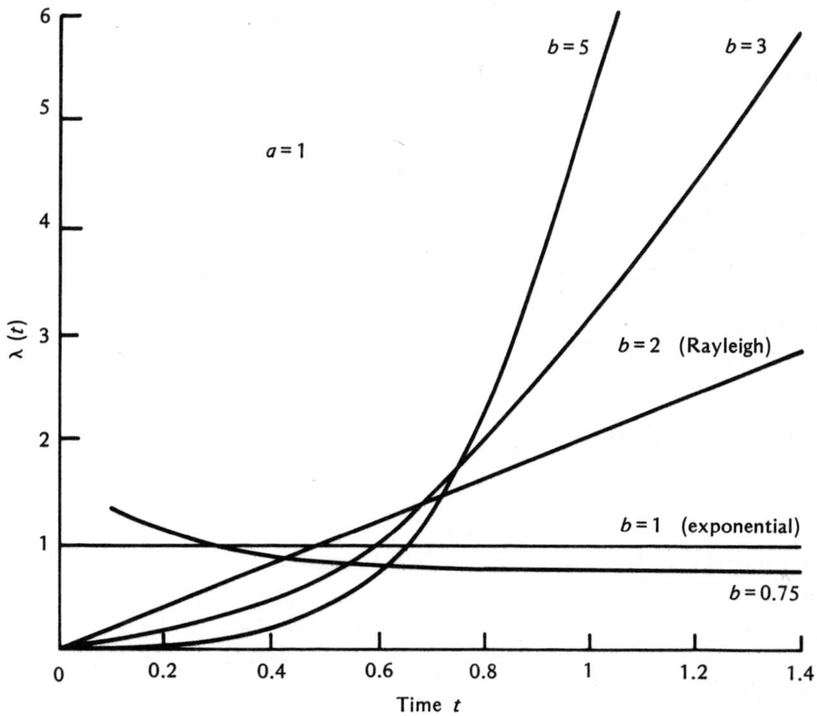

Figure 3.1 Plots of Weibull hazard function

Utilizing the given data in equation (3.4) results in:

$$\lambda(200)=\frac{3}{2500}(100)^{2-1}=0.12 \text{ failure/hour}$$

Exponential Hazard Rate

The exponential hazard rate model is used to represent the hazard rate of mechanical components. Mechanical components usually exhibit the increasing hazard rate pattern. The exponential hazard rate is defined by

$$\lambda(t)=\beta_1 e^{\beta_2 t} \tag{3.8}$$

where

t is time

β_1 and β_2 are the distribution parameters

Substituting hazard rate function (3.8) in relationship (3.2) and integrating yields the failure probability density function

$$f(t)=e^{-\alpha(e^{\beta_2 t}-1)}\cdot\beta_1 e^{\beta_2 t} \tag{3.9}$$

where

$$\alpha\equiv\beta_1/\beta_2 \tag{3.10}$$

Gamma Hazard Rate

This is another hazard rate model which has applications in reliability engineering. The hazard function of the model is given by

$$\lambda(t)=\{t^a\cdot e^{-t/\theta}\}\,/\int_t^\infty y^a\cdot e^{-y/\theta}\cdot dy \tag{3.11}$$

where

a is the shape parameter

θ is the scale parameter

t is time

This model can represent the increasing, decreasing, and constant hazard rates. In Gupta and Groll[4] the hazard function is applied to life test problems. At $a=0$ equation (3.11) reduces to a constant value. Utilizing hazard rate function (3.11) in equation (3.2) leads to the following failure probability density function:

$$f(t)=t^a e^{-t/\theta}\cdot(1/a!\theta^{a+1}) \quad \text{for } t>0 \tag{3.12}$$

Beta Hazard Rate

This hazard rate function is given by

$$\lambda(t) = \{t^a (1-t)^\theta\} \,/\, \int_t^1 y^a (1-y)^\theta \cdot dy \tag{3.13}$$

where

t is time

a, θ are the distribution parameters

The plots of equation (3.13) are given in Ireson.[3] Thus, substituting equation (3.13) in equation (3.2) and integrating leads to the following failure probability density function:

$$f(t) = \{t^a (1-t)^\theta \cdot (\alpha+\theta+1)!\} \,/\, a!\theta! \tag{3.14}$$

for $0 < t < 1$

$a > -1$

$\theta > -1$

Example 3.2

Suppose a system has three independent components—1, 2, 3—and their hazard functions are defined by equations (3.8), (3.11) and (3.13), respectively. Obtain a reliability expression for each component by utilizing relationship (3.3).

Thus, the reliability expressions for components 1, 2, and 3 are as follows:

$$R(t) = e^{-\int_0^t \beta_1 e^{\beta_2 x} dx} = e^{-\frac{\beta_1}{\beta_2}\left(e^{\beta_2 t} - 1\right)} \tag{3.15}$$

$$R(t) = e^{-\int_0^t [\{y^a e^{-y/\theta}\} / \int_y^\infty x^a e^{-x/\theta} dx]\, dy}$$

$$= \frac{1}{a!\theta^{a+1}} \int_t^\infty y^a e^{-y/\theta} \cdot dy \tag{3.16}$$

and

$$R(t) = 1 - A\, B_t\,(a+1, \theta+1) \quad \text{for } 0 < t < 1 \tag{3.17}$$

where

$$A \equiv \{(a+\theta+1)!\} / a!\theta! \tag{3.18}$$

and

$$B_t(a+1, \theta+1) \equiv \int_0^t y^a (1-y)^\theta dy \tag{3.19}$$

COMPLEX HAZARD RATE MODELS

This section presents the hazard rate model which was developed by Birnbaum and Saunders[5]. The model is sometimes known as the two-parameter fatigue-life model.

The Fatigue-Life Model

This model is used to characterize failures due to fatigue. The hazard rate, $\lambda(t)$, of the distribution is defined by

$$\lambda(t)=\frac{f(t)}{R(t)}=\frac{f(t)}{1-F(t)} \tag{3.20}$$

where

$$f(t)=\frac{k(t^2-b^2)}{t^2\left\{(t/b)^{0.5}-\left(\frac{b}{t}\right)^{0.5}\right\}}\exp\left\{-\frac{1}{2a^2}\left(\frac{t^2+b^2-2bt}{bt}\right)\right\} \tag{3.21}$$

for $a, \beta > 0; t > 0$.

$$k \equiv \{2(2\pi)^{0.5}a^2b\}^{-1} \tag{3.22}$$

$$R(t)=1-F(t)=1-\int_0^t f(x)\cdot dx \tag{3.23}$$

In equation (3.21) a denotes the shape parameter, b denotes the scale parameter, and t represents time.

Birnbaum and Saunders also report the result of the hazard rate study. According to their findings, the fatigue-life model hazard rate is nonincreasing. In addition, they established that the average hazard rate is almost nondecreasing.[5]

BATHTUB HAZARD RATE MODELS

To represent the failure behavior of many different kinds of systems and components, we can try to apply the failure distributions such as exponential, normal, Weibull, beta, or gamma. However, it's often impossible to represent mathematically the failure behavior of items which fail due to a variety of different physical causes. This is why in the field of reliability engineering the concept of the bathtub hazard rate curve is well known.

A typical bathtub hazard rate curve is shown in Figure 3.2.

Researchers in the field have verified that some systems and components follow the bathtub hazard rate pattern. The curve is divided into three parts. The first part, the decreasing hazard rate region, is sometimes called the "burn-in period." Other names for this region are break-in period, debugging period,

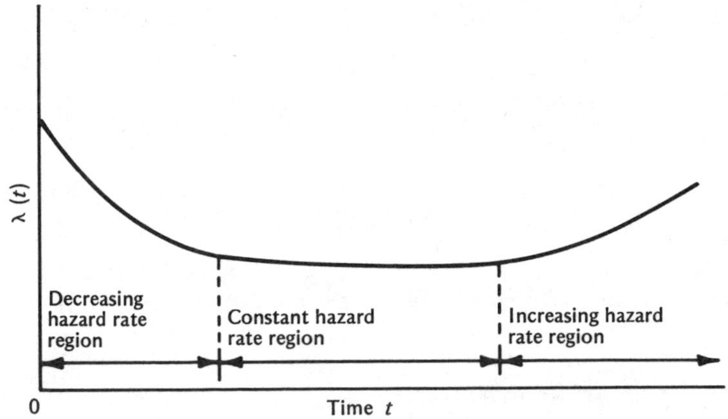

Figure 3.2 Typical bathtub hazard rate curve

and infant mortality period. Generally, failures occurring during this period are due to design and manufacturing errors.

The constant region of the curve is known as the useful life period. The failures within this region occur unpredictably or randomly.

The increasing hazard rate portion of the curve is known as the wear-out period. This region represents the failures when a system or component has aged or bypassed its useful operating life.

In order to represent the bathtub hazard rate curve researchers have proposed various functions. This section will present some of these functions and apply selective ones in order to develop redundant system reliability expressions. The following notations are associated with hazard rate models:

$R(t)$ is the reliability at time t

$\lambda(t)$ is the hazard rate

β is the scale parameter

b is the shape parameter

t_i is the ith time, for $i=1, 2$

Mathematical Models

◆ **BATHTUB HAZARD RATE MODEL I** The hazard rate for the model is:[7]

$$\lambda(t)=j\,\lambda a t^{a-1}+(1-j)\,b t^{b-1}\,\beta e^{\beta t^{b}} \tag{3.24}$$

for $a, b, \beta, \lambda > 0; 0 \leqslant j \leqslant 1; t \geqslant 0$, where

a is the shape parameter

λ is the scale parameter

The following hazard rate functions are special cases of equation (3.24):

$j=1$	Weibull
$j=0, b=1$	extreme value
$a=0.5, b=1$	bathtub curve
$a=1, b=1$	Makeham distribution

Figure 3.3 shows the plot of equation (3.24) for $j=a=0.5, b=\lambda=\beta=1$. This plot clearly indicates the existence of the bathtub hazard rate curve. The parameter estimation of the function is not an easy task. The reliability function of the model is:[7]

$$R(t)=\exp[-j\lambda t^a-(1-j)(e^{\beta t^b}-1)] \tag{3.25}$$

♦ **BATHTUB HAZARD RATE MODEL II** The model hazard rate and reliability expressions are the special cases of equations (3.24) and (3.25), respectively, for $j=0$[2,8]

$$\lambda(t)=b\,\beta(\beta t)^{b-1}\cdot e^{(\beta t)^b} \tag{3.26}$$

$$R(t)=\exp[-(e^{(\beta t)^b}-1)] \tag{3.27}$$

At $b=1$, the above two equations reduce to the one for the extreme value distribution. In additon, at $b=0.5$, equation (3.26) can represent the bathtub hazard rate curve. Parameters β and b can easily be estimated by applying the

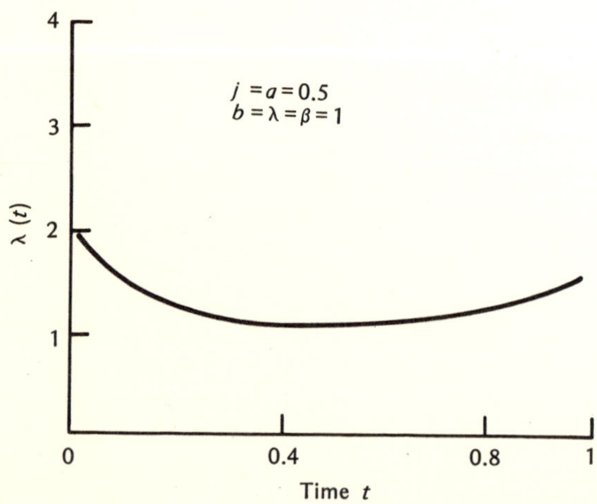

Figure 3.3 Bathtub hazard rate curve for model I

hazard plotting and maximum likelihood estimation techniques without any difficulty.[2] Figure 3.4 shows the plot of equation (3.26) for $b=0.5$. The plot shows the bathtub hazard rate curve.

◆ **BATHTUB HAZARD RATE MODEL III** Murthy gives the hazard rate and reliability functions of the model, respectively, by[9]

$$\lambda(t)=\frac{1}{a}e^{-at}+k\,p\,t^{p-1} \tag{3.28}$$

for $p \geqslant 1$ and $a, k > 0$, where p, a, and k are the model parameters.

And

$$R(t)=e^{-\left[\frac{1}{a^2}(1-e^{-at})-k\,t^p\right]} \tag{3.29}$$

Figure 3.5 shows the plot of equation (3.28) for $a=0.1$, $k=0.45$, and $p=2$. The plot exhibits the time-dependent failure rate with bathtub characteristics. Murthy uses the maximum likelihood estimation technique to estimate parameters of the hazard function.[9]

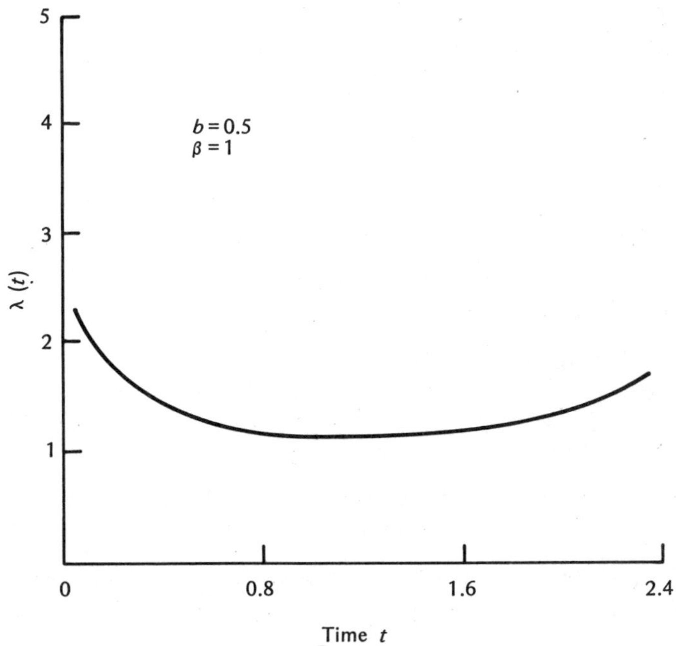

Figure 3.4 Bathtub hazard rate curve for model II

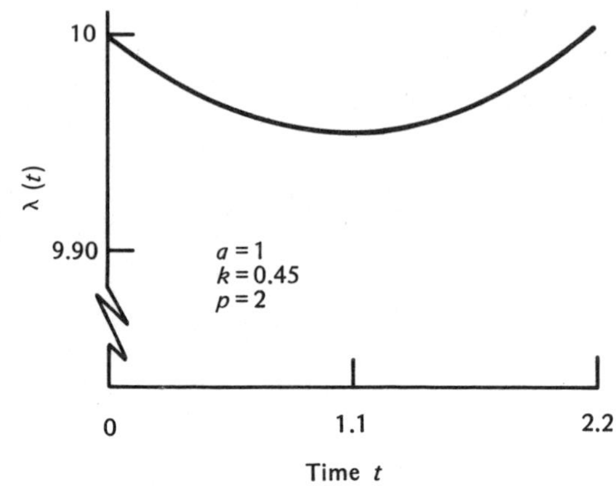

Figure 3.5 Bathtub hazard rate curve for model III

♦ **BATHTUB HAZARD RATE MODEL IV** The hazard function is defined in Shooman[10] as follows:

$$\lambda(t) = \begin{cases} c_1 - k_1 t & 0 < t \leqslant t_1 \\ c_2 - k_2(t - t_1) & t_1 < t \leqslant t_2 \\ c_3 - k_3(t - t_2) & t_2 < t \leqslant \infty \end{cases} \tag{3.30}$$

where

c_i is the ith constant, for $i = 1, 2, 3$

k_i is the ith slope, for $i = 1, 2, 3$

t_i is the ith time, for $i = 1, 2$

Equation (3.30) represents the decreasing, constant, and increasing regions of the bathtub hazard rate curve, respectively.

♦ **BATHTUB HAZARD RATE MODEL V** The hazard rate $\lambda(t)$ for the model is given in Murthy as

$$\lambda(t) = \theta_1 b_1 t^{b_1 - 1} + \theta_2 b_2 t^{b_2 - 1} \tag{3.31}$$

where θ_1 θ_2, b_1 and b_2 are the parameters of the distribution.[9]

For $b_1 < 1$ and $b_2 > 1$, equation (3.31) gives a U-shaped curve.

♦ **BATHTUB HAZARD RATE MODEL VI** Ghare and Kim define the hazard rate of this model by

$$\lambda(t) = \frac{\alpha}{t^2 + k} + n\, e^{t^{p}/q} \tag{3.32}$$

for $\alpha, p \geqslant 0$ and $k, q, n > 0$, $0 < t$, where α, p, k, q and n are the parameters.[11]

Equation (3.32) can be used to represent (approximately) the bathtub hazard rate curve. A parameter estimation procedure is given in Ghare and Kim.[11] Other hazard rate functions may be found in Murthy.[9]

Networks Composed of Components with Bathtub Hazard Rates

This section presents reliability and hazard rate expressions for the series k-out-of-n, and for identical unit standby networks, when the unit or component hazard rate is represented by models I, II and III.

♦ **SERIES NETWORK** For independent n units, the series network[10] reliability, $R_s(t)$, and the hazard rate, $h_s(t)$, when the unit hazard rate follows the hazard rates of models I, II and III, are as follows, respectively:

For bathtub hazard rate model I (equation (3.24):

$$R_s(t) = e^{-\sum_{i=1}^{n} [j\lambda_i t^a + (1-j)(e^{\beta_i t^b} - 1)]} \tag{3.33}$$

and

$$h_s(t) = \sum_{i=1}^{n} \left[j\lambda_i a t^{a-1} + (1-j)\, b t^{b-1}\, \beta_i e^{\beta_i t^b} \right] \tag{3.34}$$

At $a = 0.5$ and $b = 1$, equations (3.33) and (3.34) yield series system reliability and hazard rate expressions when the unit follows the bathtub hazard rate curve. Figure 3.6 shows the reliability plot for $j = a = 0.5$, $b = \beta = \lambda = 1$, and $n = 2$ (identical units).

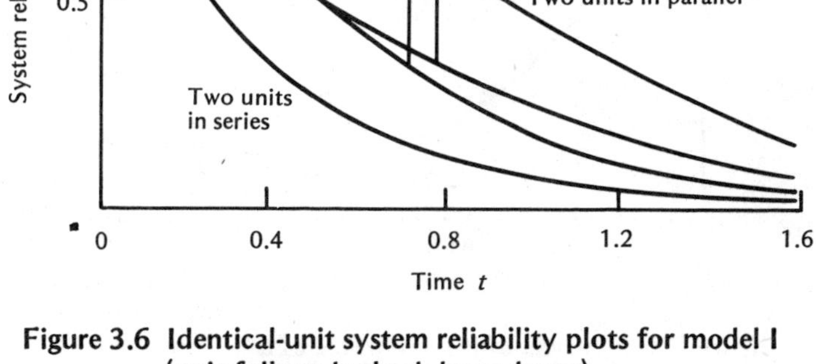

Figure 3.6 Identical-unit system reliability plots for model I (unit follows bathtub hazard rate)

For bathtub hazard rate model II (equation (3.26):

$$R_s(t) = e^{-\sum_{i=1}^{n} (e^{\beta_i t^b} - 1)} \tag{3.35}$$

and

$$h_s(t) = b \sum_{i=1}^{n} e^{\beta_i t^b} \beta_i t^{b-1} \tag{3.36}$$

Equations (3.35) and (3.36) can be used to obtain series network reliability and hazard rate expressions when a unit or component follows the bathtub hazard rate curve at $b = 0.5$. Figure 3.7 shows the reliability plot for $b = 0.5, \beta = 1$, *and* $n = 2$ (identical units).

For bathtub hazard rate model III (equation (3.28):

$$R_s(t) = e^{-\sum_{i=1}^{n} \left[\frac{1}{2a_i} (1 - e^{a_i t}) + k_i t^p\right]} \tag{3.37}$$

and

$$h_s(t) = \sum_{i=1}^{n} \left[\frac{1}{a_i} e^{-a_i t} + k_i p t^{p-1}\right] \tag{3.38}$$

Figure 3.8 shows the reliability plot for $a = 0.1, k = 0.45, p = 2$, and $n = 2$ (identical units). This plot represents the situation when a system unit follows the bathtub hazard rate curve.

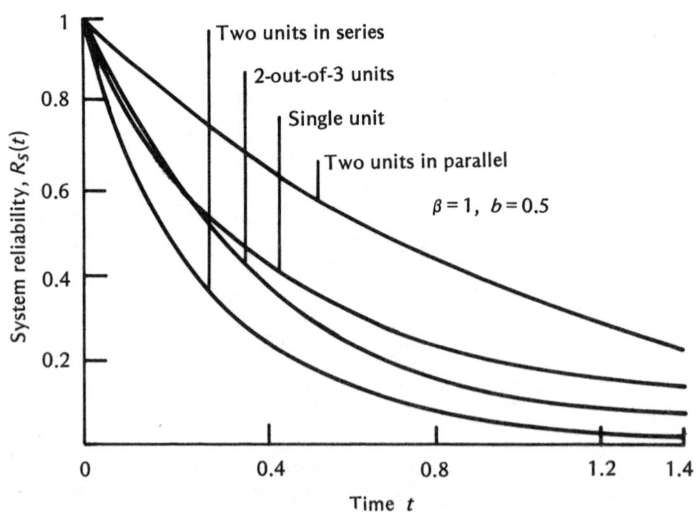

Figure 3.7 Identical-unit system reliability plots for model II (unit follows bathtub hazard rate)

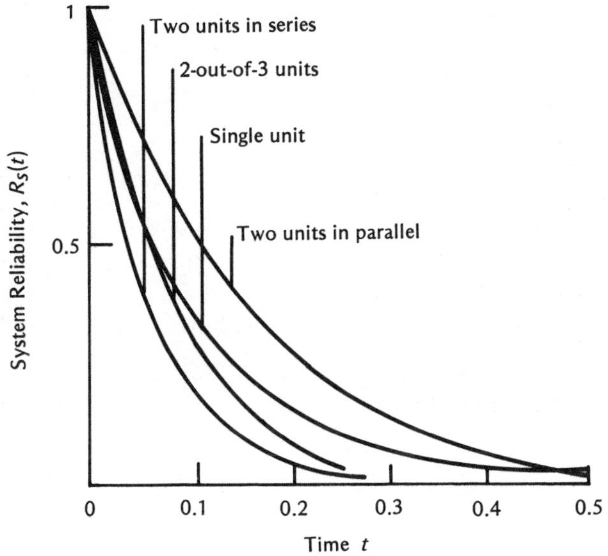

Figure 3.8 Identical-unit system reliability plots for model III (unit follows bathtub hazard rate)

♦ **K-OUT-OF-N UNIT SYSTEM** In the case of n independent identical units, the k-out-of-n units network's reliability, $R_{k/n}(t)$, at time t when the unit hazard follows models' I, II and III hazard rates, is given by the following expressions, respectively:[10]

For bathtub hazard rate model I (equation (3.24):

$$R_{k/n}(t) = \sum_{i=k}^{n} \binom{n}{i} [\exp\{-j\lambda t^a - (1-j)(e^{\beta t^b} - 1\}]^i$$

$$[1 - \exp\{-j\lambda t^a - (1-j)(e^{\beta t^b} - 1)\}]^{n-i} \quad (3.39)$$

Special cases of equation (3.39) are series ($k = n$) and parallel ($k = 1$) networks. For $a = 0.5$ and $b = 1$, the unit hazard rate in equation (3.39) satisfies the bathtub hazard curve. Figure 3.6 shows the plot of equation (3.39) for $j = a = 0.5$, $b = \beta = \lambda = 1$, $k = 2$ and $n = 3$ (identical units).

For bathtub hazard rate model II (equation (3.26):

$$R_{k/n}(t) = \sum_{i=k}^{n} \binom{n}{i} [e^{-i(e^{\beta t^b} - 1)}] [1 - e^{-(e^{\beta t^b} - 1)}]^{n-i} \quad (3.40)$$

In order to obtain identical unit series and parallel network reliability, in equation (3.40) set $k = \text{n}$ and $k = 1$, respectively. At $b = 0.5$, the system unit hazard rate follows the bathtub curve. Figure 3.7 shows the plot of equation (3.40) for $b = 0.5$, $\beta = 1$, $k = 2$ and $n = 3$ (identical units).

For bathtub hazard rate model III (equation (3.28):

$$R_{k/n}(t) = \sum_{i=k}^{n} \binom{n}{i} \left[e^{-\frac{1}{a^2}(1 - e^{-at}) - kt^p} \right]^i$$

$$\left[1 - e^{-\frac{1}{a^2}(1 - e^{-at}) - kt^p} \right]^{n-i} \tag{3.41}$$

Identical unit series and parallel network reliability can be obtained by setting $k = n$ and $k = 1$. In addition, for $a = 0.1$, $k = 0.45$, and $p = 2$ the unit hazard rate in equation (3.41) follows the bathtub curve as shown in Figure 3.5. The reliability plot of equation (3.41) for $a = 0.1, k = 0.45, p = 2, k = 2$, and $n = 3$ (identical units) is shown in Figure 3.8.

♦ **IDENTICAL UNIT STANDBY SYSTEM** Sandler gives an n unit standby system's reliability, $R_{st}(t)$, at time t as[12]

$$R_{st}(t) = \sum_{i=0}^{n-1} \frac{[\lambda_c(t)]^i}{i!} e^{-\lambda_c(t)} \tag{3.42}$$

where

$$\lambda_c(t) = \int_0^t \lambda(t)\, dt \tag{3.43}$$

To obtain the standby system reliability expressions for component bathtub hazard rate models I, II and III, substitute equations (3.24), (3.26), and (3.28), respectively, in equation (3.42) and perform the necessary steps.

Example 3.3

The hazard rate, $\lambda(t)$, of a component is described by equation (3.26). Find a reliability expression for the identical n unit standby system. Substituting equation (3.26) in equation (3.43) and integrating yields the following cumulative hazard function:

$$\lambda_c(t) = \int_0^t b\, \beta(\beta t)^{b-1}\, e^{(\beta t)^b} = \exp\,(\beta t)^b - 1 \tag{3.44}$$

Thus, substituting equation (3.44) in equation (3.43) results in:

$$R_{st}(t) = \sum_{i=0}^{n-1} \frac{\{\exp(\beta t)^b - 1\}^i}{i} \exp\{-e^{(\beta t)^b} + 1\} \tag{3.45}$$

NON-CONVENTIONAL HAZARD RATE MODELS

This section presents those hazard rate models which could not be easily categorized according to the three earlier classifications. These models can be utilized in various situations.

Hazard Rate Model I

This model was studied by Flehinger and Lewis, and the hazard rate function, $\lambda(t)$, is of the form[13]

$$\lambda(t)=\theta+b\,t^k \tag{3.46}$$

where

t is time

θ, b and k are parameters

For $k=1$ and 2, the model was studied extensively by Flehinger and Lewis.

Hazard Rate Model II

Drenick defines this hazard rate by[14]

$$\lambda(t)=\begin{cases}\theta & 0\leqslant t\leqslant t_1\\ \theta+\theta_1\,(t-t_1) & t_1\leqslant t\end{cases} \tag{3.47}$$

where

t is time

θ and θ_1 are the parameters

Hazard Rate Model III

This hazard rate is defined by Foster and Craddock as[15]

$$\lambda(t)=\beta+\theta\,e^{-\alpha t} \tag{3.48}$$

for $\beta, \theta, \alpha>0$, where β, θ, and α are the parameters.

Foster and Craddock used this model to represent equipment burn-in data.[15] Substituting equation (3.48) in equation (3.3) and integrating yields the following reliability function:

$$R(t)=\exp\left[-\left(\beta t-\frac{\theta}{\alpha}e^{-\alpha t}+\frac{\theta}{\alpha}\right)\right] \tag{3.49}$$

Foster and Craddock also used the maximum likelihood estimation procedure to estimate model parameters.[15] Models for decreasing failure rate processes may be found in Cozzolino.[16]

Hazard Rate Model IV

Shooman defines this hazard rate by a power series as[10]

$$\lambda(t)=\theta_0+\theta_1 t+\theta_2 t^2+\theta_3 t^3+\ldots+\theta_k t^k \tag{3.50}$$

where

θ's are positive or negative constant

t is time

To determine model parameters, Shooman uses the curve-fitting procedure.[10]

Hazard Rate Model V

According to Broadbent, this hazard function is known as the stange hazard rate.[17] The function is defined by

$$\lambda(t) = \theta^{\alpha}\ \alpha\ t^{\alpha-1} \tag{3.51}$$

where

t is time

θ and α are the parameters

Other hazard rate models may be found in sources listed at the end of the chapter.[18,19,20]

SUMMARY

This chapter presents various hazard rate models. These models are categorized into four classifications: (1) conventional hazard rate models, (2) complex hazard rate models, (3) bathtub hazard rate models, and (4) non-conventional hazard rate models. The first consists of well-known models such as Weibull, exponential, Rayleigh, extreme value, gamma, and beta. The second contains the fatigue-life model. The third contains seven models which can represent the well-known bathtub hazard rate curve. The last classification contains five models which have been used to represent various types of failure data.

In addition the chapter contains several redundant system mathematical models. In these models it is assumed that each system component follows the bathtub hazard rate curve.

EXERCISES

3.1. An electronic component's reliability function, $R(t)$, is defined by

$$R(t) = e^{\frac{-1}{\theta} t^2}$$

where

θ is the scale parameter

t is time

Obtain an expression for the component hazard rate.

3.2. A system's hazard rate function, $\lambda(t)$, is defined by

$$\lambda(t)=\theta^{-1}\cdot\beta t^{\beta-1}$$

where

θ and β are the parameters

t is time

Obtain an expression for the system's reliability.

3.3. Assume that in the above exercise $\theta=\beta=1$ and $t=3$. Calculate the system's unreliability for a 20-hour mission.

3.4. In equation (3.11) by fixing the value of $\theta=1$ and varying a and t, plot the hazard rate function. Compare the hazard rate curves with the curves of the Weibull hazard rate shown in Figure 3.1.

3.5. Discuss the bathtub hazard rate curve concept. In equation (3.26) by setting $\beta=1$ and varying b and t, plot curves for the hazard rate. Comment briefly on the shape of these curves.

3.6. Describe briefly the difference between the terms failure rate and hazard rate.

NOTES

1. W. Nelson, "Hazard Plotting for Incomplete Failure Data," *Quality Technology,* vol. 1 (1969): 27-52.
2. B.S. Dhillon, "Life Distributions," *IEEE Transactions on Reliability* (1981): 369-75.
3. W.G. Ireson, ed., *Reliability Handbook* (New York: McGraw-Hill, 1966), pp. 4.58-4.61.
4. S. Gupta and P. Groll, "Gamma Distribution in Acceptance Sampling Based on Life Tests" *Journal of American Statistics Association* (1961): 942-70.
5. Z.W. Birnbaum and S.C. Saunders, "A New Family of Life Distributions," *Journal of Applied Probability,* vol. 6 (1969): 319-27.
6. B.S. Dhillon, "Bathtub Hazard Rate Modeling: An Investigation" *Proceedings of the Institute of Environmental Sciences Annual Meeting* (1982): 94-98.
7. B.S. Dhillon, "A Hazard Rate Model," *IEEE Transactions on Reliability,* vol. 28 (1979): 150.
8. B.S. Dhillon, "Network Reliability Evaluation: Application of Bathtub Failure Rate Curve," *Microelectronics and Reliability,* vol. 21 (1981): 103-11.

9. V.K. Murthy, "Realistic Models for Mortality Rates and Their Estimation," #PB-250638 NTIS: (Springfield, VA: NTIS, 1976), pp. 44, 9.
10. M.L. Shooman, *Probabilistic Reliability: An Engineering Approach,* (New York: McGraw-Hill, 1968), pp. 193–196.
11. P.M. Ghare and Y.H. Kim, "An Approximate Function for the Hazard Rate Curve," *American Society for Quality Control Technical Conference Proceedings* (1970): 367–73.
12. G.H. Sandler, *System Reliability Engineering* (Englewood Cliffs, N.J.: Prentice-Hall, 1963), pp. 98.
13. B.J. Flehinger and P.A. Lewis, "Two-Parameter Lifetime Distribution for Reliability Studies of Renewal Processes," *IBM Journal of Research and Development,* vol. 3 (1959): 58–73.
14. R.F. Drenick, "Mathematical Aspects of the Reliability Problem," *Journal of Social and Industrial Applied Mathematics,* vol. 8 (1960): 125–49.
15. J.W. Foster and W.T. Craddock, "Estimating Life Parameters from Burn-in Data," *Proceedings of the Annual Reliability and Maintainability Symposium* (1974): 206–09.
16. J.M. Cozzolino, "Probabilistic Models of Decreasing Failure Rate Processes," *Naval Research Logistics Quarterly,* vol. 15 (1968): 361–74.
17. S. Broadbent, "Simple Mortality Rates," *Applied Statistics,* vol. 7 (1958): 86–95.
18. B.S. Dhillon, "Statistical Functions to Represent Various Types of Failure Data," *Microelectronics and Reliability,* vol. 20 (1980): 581–84.
19. B.S. Dhillon, "New Hazard Rate Functions," *Microelectronics and Reliability,* vol. 19 (1980): 533–34.
20. B.S. Dhillon, "Hazard Rate Models for Failure Data Analysis," *Proceedings of the* 11th *Annual Pittsburgh Modeling and Simulation Conference* (1980): 1–4.

4

Introduction to Systems Engineering and Quality Control

This chapter briefly presents the important aspects of system engineering and quality control because both of these areas are closely related to reliability and maintainability. When a customer procures a system his or her expectations from that system are that it must fulfill its required functions successfully with certain reliability. Furthermore, the system's maintainability costs in the field should be at minimum. In order to make sure that a newly designed system will be less costly to maintain and will be reliable in the field, disciplines such as reliability, maintainability, and quality control play an important role in the system development and production phases.

The word "system" is derived from the Greek word "systema," which in turn is developed from the words "syn" and "histemi." The word "syn" means "together" and "histemi" means "to set." Schlager states that the world-reknowned Bell Telephone Laboratories may have been the first to make use of the term systems engineering.[1] After some literature search it is concluded that it may have been used in the early 1940s. To date many books and articles have been published on the subject.

The history of the application of statistical methods to inspection problems goes back to 1916; this work is credited to C.N. Frazee of Bell Telephone Laboratories. In 1924, W.A. Shewhart developed the quality control charts which are still widely used in quality control work. Another important aspect of statistical quality control, acceptance sampling by the method of variables, was applied for the first time in 1934 at Bell Telephone Laboratories. Since then several researchers and authors have contributed to the discipline of quality control.

SYSTEMS ENGINEERING

Characteristics Of A System

The important characteristics of a system are as follows:

1. A system may be subdivided into subsystems.
2. Subsystems interact: subsystem's outputs are inputs to other subsystems.
3. A complex grouping of humans and machines form a system.
4. A system has an objective. The objective is vital for the system to function correctly.
5. Systems usually form hierarchy structures.
6. In order to fulfill required objectives, a system has to be designed.

Systems Classifications

According to Blanchard and Fabrycky, the systems may be classified as to the following categories:

1. Physical systems
2. Natural systems
3. Man-created systems
4. Static systems
5. Conceptual systems
6. Closed systems
7. Dynamic systems
8. Open systems[2]

Since the above categories of systems are self-explanatory, they are not discussed here. However, they are discussed in Blanchard and Fabrycky.

Systems Approach Stages

This section briefly presents the guidelines in the application of systems engineering.

Below are four systems approach stages which are generally followed to tackle a system problem:

1. Analysis
2. Design
3. Implementation
4. Operation

♦ **ANALYSIS** In this phase the preliminary analysis is performed to see what is happening and if things can be improved. In addition, the definitions of the system objectives are established and the necessary data about its required performance is collected. The stages involved in system analysis are problem formulation, project organization, system definition, data collection, and so on.

♦ **DESIGN** The system design phase is concerned with items such as forecasting, reliability, optimization, control and model building, simulation, and so on. Once the system design stage is accomplished, the implementation stage begins.

♦ **IMPLEMENTATION** There are basically two steps involved in the implementation phase: approval and construction. In the first phase the system study results are approved for their implementation by the concerned bodies. Then the system is built.

♦ **OPERATION** Once the system is built and installed in the field, the operation stage begins. This phase is concerned with properly handing over the system to the user in the field environments, retrospective appraisal of the fielded system after an adequate operation period, and so on.

Models

Models are quite commonly used to analyze systems. There are various types of models which are used in the real world, however they may be categorized into the following four classifications:

Mathematical

Analog

Schematic

Physical[2]

♦ **MATHEMATICAL** The language of mathematics is used to develop the mathematical model of a system. In other words, equations and symbols are used to describe a system. The application of nearly all mathematical models is used either to control or to predict. Some examples of mathematical models are: linear programming models, queueing theory models, inventory control models, and reliability models.

♦ **ANALOG** The Greek work "analogia," whose meaning is proportion, is the base for the word analog. The similarity in meaning is the main idea behind analog modeling. For example, economic, mechanical, etc., systems may be represented by electric circuits. Furthermore, electronic analog computers are used to model various types of systems.

♦ **SCHEMATIC** The basic idea behind the development of a schematic model is to consider an event and reduce it to an understandable diagram. The vital aspects of the existing situation can easily be described by a schematic model. This is an important advantage of such a model. A chart denoting an organizational structure or a flow process chart are examples of schematic models.

♦ **PHYSICAL** Physical models, which are basically the visual geometric equivalents, become very useful in engineering, architecture, etc. These physical models may represent an item of either same size, larger size, or smaller size. Typical examples of such models are globes, an atomic structure model, a solar system model and a building model. These four types of models are described in detail in Blanchard and Fabrycky.[2]

QUALITY CONTROL

Terminology

This section presents the definitions of the terms commonly used in quality control.

♦ **QUALITY** In short, from the user point of view, quality may be defined simply as the fitness for use. Other definitions may be degree of excellence, meeting an expectation, and so on.

♦ **QUALITY CONTROL** According to MIL-STD-109 quality control is a management function which is exercised by controlling the quality of raw materials and manufactured goods in order to prevent manufacture of defective units.

Inspection lot—a class of similar items or materials offered at one time for the purpose of inspection and acceptance.[3]

Lot, batch—a definite quantity of items produced under the same conditions.

Lot size—the quantity of items in a given lot.

Statistical Techniques

There are basically two statistical techniques which are frequently used in quality control work: acceptance sampling and process control charts.

♦ **ACCEPTANCE SAMPLING** This technique is applied either to continuous production or to individual lots.[4] The main objective of continuous sampling is to ensure a given AOQL (i.e., average outgoing quality limit). This is accomplished by 100% sampling (when loss of control is experienced or at the initial stage of the inspection process) and by alternating periods of individual units' sampling. The continuous sampling procedure is utilized where production is continuous.

On the other hand, lot-by-lot sampling randomly selects the units of a product from a lot, and the quality of the samples examined is used to make a decision whether the entire lot is to be accepted or rejected.

The advantages and disadvantages of random sampling are as follows:

Advantages

1. Economical: only a portion of the entire product population is inspected.
2. Destructive testing application: it is used to destructive testing.
3. Reduces the manpower requirement: a lesser number of inspectors are needed.
4. Reduces the handling damage to product: during inspection the handling damage is less.
5. Entire lot rejection at the maufacturer's facility: this is a motivational factor for improvement of the product.

Disadvantages

1. More documentation.
2. Increase in planning.
3. Reduction in information on the product in question. Usually more information is gained from 100% inspection as against sampling.
4. Bad lot acceptance risks.
5. Good lot rejection risks.[5]

♦ **CONTROL CHARTS** These charts are used in quality control work to keep a process under a state of control (i.e., from the standpoint of statistical control). Control charts are very beneficial in identifying causes which have led a process to an out-of-control condition. The process performance data which is utilized in the control charts usually consists of groups of measurements.

Where no standard is known, the following procedure can be followed to construct a control chart:

1. Collect data: This can be accomplished by taking a series of samples from a process in question.
2. Keep records of process changes: Records of any process changes, such as operator, changes in material and tools, must be maintained.

3. Analyze the collected data and utilize it to calculate the trial limits of the control chart.
4. Plot data on the trial control chart: This step will be helpful in determining whether any of the samples are outside the established trial control limits.[5]

The two most commonly used control charts are:

1. p-chart: A p-chart records the fraction of defectives in samples taken periodically from a process in question. In comparison to an $\overline{X}$-R chart (a chart for variables), the p-chart is not that sensitive. In addition, to ascertain causes, the p-chart is not very helpful either.
2. $\overline{X}$-R chart: This chart records jointly the samples' mean ($\overline{X}$) and range (R). The samples are collected periodically from the process in question.

These two charts are described in detail in Juran et al. and in Hayes and Romig.

Department Functions

Below are the main functions of a quality control department:

1. Development of specifications and standards of the product.
2. Customer relations in regard to product quality.
3. Cost analysis in regard to quality.
4. Analysis and evaluation of the quality data.
5. Preparation of plans for inspection.
6. Audits in regard to product.
7. Preparation of reports on quality and reporting the quality results to concerned people.[5]

Functions of the quality control department are discussed in detail in Juran et al.

SUMMARY

This chapter summarizes the introductory aspects of systems engineering and quality control. The following aspects of both of these disciplines are presented: brief histories of both subjects, system properties and classifications, stages of the system approach, classifications of system modeling, terms used in quality control, quality control statistical techniques, advantages and disadvantages of sampling, quality control charts and functions of a quality control department.

EXERCISES

4.1. Discuss briefly the history of systems engineering and of quality control.

4.2. List and describe briefly the main properties of a system.

4.3. Describe acceptance sampling and quality control charts in detail.

4.4. What are the advantages and disadvantages of sampling in comparison to 100% sampling?

4.5. Describe the role of the quality control department.

NOTES

1. K.J. Schlager, "System Engineering—Key to Modern Development," *IRE Transactions on Engineering Management*, vol. 3 (1956): 64–66.
2. B.S. Blanchard and W.J. Fabrycky, *Systems Engineering and Analysis* (Englewood Cliffs, N.J.: Prentice-Hall, 1981): pp. 6-9.
3. *Glossary and Tables for Statistical Quality Control* (Milwaukee, WI: American Society for Quality Control, 1973) pp. 24.
4. *Generic Guidelines for Quality Systems*, American National Standard. (Milwaukee, WI: American Society for Quality Control, 19—), pp. 14.
5. J.M. Juran, F.M. Gryna and R.S. Bingham, ed., *"Quality Control Handbook"* (New York: McGraw-Hill, 1979): pp. 24.2.
6. G.E. Hayes and H.G. Romig, *Modern Quality Control* (Encino, CA: Bruce: a division of Benziger & Glencoe, 1977), pp. 115-326.

5

Basic Reliability Theory

The objective of this chapter is to present reliability evaluation measures of a single component. In the field of reliability engineering various measures of a single component's reliability have to be known before one can predict the reliability of a system. Furthermore, in real life some of the components may be repairable, while others may not be. Therefore, this chapter is concerned with reliability evaluation of single repairable and single non-repairable components.

BASIC FUNCTIONS

The basic functions associated with single components are presented in this section.

By definition the failure density function, $f(t)$, is given by

$$f(t) = \lim_{\Delta t \to 0} \frac{\overline{m}_0(t) - \overline{m}_0(t+\Delta t)}{m \cdot \Delta t} \tag{5.1}$$

where

- t is time
- Δt is the finite time interval
- m is the population size of identical components put on test at time $t=0$

$m_s(t)$ is the number of components survived at time t

$\overline{m}_0(t)$ is the expected value of $m_s(t)$, which is given by $m\,R(t)=\overline{m}_0(t)$, where $R(t)$ is the component's reliability at time t

Equation (5.1) may be rewritten to the form

$$f(t)=\frac{d\,F(t)}{dt}=-\frac{1}{m}\cdot\frac{d\,\overline{m}(t)}{dt} \tag{5.2}$$

where $F(t)$ is the cumulative distribution function. Similarly, the hazard rate, $\lambda(t)$, of a component is defined by:

$$\lambda(t)=\lim_{\Delta t\to 0}\frac{\overline{m}_0(t)-\overline{m}_0(t+\Delta t)}{\overline{m}_0(t)\cdot\Delta t}=\frac{f(t)\cdot m}{\overline{m}_0(t)} \tag{5.3}$$

Since $R(t)=\overline{m}_0(t)/m$, the above equation reduces to

$$\lambda(t)=\frac{f(t)}{R(t)}=\frac{f(t)}{1-F(t)} \tag{5.4}$$

because

$$R(t)+F(t)=\int_t^\infty f(x)\,dx+\int_0^t f(x)\,dx=1 \tag{5.5}$$

Rewriting equation (5.4) into the following form results in:

$$\lambda(t)=-\frac{d}{dt}\cdot \ln R(t) \tag{5.6}$$

Integrating both sides of equation (5.6) yields:

$$\ln R(t)=-\int_0^t \lambda(t)\cdot dt \tag{5.7}$$

Therefore

$$R(t)=e^{-\int_0^t \lambda(t)\cdot dt} \tag{5.8}$$

The component's mean time to failure (MTTF) is given by:

$$\text{MTTF}=\int_0^\infty t\,f(t)\cdot dt \tag{5.9}$$

Since $dR(t)/dt=-f(t)$, the above relationship is rewritten to the following form:

$$\text{MTTF}=-\int_0^\infty t\cdot\frac{dR(t)}{dt}\cdot dt \tag{5.10}$$

Integrating equation (5.10) by parts leads to:

$$\text{MTTF}=\int_0^\infty R(t)\,dt-\{t\,R(t)\}_0^\infty \tag{5.11}$$

In order to prove that the second right-hand term of equation (5.11) is equal to zero, we rewrite that term to the following form:

$$\left[\frac{t}{R^{-1}(t)}\right]_0^\infty \tag{5.12}$$

Therefore, substituting the limits in the above relationship leads to *at* $t=0$, $t\,R(t)=0$ and *at* $t=\infty$ for a finite mean. We assume that:

$$\lim_{t\to\infty}\,[t/R^{-1}(t)]=0 \tag{5.13}$$

Thus, since the second right-hand term of equation (5.11) is proven to be equal to zero, the component's MTTF is simply given by:

$$\text{MTTF}=\int_0^\infty R(t)\,dt \tag{5.14}$$

Mean Time to Failure of a Single Component

This section presents mean time to failure of a component whose failure probability density function may be defined by various statistical distribution functions such as those below.

♦ **EXPONENTIAL DISTRIBUTION** The failure probability density function, $f(t)$, of a component is defined by

$$f(t)=\lambda\, e^{-\lambda t} \tag{5.15}$$

for $t \geqslant 0$, where

t is time

λ is the component's constant failure rate

Rearranging equation (5.5) results in:

$$R(t)=1-\int_0^t f(x)\cdot dx \tag{5.16}$$

Substituting relationship (5.15) in equation (5.16) and integrating yields:

$$R(t)=e^{-\lambda t} \tag{5.17}$$

The component's mean time to failure is obtained by utilizing equation (5.17) in equation (5.14) and integrating:

$$\text{MTTF}=\int_0^\infty e^{-\lambda t}\,dt=\frac{1}{\lambda} \tag{5.18}$$

♦ **WEIBULL DISTRIBUTION** A component's failure probability density function, $f(t)$, is defined by

$$f(t)=\frac{b}{a}(t-\theta)^{b-1}\cdot e^{-(t-\theta)^b/a} \tag{5.19}$$

for $t \geqslant \theta, a>0, \theta \geqslant 0, b>0$; where

t is time

θ is the location parameter of the distribution

b is the distribution shape parameter

a is the scale parameter

The component reliability function, $R(t)$, by utilizing relationship (5.19) in equation (5.16), results in:

$$\begin{aligned} R(t) &= 1-\frac{b}{a}\int_0^t (x-\theta)^{b-1}\cdot e^{-(x-\theta)^b/a}\,dx \\ &= e^{-(t-\theta)^b/a} \end{aligned} \tag{5.20}$$

Thus, substituting equation (5.20) in equation (5.14), setting $\theta=0$, and integrating leads to the component's

$$\begin{aligned} \text{MTTF} &= \int_0^\infty e^{-\frac{1}{a}t^b}\,dt \\ &= a^{1/b}\,\Gamma(1+b^{-1}) \end{aligned} \tag{5.21}$$

♦ **RAYLEIGH DISTRIBUTION** This and the exponential distributions are the special cases of the Weibull distribution. Therefore, single component mean time to failure can be directly obtained from equation (5.21) by setting $b=2$. Thus:

$$\text{MTTF}=\sqrt{a}\,\Gamma(1.5) \tag{5.22}$$

The above equation yields the MTTF of a component whose failure times are Rayleigh distributed.

Similarly, setting $b=1$ and $a=1/\lambda$ in equation (5.21) leads to:

$$\begin{aligned} \text{MTTF} &= \frac{1}{\lambda}\Gamma(2) \\ &= \frac{1}{\lambda} \end{aligned} \tag{5.23}$$

We should note here that equation (5.23) is same as equation (5,18). Therefore, it proves that the exponential distribution is a special case of the Weibull distribution.

♦ **GAMMA DISTRIBUTION** A component failure time's probability density function, $f(t)$, is given by

$$f(t) = (1/a!b^{a+1})\, t^a e^{-t/b} \tag{5.24}$$

for $t > 0, b > 0, a > -1$; where

t is time

a is the shape parameter

b is the scale parameter

The single component reliability function is obtained by substituting equation (5.24) in equation (5.16) and integrating:

$$R(t) = 1 - (1/a!b^{a+1}) \int_0^{\infty} t^a e^{-t/b}\, dt$$

$$= 1 - (1/a!)\, \Gamma_{t/b}(\alpha + 1) \tag{5.25}$$

where $\Gamma_{t/b}(\alpha + 1)$ denotes the incomplete gamma function.

Thus, substituting equation (5.25) in relationship (5.14) and integrating yields the component's[1]

$$\text{MTTF} = b(a + 1) \tag{5.26}$$

By setting $a = 0$ and $b = 1/\lambda$ in equation (5.26), the resulting equation is the same as for the exponential distribution [see equation (5.18)]. In other words, the exponential distribution is a special case of the gamma distribution.

♦ **UNIFORM DISTRIBUTION** A component's failure probability density function, $f(t)$, is defined by

$$f(t) = \frac{1}{\beta - \theta} \tag{5.27}$$

for $\theta < t < \beta$, where θ and β are the distribution parameters.

Substituting equation (5.27) in equation (5.16) and integrating yields:

$$R(t) = \begin{cases} 1 \\ (\beta - t)/(\beta - \theta) \\ 0 \end{cases} \tag{5.28}$$

for $0 \leqslant t \leqslant \theta, \theta < t < \beta$, and $t \geqslant \beta$.

Thus, substituting equation (5.28) in equation (5.14) and integrating yields the component's

$$\text{MTTF} = (\beta + \theta)/2 \tag{5.29}$$

Example 5.1

A component's failure times are described by the probability density function

$$f(t) = (0.002)\, e^{-0.002\, t}$$

where t is time and $\lambda = 0.002$ failures/hour.

Calculate the mean time to failure of the component. By substituting directly the value of λ in equation (5.18), the result is:

$$\text{MTTF} = \frac{1}{0.002} = 500 \text{ hours}$$

NONREPAIRABLE SINGLE COMPONENT RELIABILITY EVALUATION MODELS

This section presents three Markov models to evaluate the reliability of a single nonrepairable component.

The following assumptions are associated with the Markov models:

1. The probability of two or more occurrences in the time interval Δt is very small; therefore it is neglected.
2. Occurrences are independent.
3. The occurrence probability of a transition from, say, state i to state $(i+1)$ in the time interval Δt is given by $\lambda \Delta t$, where λ is the constant transition rate.

Model I

This Markov model represents a nonrepairable component with a constant failure rate. The state space diagram of the component is given in Figure 5.1.

The following symbols are associated with the model:

$P_i(t)$ is the probability that the component is in state i at time t, for $i = 0, 1$

λ is the component's constant failure rate

Δt is the time interval

s is the Laplace transform variable

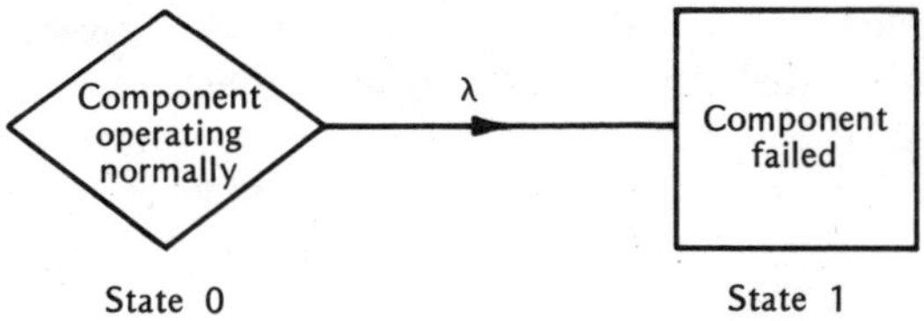

Figure 5.1 Component state-space diagram

The following transition equations are associated with Figure 5.1:

$$P_0(t+\Delta t)=P_0(t)(1-\lambda\Delta t) \tag{5.30}$$

$$P_1(t+\Delta t)=P_1(t)+P_0(t)\cdot\lambda\Delta t \tag{5.31}$$

The results of rearranging equations (5.30) and (5.31) and taking limit as $\Delta t \to 0$ are

$$\lim_{\Delta t\to 0} \frac{P_0(t+\Delta t)-P_0(t)}{\Delta t}=\frac{dP_0(t)}{dt}=-\lambda P_0(t) \tag{5.32}$$

and

$$\lim_{\Delta t\to 0} \frac{P_1(t+\Delta t)-P_1(t)}{\Delta t}=\frac{dP_1(t)}{dt}=P_0(t)\cdot\lambda \tag{5.33}$$

at $t=0, P_0(0)=1, P_1(0)=0$.

By taking the Laplace transforms of equations (5.32) and (5.33) and solving, the results are

$$P_0(s)=\frac{1}{s+\lambda} \tag{5.34}$$

and

$$P_1(s)=\frac{\lambda}{s(s+\lambda)} \tag{5.35}$$

Taking the inverse Laplace transform of equations (5.34) and (5.35) results in the following expressions:

$$P_0(t)=e^{-\lambda t} \tag{5.36}$$

and

$$P_1(t)=1-e^{-\lambda t} \tag{5.37}$$

We should note here that equation (5.36) is the same as equation (5.17), which is the component's reliability equation. The component's unreliability is given by equation (5.37).

The plots of equations (5.36) and (5.37) are shown in Figure 5.2.

Model II

This Markov model represents a situation where a component may fail in k mutually exclusive failure modes. The component's transition diagram is shown in Figure 5.3.

The following symbols were used to develop equations for the model:

k is the total number of failure modes of a component

$P_i(t)$ is the probability that component is in state i at time t, for $i = 0, 1, 2, 3, \ldots, k$

λ_i is the ith failure mode constant failure rate, for $i = 1, 2, 3, \ldots, k$

Δt is the time interval

s is the Laplace transform variable.

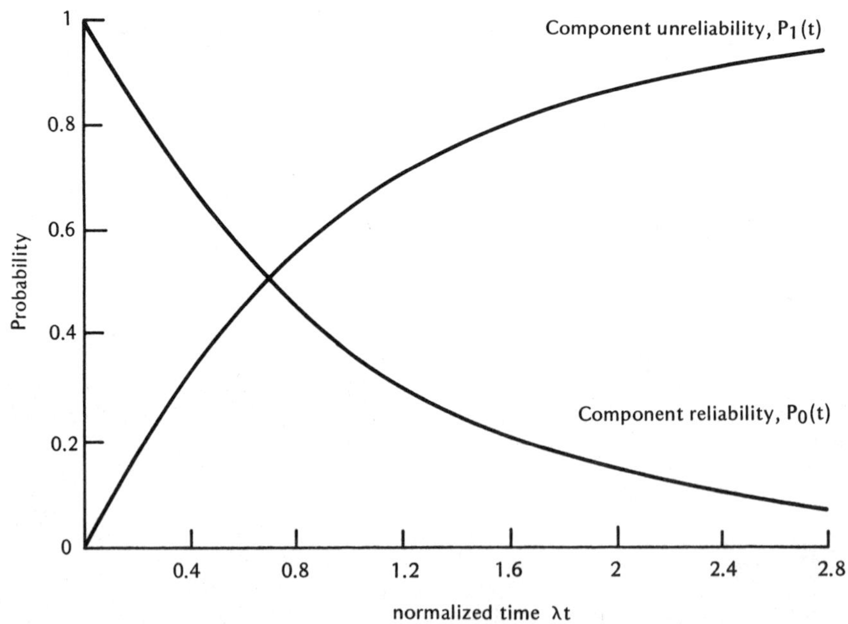

Figure 5.2 Plots of component reliability and unreliability

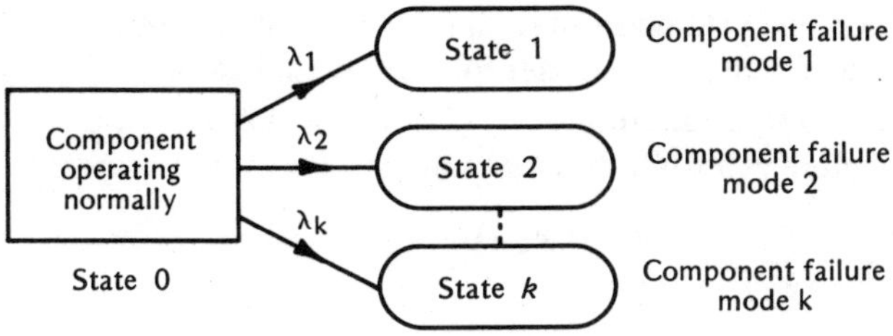

Figure 5.3 Transition diagram of a component with k failure modes

The following system of differential equations is associated with Figure 5.3:

$$\frac{dP_0(t)}{dt} = -\left(\sum_{i=1}^{k} \lambda_i\right) \cdot P_0(t) \tag{5.38}$$

$$\frac{dP_i(t)}{dt} = P_0(t) \cdot \lambda_i \tag{5.39}$$

at $t=0, P_0(0)=1, P_i(0)=0$ for $i=1,2,3,\ldots,k$.

The results of solving equations (5.38) and (5.39) with the Laplace transform technique are:

$$P_0(s) = \left(s + \sum_{i=1}^{k} \lambda_i\right)^{-1} \tag{5.40}$$

$$P_i(s) = \frac{\lambda_i}{s\left(s + \sum_{i=1}^{k} \lambda_i\right)} \quad \text{for } i=1,2,3,\ldots,k \tag{5.41}$$

Taking the inverse Laplace transforms of equations (5.40) and (5.41) leads to:

$$P_0(t) = e^{-\sum_{i=1}^{k} \lambda_i t} \tag{5.42}$$

$$P_i(t) = \frac{\lambda_i}{\sum_{i=1}^{k} \lambda_i}\left(1 - e^{-\sum_{i=1}^{k} \lambda_i t}\right) \quad \text{for } i=1,2,3,\ldots,k \tag{5.43}$$

Component reliability can be evaluated by utilizing equation (5.42). Similarly, component ith failure mode probability can be evaluated from equation (5.43).

Example 5.2

An electronic diode may fail either open or short-circuited. The open mode constant failure rate, $\lambda_1 = 0.001$ failures/day, and the short mode constant failure rate, $\lambda_2 = 0.002$ failures/day, are given. Calculate the diode's open mode and short mode failure probabilities for a 10-day mission.

The diode has two failure modes, therefore $k = 2$. The open mode and the short mode failure probabilities from equation (5.43) are, respectively:

$$P_1(t) = \frac{\lambda_1}{(\lambda_1 + \lambda_2)}\left(1 - e^{-(\lambda_1 + \lambda_2)t}\right)$$

$$P_1(10) = \frac{0.001}{0.001 + 0.002}\left\{1 - e^{-(0.001 + 0.002)(10)}\right\} = 0.0099 \tag{5.44}$$

and

$$P_2(t) = \frac{\lambda_2}{(\lambda_1 + \lambda_2)}\left(1 - e^{-(\lambda_1 + \lambda_2)t}\right)$$

$$P_2(10) = \frac{0.002}{0.001 + 0.002}\left\{1 - e^{-(0.001 + 0.002)(10)}\right\}$$

$$= 0.0197 \tag{5.45}$$

Thus, the diode mission open mode and short mode probabilities are 0.0099 and 0.0197, respectively.

Model III

This mathematical model represents a component which may fail partially or completely. In addition, from the partial failure state the component may also fail completely. The component's transition diagram is given in Figure 5.4.

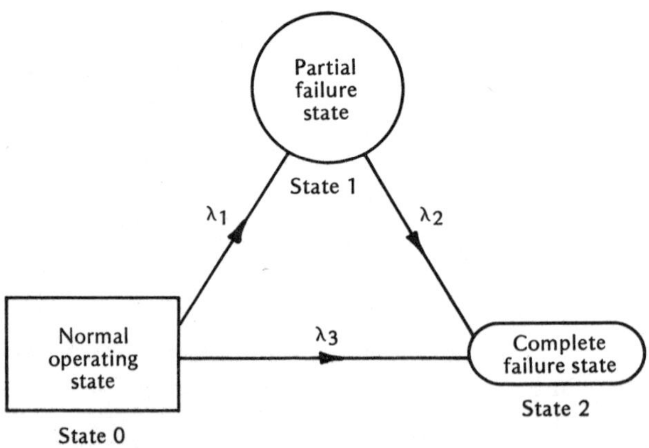

Figure 5.4 Component transition diagram

The following symbols are associated with this Markov model:

$P_i(t)$ is the probability that component is in state i at time t, for $i=0,1,2$

λ_1 is the component's constant failure rate from normal operating state to partial failure rate

λ_2 is the component's constant failure rate from partial failure state to complete failure state

λ_3 is the component's constant failure rate from normal operating state to complete failure state

Δt is the time interval

t is time

The following system of differential equations is associated with the model:

$$\frac{dP_0(t)}{dt}+(\lambda_1+\lambda_3)P_0(t)=0 \tag{5.46}$$

$$\frac{dP_1(t)}{dt}+\lambda_2 P_1(t)=\lambda_1 P_0(t) \tag{5.47}$$

$$\frac{dP_2(t)}{dt}=\lambda_2 P_1(t)+\lambda_3 P_0(t) \tag{5.48}$$

At $t=0, P_0(0)=1, P_1(0)=P_2(0)=0$.

The results of solving equations (5.46) through (5.48) are:

$$P_0(t)=e^{-(\lambda_1+\lambda_3)t} \tag{5.49}$$

$$P_1(t)=\frac{\lambda_1}{\lambda_1+\lambda_3-\lambda_2}\left(e^{-\lambda_2 t}-e^{-(\lambda_1+\lambda_3)t}\right) \tag{5.50}$$

$$P_2(t)=1-\frac{\lambda_3}{(\lambda_1+\lambda_3)}e^{-(\lambda_1+\lambda_3)t} + \frac{\lambda_1\lambda_2}{(\lambda_1+\lambda_3)(\lambda_1+\lambda_3-\lambda_2)}e^{-(\lambda_1+\lambda_3)t} - \frac{\lambda_1}{(\lambda_1+\lambda_3-\lambda_2)}e^{-\lambda_2 t} \tag{5.51}$$

The probability $P_{01}(t)$ that the component is in either an operational or a partially operational state is given by:

$$P_{01}(t)=P_0(t)+P_1(t)=e^{-(\lambda_1+\lambda_3)t}$$

$$+\frac{\lambda_1}{(\lambda_1+\lambda_3-\lambda_2)}\left(e^{-\lambda_2 t}-e^{-(\lambda_1+\lambda_3)t}\right) \tag{5.52}$$

REPAIRABLE SINGLE COMPONENT RELIABILITY EVALUATION MODELS

This section presents two Markov models of a single repairable component. The assumptions associated with the Markov technique were presented in the previous section.

Model I

This mathematical model represents a single component or a device which may fail in only one failure mode. The component or device's state-space diagram is shown in Figure 5.5.

The following assumptions are associated with the model:

1. The component's failure rate is constant.
2. The component's repair times are arbitrarily distributed.
3. The repaired component is as good as new.

The following symbols are used to develop equations for the model:

λ	is the constant failure rate of the component
$\mu(x)$, $q(x)$	are the repair rate (a hazard rate) and probability density function of repair time when component is in state 1 and has an elapsed repair time of x
$P_i(t)$	is the probability that component is in state i at time t, for $i = 0, 1$
$p_1(x,t)$	is the probability density (with respect to repair time) that the failed component is in state 1 and has an elapsed repair time of x
s	is the Laplace transform variable

By utilizing the supplementary variable technique presented in Cox and in Garg,[2,3] the following differential equations are associated with Figure 5.5:

$$\frac{dP_0(t)}{dt}+\lambda P_0(t)=\int_0^\infty p_1(x,t)\cdot\mu(x)\cdot dx \tag{5.53}$$

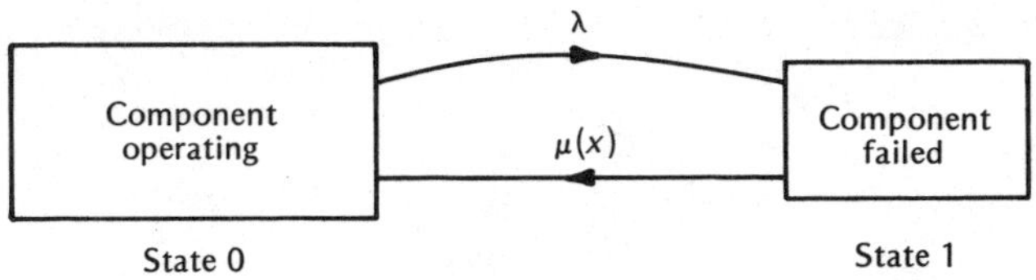

Figure 5.5 Repairable component transition diagram

$$\frac{\partial p_1(x,t)}{\partial t}+\frac{\partial p_1(x,t)}{\partial x}+\mu(x)\cdot p_1(x,t)=0 \tag{5.54}$$

$$p_1(0,t)=\lambda\cdot P_0(t) \tag{5.55}$$

at $t=0, P_0(0)=1, p_1(x,0)=0$

The result of solving equations (5.53) and (5.54) by Laplace transforms is

$$P_0(s)=\{s+\lambda-\lambda L(s)\}^{-1} \tag{5.56}$$

where

$$L(s)\equiv\int_0^\infty e^{-sx}\cdot q(x)\cdot dx \tag{5.57}$$

$$q(x)\equiv\mu(x)\cdot e^{-\int_0^x \mu(y)\cdot dy} \tag{5.58}$$

$$P_1(s)=\frac{\lambda}{\{s+\lambda-\lambda L(s)\}}\cdot\frac{\{1-L(s)\}}{s} \tag{5.59}$$

In equations (5.56) and (5.59) for known Laplace transform of the component repair time's density function, $L(s)$, generally the expressions for state probabilities $P_0(t)$ and $P_1(t)$ may be obtained.

Example 5.3

A component repair time's probability density function, $f(t)$, is defined by

$$f(t)=\mu_1 e^{-\mu_1 t} \tag{5.60}$$

where

μ_1 is the component constant repair rate

t is time

Obtain probability expressions for a component both in a normal operational state and in a failed state by utilizing equations (5.56) and (5.59), respectively.

By utilizing relationship (5.57), the Laplace transform of equation (5.60) is:

$$L(s)=\frac{\mu_1}{s+\mu_1} \tag{5.61}$$

Using equation (5.61) in equations (5.56) and (5.59) results in

$$P_0(s)=\frac{s+\mu_1}{s(s+\lambda+\mu_1)} \tag{5.62}$$

and

$$P_1(s)=\frac{\lambda}{s(s+\lambda+\mu_1)} \tag{5.63}$$

Taking the inverse Laplace transforms of equations (5.62) and (5.63) leads to:

$$P_0(t)=\frac{\mu_1}{\lambda+\mu_1}+\frac{\lambda}{\lambda+\mu_1}\, e^{-(\lambda+\mu_1)t} \tag{5.64}$$

$$P_1(t)=\frac{\lambda}{\lambda+\mu_1}\left\{1-e^{-(\lambda+\mu_1)t}\right\} \tag{5.65}$$

For very large t in equations (5.64) and (5.65), we get the component steady-state availability, A, and unavailability, UA, respectively, as follows:

$$A=P_0=\frac{\mu_1}{\lambda+\mu_1} \tag{5.66}$$

$$UA=P_1=\frac{\lambda}{\lambda+\mu_1} \tag{5.67}$$

Model II

This mathematical Markov model represents a repairable component which operates in the fluctuating weather environment.[4] In this situation, the component's failure and repair rates may be significantly different from one weather state to another. Therefore, this model takes into consideration these two factors. A typical example of such a model may be electrical components operating in an outdoor environment. The model state-space diagram is shown in Figure 5.6.

The following assumptions are associated with the model:

1. The component's failure and repair rates are constant.
2. The repaired component is as good as new.
3. The weather transition rates are constant.

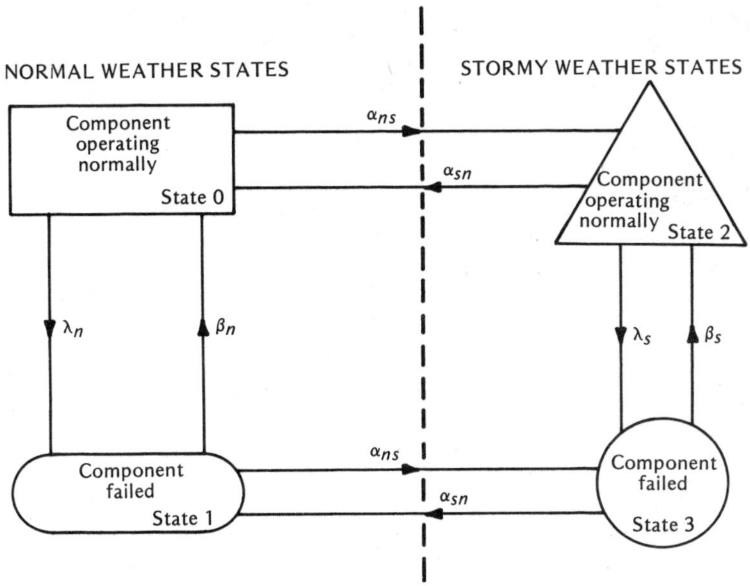

Figure 5.6 Component state-space diagram

The following symbols are associated with the model:

λ_n is the constant failure rate of the component in normal weather

λ_s is the constant failure rate of the component in stormy weather

β_n is the constant repair rate of the component in normal weather

β_s is the constant repair rate of the component in stormy weather

α_{ns} is the constant weather transition rate from normal weather to stormy weather

α_{sn} is the constant weather transition rate from stormy weather to normal weather

$P_i(t)$ is the probability that the component is in state i at time t, for $i=0$, 1,2,3

s is the Laplace transform variable

The following equations are associated with Figure 5.6:

$$\frac{dP_0(t)}{dt}+(\alpha_{ns}+\lambda_n)P_0(t)=P_1(t)\cdot\beta_n+P_2(t)\cdot\alpha_{sn} \tag{5.68}$$

$$\frac{dP_1(t)}{dt}+(\alpha_{ns}+\beta_n)P_1(t)=P_0(t)\cdot\lambda_n+P_3(t)\cdot\alpha_{sn} \tag{5.69}$$

$$\frac{dP_2(t)}{dt}+(\alpha_{sn}+\lambda_s)P_2(t)=P_0(t)\cdot\alpha_{ns}+P_3(t)\cdot\beta_s \tag{5.70}$$

$$\frac{dP_3(t)}{dt}+(\alpha_{sn}+\beta_s)P_3(t)=P_2(t)\cdot\lambda_s+P_1(t)\cdot\alpha_{ns} \tag{5.71}$$

at $t=0, P_0(0)=1$, and $P_1(0)=P_2(0)=P_3(0)=0$.

To obtain steady-state probabilities, set derivatives of equations (5.68) through (5.71) equal to zero as follows:

$$P_0(\alpha_{ns}+\lambda_n)-P_1\cdot\beta_n-P_2\cdot\alpha_{sn}=0 \tag{5.72}$$

$$P_1(\alpha_{ns}+\beta_n)-P_0\cdot\lambda_n-P_3\ \alpha_{sn}=0 \tag{5.73}$$

$$P_2(\alpha_{sn}+\lambda_s)-P_0\alpha_{ns}-P_3\cdot\beta_s=0 \tag{5.74}$$

$$P_3(\alpha_{sn}+\beta_s)-P_2\cdot\lambda_s-P_1\cdot\alpha_{ns}=0 \tag{5.75}$$

The following relationship has to be utilized to obtain expressions for P_0, P_1, P_2, and P_3:

$$P_0+P_1+P_2+P_3=1 \tag{5.76}$$

Thus, from equations (5.72) through (5.76) the component's steady-state probabilities are:

$$P_0=q_1\ \alpha_{sn}\ \{\lambda_{ns}(q_2+q_3)+\alpha_{sn}(q_4+q_1)\}^{-1} \tag{5.77}$$

where

$$q_2\equiv\beta_s\ q_5+\beta_n\alpha_{sn} \tag{5.78}$$

$$q_5\equiv\lambda_n+\alpha_{ns}+\beta_n \tag{5.79}$$

$$q_1\equiv q_6\ \beta_n+\beta_s\alpha_{ns} \tag{5.80}$$

$$q_6\equiv\lambda_s+\alpha_{sn}+\beta_s \tag{5.81}$$

$$q_3\equiv\lambda_n\alpha_{sn}+\lambda_s q_5 \tag{5.82}$$

$$q_4\equiv\lambda_n q_6+\lambda_s\alpha_{ns} \tag{5.83}$$

$$P_1=P_0\ \{\lambda_n q_6+\lambda_s\alpha_{ns}\}\ \{q_6\beta_n+\beta_s\alpha_{ns}\}^{-1} \tag{5.84}$$

$$P_2=\alpha_{sn}^{-1}\ \{q_6\beta_n+\beta_s\alpha_{ns}\}^{-1}\cdot\alpha_{ns}\ \{\beta_s q_5+\beta_n\alpha_{sn}\}\ P_0 \tag{5.85}$$

$$P_3=\alpha_{sn}^{-1}\ \{q_6\beta_n+\beta_s+\alpha_{ns}\}^{-1}\cdot\alpha_{ns}\ \{\lambda_n\alpha_{sn}+\lambda_s q_5\}\ P_0 \tag{5.86}$$

SUMMARY

This chapter presents basic functions such as failure probability density, hazard rate, reliability, and mean time to failure, in addition to various single component reliability evaluation models. Other topics discussed in the chapter are mean time to failure evaluation of a single component, nonrepairable single component reliability evaluation models, and repairable single component reliability evaluation models.

EXERCISES

5.1. A component's hazard function, $\lambda(t)$, is defined by

$$\lambda(t) = (\theta\, t^{\theta-1})/b^{\theta}$$

where

t is time

θ is the shape parameter

b is the scale parameter

Obtain an expression for the component's reliability.

5.2. For the given hazard rate function in the above exercise, obtain an expression for the component's mean time to failure.

5.3. The reliability function of a device is defined by:

$$R(t) = \exp\,[-(e^{a\,t^{\alpha}} - 1)]$$

Find the hazard rate function of the device.

5.4. An electronic part's failure times are described by a gamma probability distribution. Prove that the part's mean time to failure (MTTF) is given by

$$\text{MTTF} = \alpha(\beta + 1)$$

where

α is the scale parameter

β is the shape parameter

5.5. A fluid flow valve may fail in either open or closed mode. The open mode's constant failure and repair rates are λ_1 and μ_1, respectively. Similarly, the closed mode's constant failure and repair rates are λ_2 and μ_2, respectively. Find an expression for the valve's steady-state availability by applying the Markov modeling technique.

5.6. In equation (5.56), $L(s)$ is defined by

$$L(s)=\frac{\alpha^3}{(s+\alpha)^3}$$

where α is the distribution parameter.

Obtain an expression for $P_0(t)$ and the steady-state value of P_0 (if it exists). The symbol t denotes time.

NOTES

1. W.G. Ireson, ed., *Reliability Handbook* (New York: McGraw-Hill, 1966): pp. 4.37.
2. D.R. Cox, "The Analysis of Non-Markovian Stochastic Processes by the Inclusion of Supplementary Variables," *Proceedings Cambridge Philosophical Society,* vol. 61 (1955): 433–41.
3. R.C. Garg, "Dependability of a Complex System Having Two Types of Components," *IEEE Transactions on Reliability* vol. 12 (1963): 11–15.
4. R. Billington, *Power System Reliability Evaluation* (New York: Gordon and Breach 1970): pp. 180–183.

6

Reliability Evaluation of Systems Using Static Models

This chapter is concerned with reliability evaluation of systems whose subsystems' or components' reliabilities are constant. In the chapter title this is what is meant by the term "using static models." This type of analysis is generally a form of elementary or preliminary analysis. In this situation a complex system is represented by a block diagram which can be broken down into subsystem or component block diagrams. A typical system block diagram is shown in Figure 6.1. The small blocks denote system components.

RELIABILITY EVALUATION OF SIMPLE SYSTEMS

This section is concerned with the reliability evaluation of parallel, series, series-parallel, parallel-series, and standby systems. It is assumed that each component can be either in a successfully operating state or in a failed state.

Parallel Configuration Type I

A α unit parallel system is shown in Figure 6.2. In this configuration it is assumed that all the units are active and at least one unit is required for system success. In other words, the system fails only if all of its units malfunction.

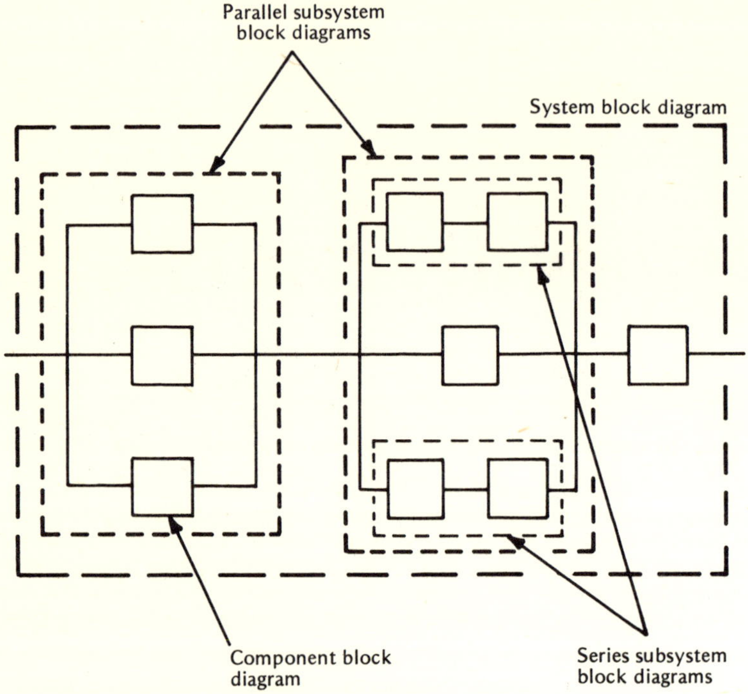

Figure 6.1 Typical system block diagram

The probability, R_p, that the parallel system operates successfully is given by:

$$R_p = P(E_1 + E_2 + \ldots + E_\alpha) \tag{6.1}$$

The right-hand term denotes probability of union of the successful events α. More clearly, E_i denotes an event that the parallel system's ith unit is functioning successfully. Since the probability of failure plus the probability of success of a system are always equal to unity, from expression (6.1) system unreliability, F_p (probability of failure), is given by:

$$F_p = 1 - R_p = 1 - P(E_1 + E_2 + \ldots + E_\alpha) \tag{6.2}$$

The above expression may be rewritten as

$$F_p = P(\bar{E}_1 \cdot \bar{E}_2 \cdot \bar{E}_3 \cdot \ldots \bar{E}_\alpha) \tag{6.3}$$

where the right-hand term denotes the probability of intersection of the α unsuccessful events. When the unit failures are independent, expression (6.3) simplifies to

$$F_p = P(\bar{E}_1) \cdot P(\bar{E}_2) \cdot P(\bar{E}_3) \cdot \ldots P(\bar{E}_\alpha) \tag{6.4}$$

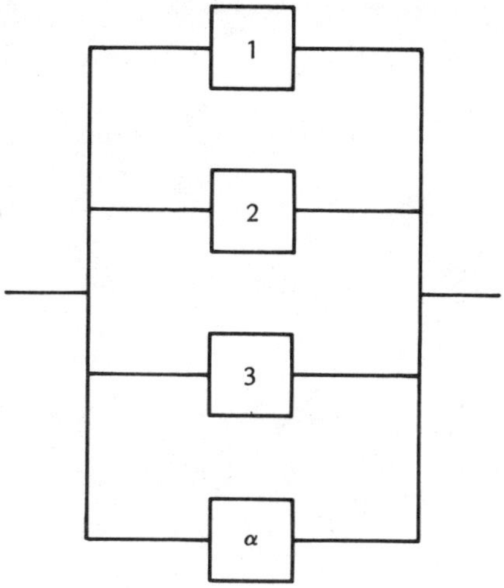

Figure 6.2 Parallel system composed of α units

where $P(\bar{E}_i)$ denotes the failure probability of unit i, for $i = 1, 2, 3, \ldots, \alpha$.

If we let $F_i = P(\bar{E}_i)$, equation (6.4) is rewritten to the following form:

$$F_p = \prod_{i=1}^{\alpha} F_i \tag{6.5}$$

Substracting equation (6.6) from unity yields the parallel system's reliability:

$$R_p = 1 - \prod_{i=1}^{\alpha} F_i \tag{6.6}$$

For identical units, equation (6.6) reduces to:

$$R_p = 1 - F^{\alpha} \tag{6.7}$$

This equation's plots are shown for $\alpha = 1, 2$, and 3 in Figure 6.3. It can be seen clearly from the reliability curves that as the total number of units in the system increases, system reliability increases accordingly.

Example 6.1

A parallel system is composed of four independent and active units. The unreliability of units 1, 2, 3, and 4 is 0.4, 0.3, 0.2, and 0.1, respectively. Calculate the system's reliability.

Utilizing the data in equation (6.6) results in:

$$R_p = 1 - F_1 \cdot F_2 \cdot F_3 \cdot F_4 = 1 - (0.4)(0.3)(0.2)(0.1)$$

$$= 0.9976$$

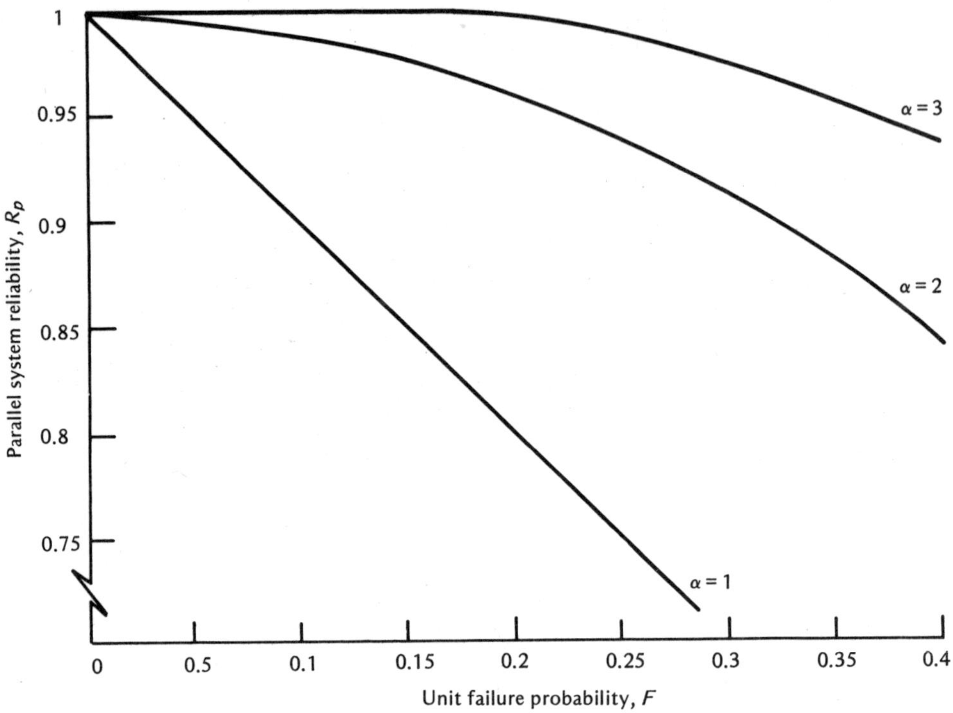

Figure 6.3 Parallel system reliability curves

Therefore, the system's reliability is 0.9976.

Series Configuration

Figure 6.4 shows a series system diagram. If any one of the units fails the system fails. In other words, all the units in the series system have to function successfully for the system's success.

The k unit series system's probability of success (reliability), P_s, is given by

$$P_s = P(E_1 \cdot E_2 \cdot E_3 \cdot \ldots E_k) \tag{6.8}$$

where the right-hand term denotes the probability of intersection of the k successful events. E_i denotes the event i that the series system's ith unit is operating normally, for $i = 1, 2, 3, \ldots, k$.

From equation (6.8), the series system's reliability, R_s, is rewritten to the following form:

$$R_s = P_s = P(E_1) \cdot P(E_2/E_1) \cdot P(E_3/E_1 \cdot E_2) \ldots P(E_k/E_1 \cdot E_2 \ldots E_{k-1}) \tag{6.9}$$

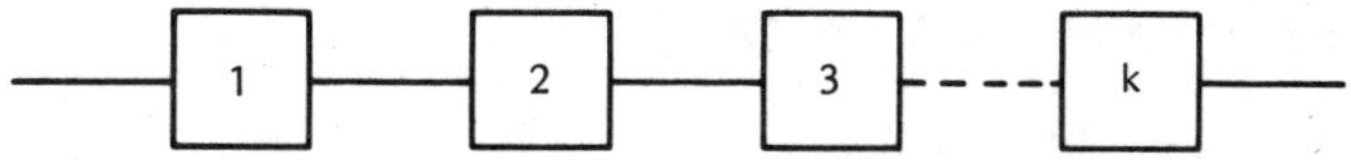

Figure 6.4 Series system

The above equation consists of conditional probabilities. For example, $P(E_2/E_1)$ signifies the probability of unit 2 functioning given that unit 1 is operating. If all the units fail independently, then equation (6.9) simplifies to:

$$R_s = P(E_1) \cdot P(E_2) \cdot P(E_3) \ldots P(E_k) \tag{6.10}$$

If we let $R_i = P(E_i)$ in equation (6.10), the resulting expression is

$$R_s = \prod_{i=1}^{k} R_i \tag{6.11}$$

where R_i is the ith unit's reliability, for $i = 1, 2, 3, \ldots, k$.

In the case of $R_i > 0.95$ for all elements in equation (6.11), system reliability may be approximated by the formula

$$R_s = 1 - \sum_{i=1}^{k} F_i \tag{6.12}$$

where F_i is the ith unit failure probability.

For identical units, equation (6.12) simplifies to:

$$R_s = 1 - kF \tag{6.13}$$

Example 6.2

Five independent electrical components form a series network. Component's 1, 2, 3, 4 and 5 failure probabilities are 0.05, 0.04, 0.03, 0.02, and 0.04, respectively. Calculate the system's reliability by using the approximated formula. Compare the result with the result obtained by using the exact formula.

Utilizing the given data in approximated equation (6.12) results in:

$$R_s = 1 - (0.05 + 0.04 + 0.03 + 0.02 + 0.04) = 0.84$$

Using the data in equation (6.1) leads to the exact system reliability result:

$$R_s = (1 - F_1)(1 - F_2)(1 - F_3)(1 - F_4)(1 - F_5)$$

$$= 0.8323$$

The above results indicate that the approximated formula has predicted optimistic system reliability.

Parallel Configuration Type II

This configuration is exactly the same as parallel configuration type I, with one exception: instead of requiring at least one unit for the system's success, now at least k units out of α units are needed for the system to function successfully. For identical units, the parallel configuration type II reliability, $R_{k/\alpha}$ is given by

$$R_{k/\alpha} = \sum_{i=k}^{\alpha} \binom{\alpha}{i} (1 - R)^{\alpha-i} \cdot R^i \quad (6.14)$$

where R is the unit's reliability.

$$\binom{\alpha}{i} = \frac{\alpha!}{i!(\alpha - i)!} \quad (6.15)$$

Figure 6.5 shows the plots of equation (6.14) for $k=1, \alpha=3$ (three-unit parallel system); $k=3$, $\alpha=3$ (three-unit series system); and $k=2$, $\alpha=3$ (2-out-of-3 units sytem). It can be seen from these plots that the system's reliability is highest when only one unit out of three units is required for system success.

Example 6.3

A parallel system is composed of three independent and active units. At least two units must be functioning successfully for system success. The reliability

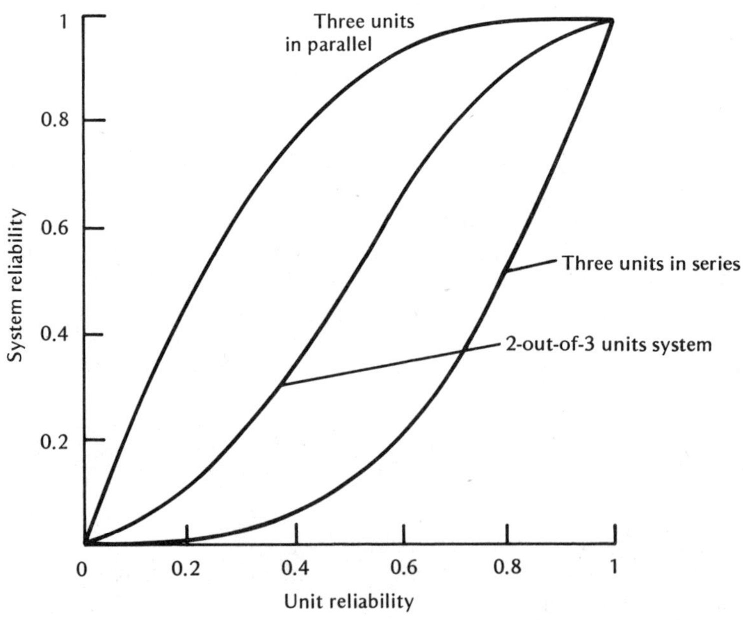

Figure 6.5 Reliability plots of a three-unit system

of units 1, 2, and 3 is 0.8, 0.9, and 0.7, respectively. Calculate the system's reliability.

Using the binomial formula for three nonidentical units we get

$$(R_1+F_1)(R_2+F_2)(R_3+F_3)=1 \tag{6.16}$$

where

R_i is the ith unit's reliability, for $i=1, 2, 3$

F_i is the ith unit's unreliability, for $i=1, 2, 3$

Expanding the left-hand side of equation (6.16), leads to

$$R_1R_2R_3+R_1R_3F_2+R_2R_3F_1+R_1R_2F_3+R_1F_2F_3+R_2F_1F_3 \\ +F_1F_2R_3+F_1F_2F_3 \tag{6.17}$$

Since at least two units operating normally are needed for system success, the sum of the first four terms yields the system's reliability

$$R_{2/3}=R_1R_2R_3+R_1R_3F_2+R_2R_3F_1+R_1R_2F_3 \tag{6.18}$$

Since $(R_1+F_1)=1$, $(R_2+F_2)=1$, and $(R_3+F_3)=1$, equation (6.18) is rewritten to the following form:

$$R_{2/3}=R_1R_2R_3+R_1R_3(1-R_2)+R_2R_3(1-R_1)+R_1R_2(1-R_3) \tag{6.19}$$

Utilizing the data in equation (6.19) results in:

$$\begin{aligned} R_{2/3} &= (0.8)(0.9)(0.7)+(0.8)(0.7)(1-0.9)+(0.7)(0.9)(1-0.8) \\ &\quad +(0.8)(0.9)(1-0.7) \\ &= 0.504+0.056+0.126+0.216 \\ &= 0.902 \end{aligned}$$

Series-Parallel Configuration

In the series-parallel network in Figure 6.6 the network or system is composed of k independent and active subsystems or networks in a series. If any one of these subsystems fails, the entire system fails. Each subsystem contains r number of independent units in parallel. From equation (6.6) the jth parallel subsystem's reliability, R_{pj}, is

$$R_{pj}=1-\prod_{i=1}^{r} F_{ji} \tag{6.20}$$

where F_{ji} is the jth subsystem ith unit's unreliability.

Thus, substituting equation (6.20) in equation (6.11) leads to the following series-parallel network reliability:

$$R_{sp} = \prod_{j=1}^{k} R_{pj} = \prod_{j=1}^{k} \left(1 - \prod_{i=1}^{r} F_{ji}\right) \tag{6.21}$$

For identical subsystems, equation (6.21) simplifies to

$$R_{sp} = \{1 - F^r\}^k \tag{6.22}$$

where F is the unit's unreliability.

Example 6.4

A system is composed of two independent, identical, and active subsystems in a series. Each subsystem consists of two identical units in parallel. The unit's failure probability is 0.2. Calculate the system's reliability.

Utilizing the data given in equation (6.22) yields:

$$R_{sp} = \{1 - (0.2)^2\}^2$$

$$= 0.9216$$

Parallel-Series Configuration

The block diagram of the configuration is shown in Figure 6.7. Basically, the network is composed of r independent and active subsystems in parallel. Each series subsystem contains k independent units. Only one subsystem functioning successfully is needed for system success.

The reliability, R_{si}, of subsystem j from equation (6.11) is

$$R_{sj} = \prod_{j=1}^{k} R_{ji} \tag{6.23}$$

where R_{ji} denotes the jth subsystem's ith unit's reliability.

Substituting equation (6.23) in equation (6.6) leads to the following parallel-series network reliability expression:

$$R_{ps} = 1 - \prod_{j=1}^{r} (1 - R_{sj})$$

$$= 1 - \prod_{j=1}^{r} \left(1 - \prod_{i=1}^{k} R_{ji}\right) \tag{6.24}$$

For identical subsystems, the above expression becomes

$$R_{ps} = 1 - (1 - R^k)^r \tag{6.25}$$

where R is the unit's reliability.

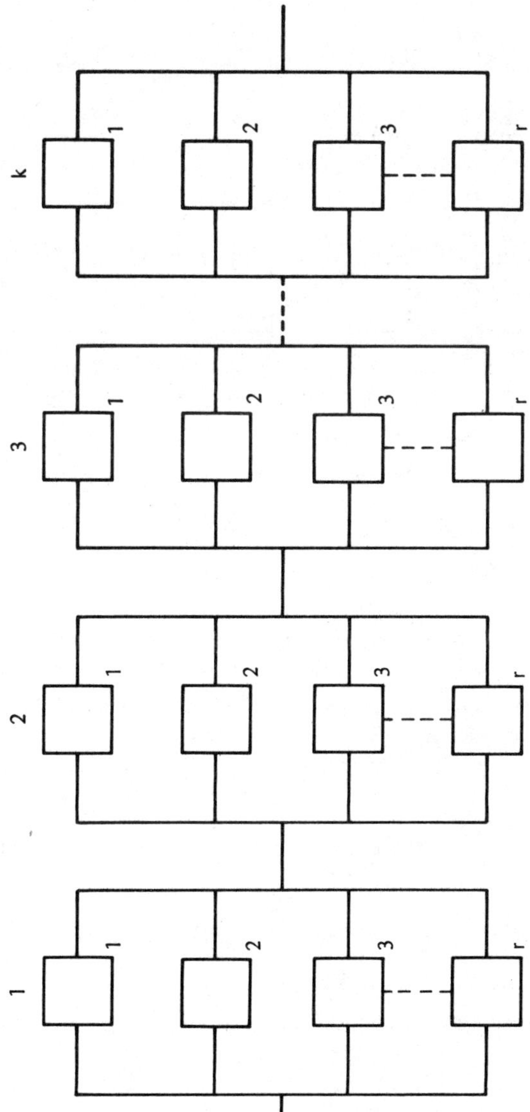

Figure 6.6 Series-parallel network

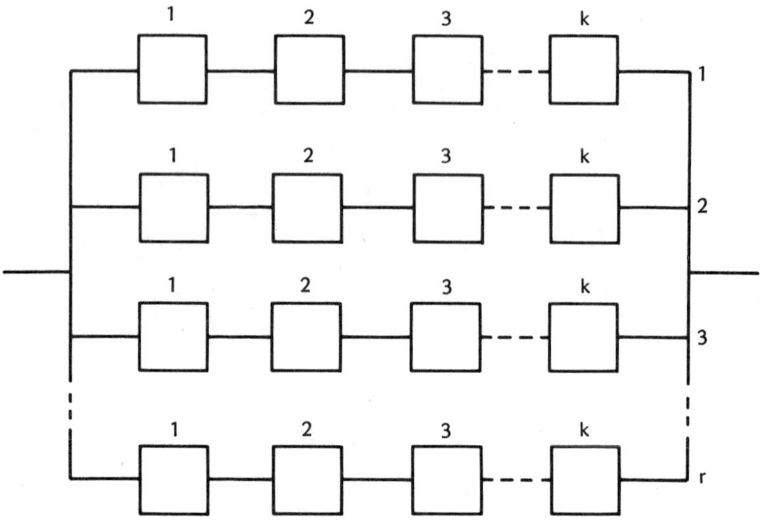

Figure 6.7 Parallel-series network

Example 6.5

A parallel system is composed of three independent, identical, and active subsystems. At least one subsystem is required to function normally for system success. Each subsystem is composed of three independent units in a series. The unit's reliability is 0.7. Calculate the system's reliability.

Substituting this data into equation (6.25) yields the system's reliability:

$$R_{ps} = 1 - \{1 - (0.7)^3\}^3$$

$$= 0.7164$$

Standby System

The diagram of a two-unit standby system is given in Figure 6.8. The diagram shows two units (one operating and the other on standby) and one switch. As soon as the operating unit fails, the standby unit is switched in. However, the switch may fail in two failure modes: activate prematurely, or fail to activate when it should.

The system may fail in the following three ways:

1. The switch correctly switches in unit 2 when unit 1 fails, nevertheless unit 2 fails.
2. Unit 1 is operating normally, however the switch activates prematurely and the standby (unit 2) fails.

3. The operating unit fails and the switch fails to switch in the standby unit.[1]

Thus system unreliability, F_{ss}, is expressed as

$$F_{ss} = R_1 \cdot F_2 \cdot F_3' + F_1 F_2 R_3 + F_1 F_3 \qquad (6.26)$$

where

- R_1 is the reliability of operating unit 1
- F_1 is the unreliability of operating unit 1
- F_2 is the unreliability of standby unit 2.
- F_3 is the probability of switch failure (failed to activate when needed)
- F_3' is the probability of premature switch activation
- R_3 is the switch's reliability which is given by $(1 - F_3)$

To obtain an expression for system reliability, R_{ss}, subtract equation (6.26) from unit as follows:

$$R_{ss} = 1 - \{R_1 F_2 F_3' + F_1 F_2 R_3 + F_1 F_3\} \qquad (6.27)$$

Example 6.6

A standby system consists of two identical units and one switch. Each unit's reliability is 0.85, and the switch's probability of failure when needed is 0.02. In addition, the probability of premature switch activation is 0.06. Calculate the system's reliability.

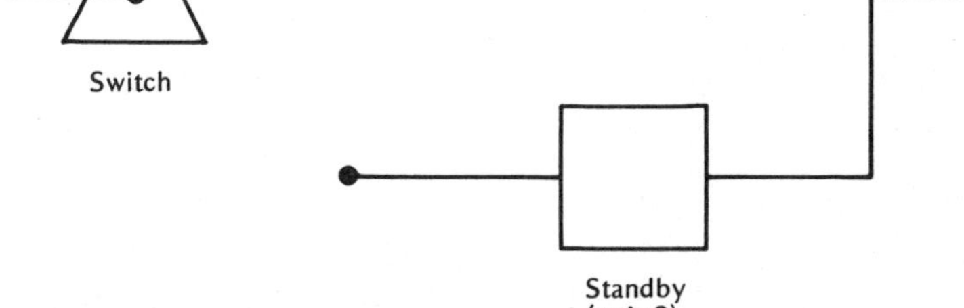

Figure 6.8 Two-unit standby system

Substituting the above data into equation (6.27) yields:

$$R_{ss} = 1 - \{(0.85)(0.15)(0.06) + (0.15)^2 (0.98) + (0.15)(0.02)\}$$

$$= 0.967$$

RELIABILITY EVALUATION OF COMPLEX SYSTEMS

This section is concerned with reliability evaluation of complex systems composed of one and two failure mode devices.

Complex System Type I

This is simply a five-unit bridge network whose block diagram is shown in Figure 6.9. The network is neither a series network nor a parallel network; therefore, equations developed in previous sections of this chapter cannot be directly applied to the bridge network to evaluate its reliability. However, the delta-star and decomposition approaches can be used to evaluate the reliability of such a network.[2,3] Here we will evaluate its reliability by utilizing the decomposition procedure.

In this approach a complex reliability system is decomposed into simpler subsystems with a conditional probability theorem which is applied successively to each subsystem. To obtain the complex system's reliability, the end results of the subsystems' probability are combined.

The starting point of the technique is selection of the key element (unit or component), say, E_c. Once this is decided, then the complex system reliability,

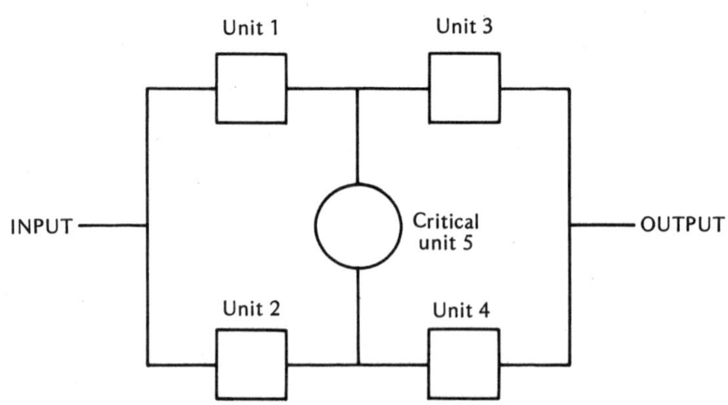

Figure 6.9 Bridge network

R_{cs}, expression can be written in terms of E_c. Complex system reliability is given by

$$R_{cs} = P(E_c) \cdot P(\text{complex system good}/E_c \text{ good}) + P(\bar{E}_c) \cdot P(\text{complex system good}/E_c \text{ bad}) \quad (6.28)$$

where

$P(\text{complex system good}/E_c \text{ good})$	is the system's probability of success when the key element is 100% reliable.
$P(\text{complex system good}/E_c \text{ bad})$	is the system's probability of success when the key element is 100% bad (assume it is removed from the complex system)
$P(E_c)$	is the key element's probability of success
$P(\bar{E}_c)$	is the key element's probability of failure

Now, if we assume that in Figure 6.9 key element E_c is the critical unit 5, by utilizing expressions (6.28), (6.21), and (6.24) the following bridge system reliability, R_{cs}, results

$$R_{cs} = R_5 [1-(1-R_1)(1-R_2)] [1-(1-R_3)(1-R_4)] + (1-R_5) [1-(1-R_1R_3)(1-R_2R_4)] \quad (6.29)$$

where

R_5 is the key element's (critical unit 5) reliability

R_i is the ith bridge unit's reliability, for $i = 1, 2, 3, 4$

For identical elements, equation (6.29) reduces to:

$$R_{cs} = 2R^5 - 5R^4 + 2R^3 + 2R^2 \quad (6.30)$$

The plot of equation (6.30) is shown in Figure 6.10, along with a plot of equation (6.7) for $\alpha = 5$. Both of these curves show that system reliability is greater when five identical units form a parallel configuration than when they form a bridge configuration.

Example 6.7

Figure 6.9 shows a five independent electrical unit bridge network. Units' 1, 2, 3, 4, and 5 reliabilities are 0.9, 0.8, 0.7, 0.9, and 0.8, respectively. Find the bridge system's reliability.

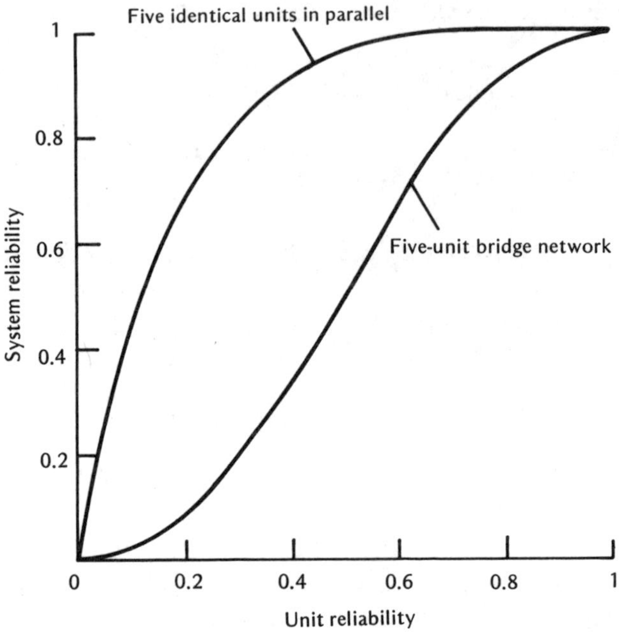

Figure 6.10 System reliability plot

By substituting the given data into equation (6.29), the system's reliability is:

$$R_{cs} = 0.9\,[1-(1-0.9)(1-0.8)]\;[1-(1-0.7)(1-0.9)] + (1-0.9)$$
$$[1-\{1-(0.9)(0.7)\}\;\{1-(0.8)(0.9)\}]$$
$$= 0.9(0.98)(0.97) + 0.1(0.8964)$$
$$= 0.7659$$

Complex System Type II

This network is composed of independent series and parallel configurations. Each independent unit of the network may fail in two mutually exclusive failure modes, say, open mode and short mode. A typical example of such a unit is an electronic diode. The network diagram is given in Figure 6.11.

In the figure the symbols F_{0i} and F_{si} denote the ith unit's open mode and short mode failure probabilities, respectively, for $i = 1, 2, 3, \ldots, 7$. The relationship below is used to compute two failure mode unit series and parallel network reliabilities

$$\prod_{i=1}^{k} (R_i + F_{0i} + F_{si}) = 1 \tag{6.31}$$

where

k is the number of units

R_i is the ith unit's reliability

Expression (6.31) is for nonidentical k units. However, for identical k units that expression simplifies to:

$$(R + F_0 + F_s)^k = 1 \tag{6.32}$$

For $k = 2$, the left-hand side of equation (6.32) becomes:

$$(R + F_0 + F_s)^2 = R^2 + 2RF_s + 2RF_0 + F_0^2 + 2F_0F_s + F_s^2 \tag{6.33}$$

In the case of a series network, the two-unit system reliability, R_{ss}, from the first two right-hand terms of equation (6.33) is:

$$R_{ss} = R^2 + 2RF_s \tag{6.34}$$

The above equation is based on the fact that if one of the electrical components (electronic diode) of a series network fails in short mode, the series system can still operate normally because the current can still pass through the short-circuited component.

Since

$$R + F_0 + F_s = 1 \tag{6.35}$$

substituting from the above relationship for R in equation (6.34) leads to:

$$R_{ss} = (1 - F_0)^2 - F_s^2 \tag{6.36}$$

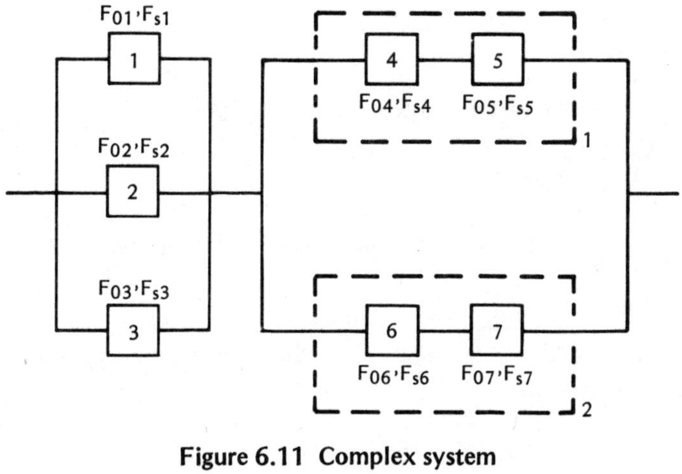

Figure 6.11 Complex system

Similarly, for k independent units in a series, the system reliability from equation (6.36) is generalized to the following form:[2]

$$R_{ss} = (1 - F_0)^k - F_s^k \tag{6.37}$$

For nonidentical k units, the above equation becomes:

$$R_{ss} = \prod_{i=1}^{k} (1 - F_{0i}) - \prod_{i=1}^{k} F_{si} \tag{6.38}$$

Similarly, from equation (6.33) for nonidentical k component series network, open mode failure probability, F_{s0}, and short mode failure probability, F_{ss}, are given by

$$F_{s0} = 1 - \prod_{i=1}^{k} (1 - F_{0i}) \tag{6.39}$$

and

$$F_{ss} = \prod_{i=1}^{k} F_{si} \tag{6.40}$$

Because of duality, the corresponding parallel network formulas from equations (6.38) through (6.40) are as follows:

$$R_{ps} = \prod_{i=1}^{m} (1 - F_{si}) - \prod_{i=1}^{m} F_{0i} \tag{6.41}$$

where

m is the number of units in parallel

R_{ps} is the parallel system's reliability

$$F_{p0} = \prod_{i=1}^{m} F_{0i} \tag{6.42}$$

where F_{p0} is the parallel network's open mode failure probability; and

$$F_{ps} = 1 - \prod_{i=1}^{m} (1 - F_{si}) \tag{6.43}$$

where F_{ps} is the parallel network's short mode failure probability.

Example 6.8

Obtain an expression for the reliability of the independent component network shown in Figure 6.11.

In this figure two series subsystems, 1 and 2, are shown in dotted lines and their open mode and short mode failure probabilities utilizing equations (6.39) and (6.40), respectively, are as follows:

Series Subsystem 1

$$F_{s01} = 1 - (1 - F_{04})(1 - F_{05}) \tag{6.44}$$

$$F_{ss1} = F_{s4} \cdot F_{s5} \tag{6.45}$$

where

F_{s01} is subsystem 1's open mode failure probability

F_{ss1} is subsystem 1's short mode failure probability

Series Subsystem 2

$$F_{s02} = 1 - (1 - F_{06})(1 - F_{07}) \tag{6.46}$$

$$F_{ss2} = F_{s6} \cdot F_{s7} \tag{6.47}$$

where

F_{s02} is subsystem 2's open mode failure probability

F_{ss2} is subsystem 2's short mode failure probability

Thus, the network in Figure 6.11 is reduced to the one shown in Figure 6.12.

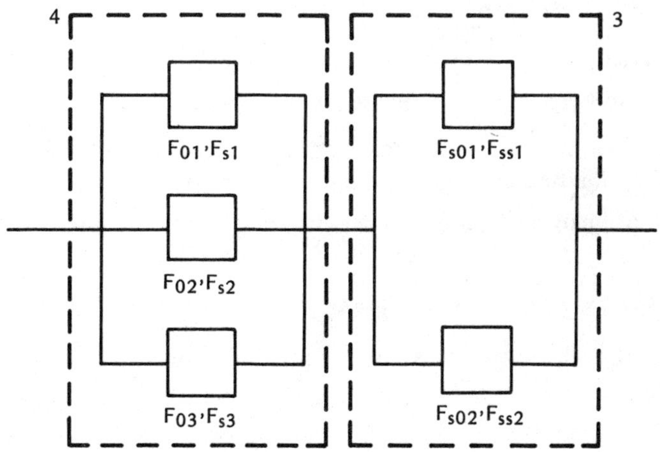

Figure 6.12 Reduced network

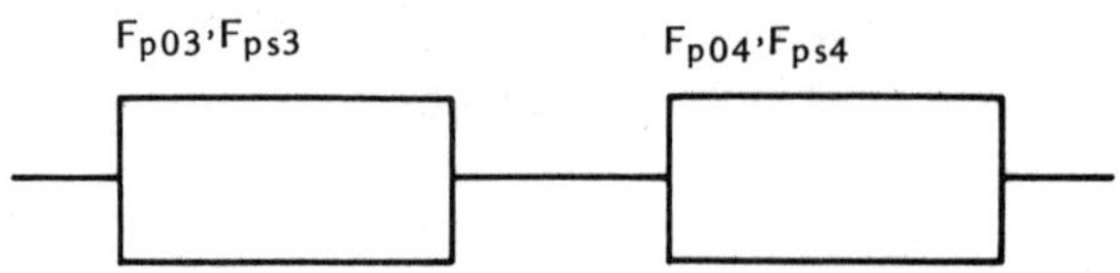

Figure 6.13 Simplified series network

In Figure 6.12 parallel subsystems 3 and 4 are shown in dotted lines and their open mode and short mode failure probabilities utilizing equations (6.42) and (6.43), respectively, are as follows:

Parallel Subsystem 3

$$F_{p03} = F_{s01} \cdot F_{s02} \tag{6.48}$$

$$F_{ps3} = 1 - (1 - F_{ss1})(1 - F_{ss2}) \tag{6.49}$$

where

F_{p03} is subsystem 3's open mode failure probability

F_{ps3} is subsystem 3's short mode failure probability

Parallel Subsystem 4

$$F_{p04} = F_{01} \cdot F_{02} \cdot F_{03} \tag{6.50}$$

$$F_{ps4} = 1 - (1 - F_{s1})(1 - F_{s2})(1 - F_{s3}) \tag{6.51}$$

where

F_{p04} is subsystem 4's open mode failure probability

F_{ps4} is subsystem 4's short mode failure probability

Thus, utilizing the results of equations (6.48) through (6.51) Figure 6.12's network is simplified to the one given in Figure 6.13.

By utilizing equation (6.38), the reliability, R_{ts}, of the network in Figure 6.13 is given by:

$$R_{ts} = (1 - F_{p03})(1 - F_{p04}) - F_{ps3} \cdot F_{ps4} \tag{6.52}$$

Therefore, the reliability of the network given in Figure 6.11 can be calculated by utilizing equation (6.52).

SUMMARY

This chapter covers the reliability evaluation of networks whose components' reliabilities are constant. The following types of systems are analyzed: series, parallel, series-parallel, parallel-series, standby, bridge, and two failure mode networks. In addition, the decomposition and network reduction techniques are presented.

EXERCISES

6.1. A series system is composed of 10 independent and identical components. Each component's failure probability is 0.09. Calculate the system's reliability.

6.2. A system is composed of four independent active units forming a parallel configuration. At least three units are needed for system success. Unit's 1, 2, 3, and 4 reliabilities are 0.9, 0.95, 0.85, and 0.8, respectively. Calculate the probability of system failure.

6.3. Develop an expression for the system reliability of the independent unit network shown in Figure 6.14. In the diagram, R_i denotes the ith unit's reliability, for $i = 1, 2, \ldots, 8$.

6.4. Calculate the unreliability of the network given in Figure 6.15. Each unit's reliability is given in the network block diagram.

6.5. A parallel network is composed of five identical and independent two failure mode (open and short) devices. Each device's open and short mode failure probabilities are 0.05 and 0.02, respectively. Calculate the network's unreliability.

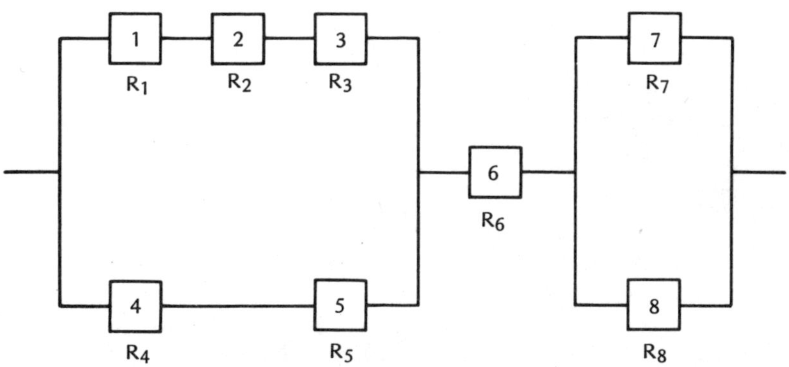

Figure 6.14 Reliability network

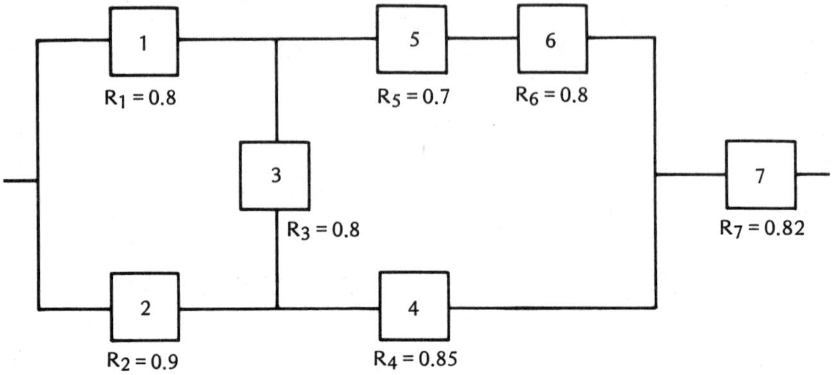

Figure 6.15 Complex network

NOTES

1. *Quality Assurance-Reliability Handbook*, AMCP 702-3. (Headquarters, U.S. Army Material Command, Oct. 1968), pp. D6–D13.
2. B.S. Dhillon, *The Analysis of the Reliability of Multi-State Device Networks*, Ph.D. thesis (1975), pp. 121–130.
3. M.L. Shooman, *Probabilistic Reliability: An Engineering Approach* (New York: McGraw-Hill, 1968), pp. 135–136.

7

Reliability Tools

The objective of this chapter is twofold. The first is to perform time-dependent analysis of selective networks presented in chapter 6. The time-dependent analysis is very important because generally it is assumed that an item's reliability is a function of time, i.e., with use the item's reliability decreases. The second objective is to present selected reliability topics such as reliability growth modeling, software reliability modeling, confidence limits for mean time between failures, Markov modeling, and system reliability evaluation with the joint-density function approach.

TIME-DEPENDENT ANALYSIS OF RELIABILITY NETWORKS

This section presents the time-dependent reliability analysis of certain networks presented in chapter 6. From chapter 3 the time-dependent reliability, $R(t)$, of an item is given by

$$R(t)=e^{-\int_0^t \lambda(x)\cdot dx} \tag{7.1}$$

where

t is time

$\lambda(t)$ is the item's hazard rate or the instantaneous failure rate

Also from chapter 3, the mean time to failure, MTTF, is defined by

$$\text{MTTF}=\int_0^\infty R(t)\,dt \tag{7.2}$$

Equation (7.2) developed in Laplace transform is as follows:[1]

$$\mathrm{MTTF} = \lim_{t \to \infty} \left[\int_0^t R(x) \cdot dx \right] \tag{7.3}$$

The Laplace transform of the term given in brackets in equation (7.3) is

$$\mathcal{L} \left[\int_0^t R(x) \cdot dx \right] = \frac{r(s)}{s} \tag{7.4}$$

where

s is the Laplace transform variable

$r(s)$ is the Laplace transform of the reliability function $R(t)$

The Laplace transform of the final value theorem is

$$\lim_{t \to \infty} f(t) = \lim_{s \to 0} s\, F(s) \tag{7.5}$$

where

$f(t)$ is a function

$F(s)$ is the Laplace transform of function $f(t)$

Thus, substituting relationships (7.4) and (7.5) in equation (7.3) results in:

$$\mathrm{MTTF} = \lim_{s \to 0} r(s) \tag{7.6}$$

Example 7.1

An item's hazard rate is defined by the function

$$\lambda(t) = (k\, t^{k-1})/\theta \tag{7.7}$$

where

k is the shape parameter

θ is the scale parameter

t is time

Obtain an expression for the item's reliability and mean time to failure.

The result of substituting equation (7.7) in equation (7.1) and integrating is:

$$R(t) = e^{-\frac{1}{\theta} \int_0^t (k\, t^{k-1})\, dt}$$

$$= e^{-\frac{1}{\theta} t^k} \tag{7.8}$$

Thus, substituting equation (7.8) in equation (7.2) and integrating leads to item mean time to failure:

$$\text{MTTF} = \int_0^\infty e^{-\frac{1}{\theta}t^k}\,dt$$
$$= \frac{\Gamma(1/k)}{k\left(\frac{1}{\theta}\right)^{1/k}} \tag{7.9}$$

Example 7.2

An item's failure rate, λ, is $\lambda = 0.007$ failures/hour. Calculate the item's reliability for a 50-hour mission. Assume that the item starts operating at time $t = 0$.

By setting $k = 1$ in equation (7.8), the item with constant failure rate, reliability is:

$$R(t) = e^{-1/\theta\, t} \tag{7.10}$$

For $t = 50$ hours, $\lambda = 1/\theta = 0.007$ failures/hour, equation (7.10) yields the item's reliability:

$$R(100) = e^{-(0.007)\,(50)}$$
$$= 0.7047$$

Series Network

A k-unit series system's reliability from equation (6.11) is

$$R_s = \prod_{i=1}^{k} R_i(t) \tag{7.11}$$

where $R_i(t)$ is the time, t, dependent ith component's reliability.

If all the system's components have constant failure rates, then substituting equation (7.10) for the ith component in equation (7.11) results in

$$R_s(t) = \prod_{i=1}^{k} e^{-\frac{1}{\theta_i}t} \tag{7.12}$$

where θ_i is the ith component's mean time to failure.

Substituting equation (7.12) in equation (7.2) and integrating yields the series system's mean time to failure:

$$\text{MTTF} = \int_0^\infty \left(\prod_{i=1}^{k} e^{-\frac{1}{\theta_i}t}\right) dt$$
$$= \left(\sum_{i=1}^{k} \frac{1}{\theta_i}\right)^{-1} \tag{7.13}$$

If we let $\lambda_i = 1/\theta_i$, the constant failure rate of the ith component in equation (7.13) results in:

$$\text{MTTF} = \left(\sum_{i=1}^{k} \lambda_i \right)^{-1} \tag{7.14}$$

Other mathematical models useful for series systems are discussed below.

♦ **MODEL I** This model approximates the result of equation (7.12) by assuming that

$$\left(\sum_{i=1}^{k} \theta_i^{-1} t \right) << 1.^2$$

Therefore, the formula to approximate series system reliability, $R_s(t)$, simply is:

$$R_s(t) \cong 1 - \sum_{i=1}^{k} \theta_i^{-1} t \tag{7.15}$$

This formula yields good approximation when $(1/\theta_i)\, t \leqslant 0.05$.

♦ **MODEL II** This model presents an alternative method to develop series system reliability equation (7.12). This approach utilizes the well-known Markov modeling technique. The following basic assumptions are associated with the model:

1. Component failures are statistically independent.
2. Component failure rates are constant.
3. System components are nonrepairable.
4. In a small time interval, the probability of an occurrence from one system state to another is given by $\lambda\, \Delta t$, where Δt is the time interval and λ is the system's constant failure rate.
5. The probabilities of two or more transition occurrences in Δt are very small and therefore are neglected.

The following symbols are associated with the model:

- $P_0(t)$ is the probability that the series system is in state 0 at time t, i.e., it is operating successfully.
- $P_f(t)$ is the probability that at time t the series system is in state f, the failed state of the system (it is not operating at all).
- k is the number of components in the system.
- λ_i is the ith component's constant failure rate, for $i = 1, 2, 3, 4, \ldots, k$.
- s is the Laplace transform variable.

Δt is the time interval.

The system state-space diagram is given in Figure 7.1. The following equations are associated with the figure:

$$P_0(t+\Delta t)=P_0(t)\left\{1-\left(\sum_{i=1}^{k}\lambda_i\right)\Delta t\right\} \tag{7.16}$$

$$P_f(t+\Delta t)=P_f(t)+P_0(t)\cdot\left(\sum_{i=1}^{k}\lambda_i\right)\Delta t \tag{7.17}$$

Rearranging equations (7.16) and (7.17) results in:

$$\frac{P_0(t+\Delta t)-P_0(t)}{\Delta t}=-P_0(t)\cdot\sum_{i=1}^{k}\lambda_i \tag{7.18}$$

$$\frac{P_f(t+\Delta t)-P_f(t)}{\Delta t}=P_0(t)\cdot\sum_{i=1}^{k}\lambda_i \tag{7.19}$$

Taking the limit of equations (7.18) and (7.19) as Δt approaches zero leads to

$$\frac{dP_0(t)}{dt}=-P_0(t)\cdot\sum_{i=1}^{k}\lambda_i \tag{7.20}$$

$$\frac{dP_f(t)}{dt}=P_0(t)\cdot\sum_{i=1}^{k}\lambda_i \tag{7.21}$$

at $t=0, P_0(0)=1$, and $P_f(0)=0$.

The results of taking the Laplace transforms of differential equations (7.20) and (7.21) are:

$$sP_0(s)-P_0(0)\cdot=-P_0(s)\cdot\sum_{i=1}^{k}\lambda_i \tag{7.22}$$

$$sP_f(s)-P_f(0)=P_0(s)\cdot\sum_{i=1}^{k}\lambda_i \tag{7.23}$$

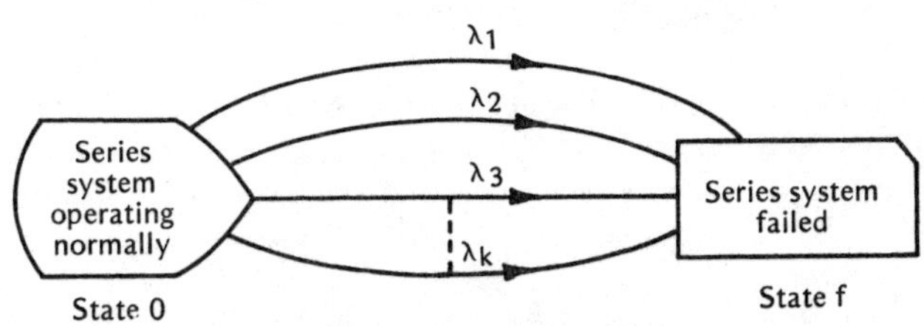

Figure 7.1 Series system transition diagram

Utilizing initial conditions in equations (7.22) and (7.23) and then solving leads to:

$$P_0(s) = \left(s + \sum_{i=1}^{k} \lambda_i\right)^{-1} \tag{7.24}$$

$$P_f(s) = \left(\sum_{i=1}^{k} \lambda_i\right) \left\{s\left(s + \sum_{i=1}^{k} \lambda_i\right)\right\}^{-1} \tag{7.25}$$

Taking the inverse Laplace transforms of equations (7.24) and (7.25) yields the following system-state probability equations:

$$P_0(t) = e^{-\sum_{i=1}^{k} \lambda_i t} \tag{7.26}$$

$$P_f(t) = 1 - e^{-\sum_{i=1}^{k} \lambda_i t} \tag{7.27}$$

If we let $\lambda_i = 1/\theta_i$ in equation (7.26), the equation becomes

$$P_0(t) = e^{-\left(\sum_{i=1}^{k} \frac{1}{\theta_i}\right) t} \tag{7.28}$$

Therefore, the above equation is the same as equation (7.12) which is for series system reliability.

♦ **MODEL III** This model examines the reliability of a series system whose components' failure rates are nonconstant. Therefore, in this model it is assumed that the jth series component's hazard rate, $\lambda_j(t)$, is defined by[1,3]

$$\lambda_j(t) = \lambda_j + \theta_j t^\beta \tag{7.29}$$

where t is time, and θ_j, λ_j and β are the constants.

Thus, substituting equation (7.29) in equation (7.1) and integrating leads to the jth component's reliability:

$$R_j(t) = e^{-[\lambda_j t + \{\theta_j t^{\beta+1}\} / (\beta+1)]} \tag{7.30}$$

The result of utilizing equation (7.30) in equation (7.11) is:

$$R_s(t) = \prod_{i=1}^{k} \exp\left[-(\lambda_j t + \{\theta_j t^{\beta+1}\} / (\beta+1)\right]$$

$$= \exp\left[-\left\{\sum_{j=1}^{k} \lambda_j t + \left(t^{\beta+1} \sum_{j=1}^{k} \theta_j\right) / (\beta+1)\right\}\right] \tag{7.31}$$

Now let

$$\lambda_{t0t} = \sum_{j=1}^{k} \lambda_j \tag{7.32}$$

$$\theta_{t0t} = \sum_{j=1}^{k} \theta_j \tag{7.33}$$

$$\Gamma = t\,\lambda_{t0t} \tag{7.34}$$

Thus, equation (7.31) is rewritten to the following form:

$$R_s(t) = \exp\left[-\left\{\Gamma + \frac{\theta_{t0t}\,\Gamma^{(\beta+1)}}{(\beta+1)\,\lambda_{t0t}\cdot\lambda_{t0t}^{\beta}}\right\}\right] \tag{7.35}$$

For a very large value of k (in other words, the system has a very large number of components in series), we assume:

$\lambda_{t0t} \to \infty$

$\{\theta_{t0t}/(\beta+1)\,\lambda_{t0t}\}$ is bounded

Thus, for a very large value of k in equation (7.35), the series system's reliability, $R_s(t)$, reduces to:

$$R_s(t) = e^{-\Gamma} = e^{-(\lambda_{t0t})\,t} \tag{7.36}$$

The above equation states that for a very large number of components with nonconstant failure rates (as defined in the model), reliability, $R_s(t)$, is simply given by the same reliability equation (7.12) as for the series system components with constant failure rates.

Parallel Network

The reliability of a parallel network from equation (6.6) is given by

$$R_p(t) = 1 - \prod_{i=1}^{\alpha} F_i(t) \tag{7.37}$$

where

$F_i(t) = 1 - R_i(t)$	is the ith unit's time, t, dependent unreliability
$R_i(t)$	is the ith unit's time-dependent reliability
α	is the number of units in parallel configuration

For constant failure rate, the *i*th unit's reliability from equation (7.10) is

$$R_i(t) = e^{-\lambda_i t} \tag{7.38}$$

where

$\lambda_i = 1/\theta_i$ is the *i*th component's constant failure rate

θ_i is the *i*th component's mean time to failure

Thus, utilizing equation (7.38) in equation (7.37) results in:

$$R_p(t) = 1 - \prod_{i=1}^{\alpha} (1 - e^{-\lambda_i t}) \tag{7.39}$$

If the value of $(\lambda_i t) \leqslant 0.05$, the following approximation formula results from equation (7.39):

$$R_p(t) \cong 1 - \prod_{i=1}^{\alpha} \lambda_i t^a \tag{7.40}$$

For identical components, the above equation simplifies to

$$R_p(t) \cong 1 - (\lambda t)^{\alpha} \tag{7.41}$$

Three models associated with the parallel configuration are described below.

♦ **MODEL I** This model is concerned with developing network reliability equation (7.39) by utilizing the Markov technique. First of all, for simplicity, we assume that there are only two identical and independent units forming the parallel network. For this condition the system (network) transition diagram is given in Figure 7.2.

The assumptions associated with the Markov modeling were stated earlier in the chapter, and the following symbols were used to develop this mathematical model:

$P_i(t)$ is the probability that the parallel system is in state i at time t, for $i = 0$ (both units operating normally), $i = 1$ (one unit operating normally, other failed), $i = 2$ (both units failed)

λ is the unit constant failure rate

s is the Laplace transform variable

The following differential equations are associated with Figure 7.2:

$$\frac{dP_0(t)}{dt} + 2\lambda P_0(t) = 0 \tag{7.42}$$

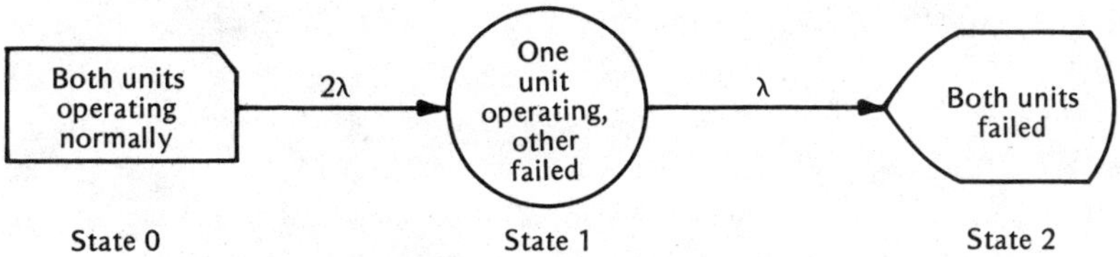

Figure 7.2 Two identical unit parallel system transition diagram

$$\frac{dP_1(t)}{dt}+\lambda P_1(t)=P_0(t)\cdot 2\lambda \tag{7.43}$$

$$\frac{dP_2(t)}{dt}=P_1(t)\cdot \lambda \tag{7.44}$$

at $t=0, P_0(0)=1, P_1(0)=P_2(0)=0.$

Taking the Laplace transforms of equations (7.42) through (7.44) and utilizing the initial conditions yields:

$$sP_0(s)-1+2\lambda P_0(s)=0 \tag{7.45}$$

$$sP_1(s)+\lambda P_1(s)=P_0(s)\cdot 2\lambda \tag{7.46}$$

$$sP_2(s)=P_1(s)\cdot \lambda \tag{7.47}$$

Rearranging equations (7.45) through (7.47) results in:

$$P_0(s)=(s+2\lambda)^{-1} \tag{7.48}$$

$$P_1(s)=2\lambda\ [(s+2\lambda)(s+\lambda)]^{-1} \tag{7.49}$$

$$P_2(s)=2\lambda^2\ [s(s+2\lambda)(s+\lambda)]^{-1} \tag{7.50}$$

The inverse Laplace transforms of equations (7.48) through (7.50) are:

$$P_0(t)=e^{-2\lambda t} \tag{7.51}$$

$$P_1(t)=2(e^{-\lambda t}-e^{-2\lambda t}) \tag{7.52}$$

$$P_2(t)=1-e^{-2\lambda t}+2e^{-\lambda t} \tag{7.53}$$

Adding equations (7.51) and (7.52) yields the following parallel system reliability:

$$R_p(t)=P_0(t)+P_1(t)=e^{-2\lambda t}+2(e^{-\lambda t}-e^{-2\lambda t})$$

$$=2e^{-\lambda t}-e^{-2\lambda t} \tag{7.54}$$

Rewriting equation (7.54) results in:

$$R_p(t)=1-(1-e^{-\lambda t})^2 \tag{7.55}$$

Note that for identical units and $\alpha=2$ in equation (7.39) we get the same result as equation (7.55). Similarly, for a three identical unit parallel system the Markov technique yields the following system reliability result:

$$R_p(t)=1-(1-e^{-\lambda t})^3 \tag{7.56}$$

Therefore, for α identical unit parallel system the reliability is:

$$R_p(t)=1-(1-e^{-\lambda t})^\alpha \tag{7.57}$$

Finally, for nonidentical units, equation (7.57) becomes:

$$R_p(t)=1-\prod_{i=1}^{\alpha}(1-e^{-\lambda_i t}) \tag{7.58}$$

Example 7.3

Three independent and identical electric generators form a parallel system. Assume that all the generators start operating at time $t=0$ and at least one generator is needed for system success. Calculate the system's reliability for a 200-hour mission. Each generator's failure rate is 0.002 failures/hour.

Using the given data in equation (7.57) yields:

$$R_p(200)=1-\{1-e^{-(0.002)(200)}\}^3$$

$$=0.9642$$

Therefore, the parallel system's reliability is 0.9642.

♦ **MODEL II** This model is concerned with developing parallel system mean time to failure (MTTF) and variance of the time-to-failure distribution formulas. In this model it is assumed that the system component's failure rates are constant.

Substituting equation (7.58) in equation (7.2) and integrating results in:

$$\text{MTTF}=\int_0^\infty \left\{1-\prod_{i=1}^{\alpha}(1-e^{-\lambda_i t})\right\} dt$$

$$\text{MTTF}=\sum_{i=1}^{\alpha}\frac{1}{\lambda_i}-\sum_{i=1}^{\alpha-1}\sum_{k=i+1}^{\alpha}\frac{1}{\lambda_k+\lambda_i}+\ldots+\frac{(-1)^{\alpha-1}}{\sum_{i=1}^{\alpha}\lambda_i} \tag{7.59}$$

For identical units, equation (7.59) reduces to:

$$\text{MTTF} = \frac{1}{\lambda} \sum_{i=1}^{\alpha} i^{-1} \tag{7.60}$$

In Sandler, the variance of the time to failure, σ^2, is[4]

$$\sigma^2 = \int_0^\infty t^2 f(t) \cdot dt - (\text{MTTF})^2 \tag{7.61}$$

where

$f(t)$ is the failure probability density function

t is time

An alternative formula to find variance of time to failure is

$$\sigma^2 = -2 \lim_{s \to 0} R'(s) - \left\{ \lim_{s \to 0} R(s) \right\}^2 \tag{7.62}$$

where

$R(s)$ is the Laplace transform of the reliability function

s is the Laplace transform variable

$(')$ is the differentiation with respect to s

According to Sandler, taking the Laplace transform of equation (7.57) and then utilizing it in equation (7.62) results in:[4]

$$\sigma^2 = \sum_{i=1}^{\alpha} (i\lambda)^{-2} \tag{7.63}$$

Example 7.4

Three independent and identical motors (units) form a parallel configuration. Each unit's constant failure rate is 0.008 failures/hour. Find the parallel network mean time to failure (MTTF) and variance of the time-to-failure. By substituting the given data into equation (7.60), we get:

$$\text{MTTF} = \frac{1}{(0.008)} \cdot \sum_{i=1}^{3} \frac{1}{i}$$

$$= \frac{1}{(0.008)} \left\{ 1 + \frac{1}{2} + \frac{1}{3} \right\}$$

$$= 229.17 \text{ hours}$$

Similarly, utilizing the given data in equation (7.63) leads to:

$$\sigma^2 = \sum_{i=1}^{3} (i\lambda)^{-2} = \frac{1}{\lambda^2} + \frac{1}{(2\lambda)^2} + \frac{1}{(3\lambda)^2}$$

$$= \frac{1}{(0.008)^2} + \frac{1}{\{2(0.008)\}^2} + \frac{1}{\{3(0.008)\}^2}$$

$$= 15{,}625 + 3{,}906.25 + 1{,}736.11$$

$$= 21{,}267.36 \text{ hours}$$

♦ **MODEL III** This model is concerned with measuring the dispersion around a mean value (MTTF of a system). This means finding the coefficient of variation, Υ, for a system which is defined by

$$\Upsilon = \frac{\text{standard deviation}}{\text{mean time to failure}} \tag{7.64}$$

Note that the standard deviation is obtained by taking the square root of the variance, σ^2. Thus, for an identical unit parallel system, substituting equations (7.60) and (7.63) in equation (7.64) yields:

$$\Upsilon = \left(\frac{1}{\lambda^2} \sum_{i=1}^{\alpha} i^{-2}\right)^{1/2} \Big/ \left(\lambda^{-1} \sum_{i=1}^{\alpha} i^{-1}\right)$$

$$= \left(\sum_{i=1}^{\alpha} i^{-2}\right)^{1/2} \Big/ \sum_{i=1}^{\alpha} i^{-1} \tag{7.65}$$

When one adds more units in parallel, the value of Υ decreases.

Series-Parallel Network

The time, t, dependent reliability, $R_{sp}(t)$, of a series-parallel network from equation (6.21) is given by:

$$R_{sp}(t) = \prod_{j=1}^{k} \left\{1 - \prod_{i=1}^{r} F_{ji}(t)\right\} \tag{7.66}$$

For the constant failure rates of components [utilizing equation (7.10)]

$$F_{ji}(t) = 1 - R_{ji}(t) = 1 - e^{-\lambda_{ji} t} \tag{7.67}$$

where

$R_{ji}(t)$ is the jth subsystem's ith unit reliability at time t

λ_{ji} is the jth subsystem's ith unit constant failure rate

Substituting equation (7.67) in equation (7.66) results in:

$$R_{sp}(t) = \prod_{j=1}^{k} \{1 - \prod_{i=1}^{r} \{1 - e^{-\lambda_{ji}t}\}\} \tag{7.68}$$

For identical components and subsystems, utilizing equation (7.68) in equation (7.2) and integrating yields the network's mean time failure:[5]

$$\text{MTTF} = \int_0^\infty \{1 - (1 - e^{-\lambda t})^r\}^k \, dt$$

$$= \left[\sum_{j=1}^{k} \left\{ (-1)^{j+1} \binom{k}{j} \sum_{i=1}^{jr} i^{-1} \right\} \right] \lambda^{-1} \tag{7.69}$$

Example 7.5

An independent unit series-parallel system contains two identical subsystems in series. Each subsystem consists of two identical units in parallel. Each unit's constant failure rate is 0.001 failures/hour. Compute the system's mean time to failure.

According to specified data, $\lambda = 0.001$ failures/hour, $k = 2$, and $r = 2$. Thus substituting the above data in equation (7.69) leads to:

$$\text{MTTF} = \left[\sum_{j=1}^{2} \left\{ (-1)^{j+1} \binom{2}{j} \sum_{i=1}^{j2} i^{-1} \right\} \right] (0.001)^{-1}$$

$$\text{MTTF} = \frac{11}{12} (0.001)^{-1}$$

$$= 916.67 \text{ hours}$$

Parallel-Series Network

From equation (6.24), the time-dependent reliability, $R_{ps}(t)$, of a parallel-series system is

$$R_{ps}(t) = 1 - \prod_{j=1}^{r} \left\{ 1 - \prod_{i=1}^{k} R_{ji}(t) \right\} \tag{7.70}$$

where $R_{ji}(t)$ denotes the jth subsystem ith unit's reliability at time t.

For the components' constant failure rates, we utilize equation (7.67) in equation (7.70) to get

$$R_{ps}(t) = 1 - \prod_{j=1}^{r} \left\{ 1 - \prod_{i=1}^{k} e^{-\lambda_{ji}t} \right\} \tag{7.71}$$

where λ_{ji} is the jth subsystem ith component's (unit) constant failure rate.

For identical components and subsystems, substituting equation (7.71) in equation (7.2) and integrating leads to the following mean time to failure result:

$$\mathrm{MTTF} = \int_0^\infty \left[1 - \left\{1 - e^{-k\lambda t}\right\}^r\right] dt$$

$$= \left(\sum_{j=1}^{r} j^{-1}\right) (k\lambda)^{-1} \tag{7.72}$$

Example 7.6

Suppose that in equation (7.72) $r = 2$, $k = 3$, and $\lambda = 0.002$ failures/hour. Find the network mean time to failure.

Thus, substituting the specified data into equation (7.72) leads to the following end result:

$$\mathrm{MTTF} = \left(\sum_{j=1}^{2} j^{-1}\right) \{3(0.002)\}^{-1}$$

$$= \frac{3}{2} \cdot \frac{1}{3(0.002)} = 250 \text{ hours}$$

Partially Redundant System

This is a α active identical unit parallel system. However, in this case at least k units operating successfully are needed for system success. Therefore, from equation (6.14), the time-dependent system reliability, $R_{k/\alpha}(t)$, is

$$R_{k/\alpha}(t) = \sum_{i=k}^{\alpha} \binom{\alpha}{i} \{1 - R(t)\}^{\alpha - i} \cdot \{R(t)\}^i \tag{7.73}$$

where $R(t)$ is the unit's time-dependent reliability.

For constant failure rates of units, substitute for $R(t)$ from equation (7.10) in equation (7.73) so that

$$R_{k/\alpha}(t) = \sum_{i=k}^{\alpha} \binom{\alpha}{i} \left\{1 - e^{-\frac{1}{\theta}t}\right\}^{\alpha - i} \left\{e^{-\frac{1}{\theta}t}\right\}^i \tag{7.74}$$

where $\theta = 1/\lambda$ is the component mean time to failure, and λ denotes the component constant failure rate.

Plots of equation (7.74) are shown in Figure 7.3 for $k = 1, \alpha = 3, k = \alpha = 1$; and $k = 2, \alpha = 3, k = \alpha = 3$.

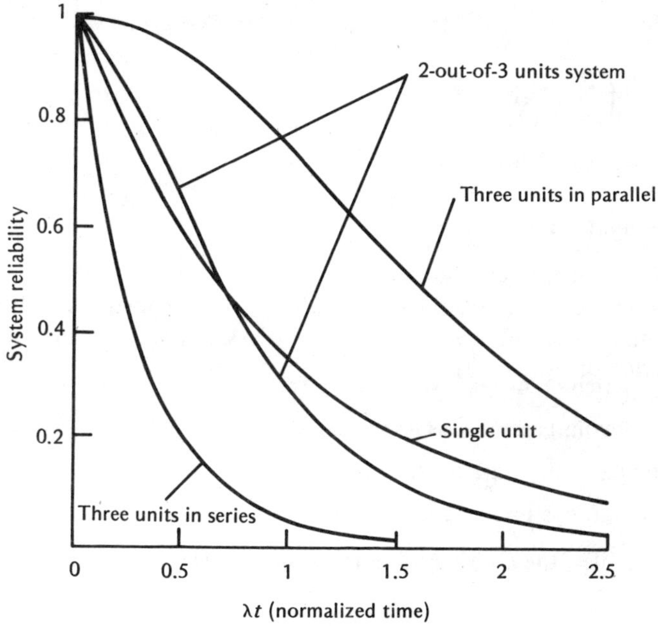

Figure 7.3 System reliability plots

Thus, substituting equation (7.74) in equation (7.2) and integrating yields the following system mean time to failure formula:

$$\text{MTTF} = \sum_{i=k}^{\alpha} \binom{\alpha}{i} \int_0^\infty \left\{1 - e^{-\frac{1}{\theta}t}\right\}^{\alpha-i} \left\{e^{-\frac{1}{\theta}t}\right\}^{i} dt$$

$$= \left(\sum_{i=k}^{\alpha} i^{-1}\right) \theta \tag{7.75}$$

Example 7.7

A system consists of four active, independent, and identical units forming a parallel configuration. At least three units operating successfully are required for system success. Each unit's constant failure rate (λ) is 0.003 failures/hour. Calculate the system mean time to failure.

Each unit mean time to failure is:

$$\theta = \frac{1}{\lambda} = \frac{1}{0.003} = 333.3 \text{ hours}$$

Thus, substituting the specified data in equation (7.75) yields:

$$\text{MTTF} = \left(\sum_{i=3}^{4} i^{-1} \right) (333.3)$$

$$= 194.425 \text{ hours}$$

Standby System

This arrangement represents a situation where one unit is operating, and $(k - 1)$ number of units are on standby. The system consists of k number of identical units. The following assumptions are associated with the model:

1. The switching mechanism never fails.
2. Standby units remain as good as new.
3. The unit failures are independent.
4. Each unit's failure rate is constant.

From Sandler, the k unit system reliability, $R_s(t)$, at time t is given by[4]

$$R_s(t) = e^{-\lambda t} \sum_{j=0}^{k-1} (\lambda t)^j / (j!) \tag{7.76}$$

where λ is the constant failure rate of each unit.

The results of substituting equation (7.76) in equation (7.2) and then integrating are:

$$\text{MTTF} = \int_0^\infty e^{-\lambda t} \left[\sum_{j=0}^{k-1} (\lambda t)^j / (j!) \right] dt$$

$$= \frac{k}{\lambda} \tag{7.77}$$

Taking the Laplace transform of equation (7.76) and then utilizing it in equation (7.62) leads to the following variance of the time to failure formula:

$$\sigma^2 = k/\lambda^2 \tag{7.78}$$

Therefore

$$\sigma = \sqrt{k}/\lambda \tag{7.79}$$

By substituting equations (7.77) and (7.79) in equation (7.64) we get:

$$\Upsilon = \sqrt{k}/k \tag{7.80}$$

where Υ is the coefficient of variation.

Example 7.8

A standby system consists of three identical pumps (units). One unit is operating and the remaining two units are on standby. Each unit's constant failure rate (λ) is 0.006 failures/hour. By utilizing equation (7.76), calculate system reliability for a 200-hour mission.

By utilizing the specified data, we get

$$R_s(200)=e^{-(0.006)\,(200)}\sum_{j=0}^{2}\{(0.006)\,(200)\}^{j}/j!$$

$$R_s(200)=e^{-(0.006)\,(200)}\left[1+\frac{(0.006)\,(200)}{1!}+\frac{\{(0.006)\,(200)\}^2}{2!}\right]$$

$$=0.3012\,[1+1.2+0.72]$$

$$=0.8795$$

System reliability is 0.8795.

SYSTEM RELIABILITY EVALUATION BY USING THE JOINT-DENSITY-FUNCTION APPROACH

This is another approach by which to evaluate the reliability of redundant networks, especially when components' or units' hazard rates are nonconstant.[1] This procedure is demonstrated by analyzing a two nonidentical unit standby system. Each unit's failure rate is constant. Other assumptions associated with this system are discussed in the section on standby systems. The failure rates of the operating and standby units are denoted by λ_0 and λ_s, respectively. We assume that for the first failure, the failure time is t_f. Therefore, the first failure density function, $f_1(t_1)$, is defined by:

$$f_1(t_1)=\lambda_0\,e^{-\lambda_0 t_1}\quad \text{for } 0<t_1<t \tag{7.81}$$

Similarly, the second failure time is t, and the dependent probability density function, $f_2(t/t_1)$, is defined by

$$f_2(t/t_1)=\lambda_s\,e^{-\lambda_s(t-t_1)}\quad \text{for } 0<t_1<t \tag{7.82}$$

We should note here that the standby system failure is a function of t_1 and t. Therefore, the joint density function,

$$f(t,t_1)=f_1(t_1)\cdot f_2(t/t_1) \tag{7.83}$$

Thus, substituting functions (7.81) and (7.82) in equation (7.83) and then integrating it over the interval $[0,t]$ leads to the following marginal density function:

$$f(t)=\int_0^t (\lambda_0 e^{-\lambda_0 t_1})\{\lambda_s e^{-\lambda_s(t-t_1)}\}\, dt_1$$

$$=A(e^{-\lambda_s t}-e^{-\lambda_0 t}) \tag{7.84}$$

where

$$A\equiv\lambda_0\lambda_s/(\lambda_0-\lambda_s). \tag{7.85}$$

The cumulative distribution function, $F(t)$, is obtained by integrating equation (7.84) over the time interval $[0,t]$ as follows:

$$F(t)=A\int_0^t (e^{-\lambda_s t}-e^{-\lambda_0 t})\,dt$$

$$=A\left\{\frac{e^{-\lambda_0 t}}{\lambda_0}-\frac{e^{-\lambda_s t}}{\lambda_s}\right\} \tag{7.86}$$

Thus, subtracting equation (7.86) from unity yields the system reliability:

$$R_s(t)=1-F(t)=\frac{\lambda_0}{(\lambda_0-\lambda_s)}\cdot e^{-\lambda_s t}-\frac{\lambda_s}{(\lambda_0-\lambda_s)}\cdot e^{-\lambda_0 t} \tag{7.87}$$

For identical units $\lambda_0=\lambda_s=\lambda$; therefore, substituting λ for λ_0 and λ_s in equation (7.87) yields an indeterminate result. Now we can only proceed further by utilizing the L' Hospital's rule. Differentiating the top and bottom of equation (7.87) with respect to λ_s and then letting $\lambda_s=\lambda_0=\lambda$ yields:

$$R_s(t)=(1+\lambda t)\,e^{-\lambda t} \tag{7.88}$$

After setting $k=2$ in equation (7.76), the resulting expression is the same as equation (7.88).

CONFIDENCE LIMITS FOR MEAN TIME BETWEEN FAILURES

This section discusses how to determine mean time between failures confidence limits when failure times are exponentially distributed. The confidence limits (upper and lower) indicate the value of a parameter being in an interval with certain confidence probability. For example, when testing a sample of components for t hours in which k failures occur, the expected mean time between failures (MTBF) will be given by t/k. This statement gives an incomplete picture because it does not provide any surety of measurement. However, it would be more meaningful to say that after testing for t hours k number of failures occur;

therefore, the actual MTBF with certain confidence lies between specific upper and lower limits.

To compute the MTBF confidence interval, the χ^2 (chi-square) distribution is used. Generally, the following symbol is used to obtain chi-square values

$\chi^2(p, fd)$

where

- p is a quantity which is a function of the confidence coefficient
- fd is the degrees of freedom

The following symbols are used in the formulas to follow:

- f is the accumulated number of failures at time t^*, where t^* denotes the life test termination time
- f^* is the number of failures which were preassigned
- m is the quantity of components which were put on test at zero time ($t=0$)
- β is the mean time between failures or mean life
- p is the acceptable error risk
- $1-p$ is the level of confidence

To estimate confidence intervals there are two cases to consider: (1) the test is terminated at a specified time, t^*, and (2) the test is terminated at a specified number of failures.

Therefore, for both cases, to compute upper and lower limits the following formulas can be used:[5]

First case (test terminated at time t^*)

$$\left(\frac{2\Gamma}{\chi^2\left(\frac{p}{2}, 2f+2\right)}, \frac{2\Gamma}{\chi^2\left\{\left(1-\frac{p}{2}\right), 2f\right\}} \right) \tag{7.89}$$

lower limit upper limit

Second case (test terminated at specified failures, f^*)

$$\left(\frac{2\Gamma}{\chi^2\left(\frac{p}{2}, 2f\right)}, \frac{2\Gamma}{\chi^2\left\{\left(1-\frac{p}{2}\right), 2f\right\}} \right) \tag{7.90}$$

lower limit upper limit

The type of test determines the value of Γ, for example, when a failure (failed unit) is replaced or repaired (replacement tests), the value of Γ is given by:

$$\Gamma = m\,t^* \tag{7.91}$$

Similarly, for the nonreplacement test the value of Γ is given by

$$\Gamma = (m - f)t^* + \sum_{j=1}^{f} T_j \tag{7.92}$$

where T_j denotes the jth failure time.

The values of $\chi^2(p, fd)$ are tabulated in Table 7.1.

Example 7.9

Fifteen components were put on test at time $t = 0$, and testing was terminated when the eighth failure occured. That failure (eighth) was observed at the 100th hour of testing. Calculate the components' mean time between failures (mean life) and mean life upper and lower confidence limits with 90% confidence level.

Table 7.1. Chi-square distribution

Degree of freedom	*Probability*					
	0.975	0.95	0.90	0.05	0.025	0.01
2	0.05	0.10	0.21	5.99	7.38	9.21
4	0.48	0.71	1.06	9.45	11.14	13.28
6	1.24	1.64	2.20	12.59	14.45	16.81
8	2.18	2.73	3.49	15.51	17.53	20.09
10	3.25	3.94	4.87	18.31	20.48	23.21
12	4.40	5.23	6.30	21.03	23.34	26.22
14	5.63	6.57	7.79	23.69	26.12	29.14
16	6.91	7.96	9.31	26.30	28.85	32.00
18	8.23	9.39	10.87	28.87	31.53	34.81
20	9.59	10.85	12.44	31.41	34.17	37.57

Assume that when a component failure occurred, it was repaired back to its as good as new state. Therefore, from equation (7.91)

$$\Gamma = m\,t^* = 15 \times 100 = 1500 \text{ hours}$$

The estimated mean life of components is

$$\hat{\beta} = \frac{\Gamma}{f^*} = \frac{1500}{8} = 187.5 \text{ hours}$$

Similarly

$$p = 1 - \text{confidence level}$$

$$= 1 - 0.90 = 0.1$$

and

$$2f = 2(8) = 16$$

Thus, substituting for p, $2f$, and Γ in equation (7.90) and utilizing Table 7.1 yields the following upper and lower confidence limits:

$$\text{upper limit} = \frac{2\Gamma}{\chi^2 \left\{\left(1 - \frac{p}{2}\right), 2f\right\}}$$

$$= \frac{2(1500)}{\chi^2(0.95,16)} = \frac{2(1500)}{7.96} = 376.9 \text{ hours}$$

$$\text{lower limit} = \frac{2\Gamma}{\chi^2(0.05,16)} = \frac{2(1500)}{26.30} = 114.07 \text{ hours}$$

Now we may say with 90% confidence probability that the components' true mean life will lie within (114.07 hours and 376.9 hours). In other words

$$114.07 \leqslant \beta \leqslant 376.9$$

Example 7.10

Twenty-five components were put on a test at time $t = 0$. It was a nonreplacement test and was terminated after 90 hours.

During that period five components failed after 20, 40, 30, 70, and 80 hours of operation, respectively. Calculate the components' mean times between failures (mean life) and mean life upper and lower confidence limits with 95% confidence level.

Substituting the given data in equation (7.92) results in:

$$\Gamma = (25 - 5)\,90 + [20 + 40 + 30 + 70 + 80]$$

$$= 1800 + 240 = 2040 \text{ hours}$$

Therefore, the estimated mean time between failures is:

$$\hat{\beta} = \frac{2040}{5} = 408 \text{ hours}$$

Substituting the given data in equation (7.89) and utilizing Table 7.1 yields the following lower limit value:

$$\text{lower limit} = \frac{2(2040)}{\chi^2(0.025,12)} = \frac{4080}{23.34} = 174.81 \text{ hours}$$

Similarly,

$$\text{upper limit} = \frac{2(2040)}{\chi^2(0.975,10)} = \frac{4080}{3.25} = 1255.39 \text{ hours}$$

The mean life will lie between 174.81 and 1255.39 hours with 95% confidence probability.

RELIABILITY GROWTH MODELING

Reliability growth modeling, another important area of reliability engineering, is concerned with monitoring the reliability growth of a product. Clarke defines the reliability growth as a continuing reduction in an item's actual hazard rate that will approach the inherent targeted value during the product design and development phase.[6] The following are Mead's main reasons for product reliability growth:

1. Correcting faults in an item's design, manufacturing, and so on
2. Identification of bad components by operating the newly developed product
3. Increased operator skill and familiarization[7]

A mathematical model developed by Duane in 1962 to monitor product reliability growth is one of the commonly used models.[8] The equation of the model is defined by

$$\lambda_k = \frac{f}{t} = \theta\, t^{-b} \tag{7.93}$$

where

t is the total test time in hours

f is the number of failures during time t

θ is a parameter which depends on design objective, design complexity, design margin, and so on

b is the growth rate

λ_k is the cumulative failure rate

To estimate θ and b, we take logarithms of equation (7.93) as follows:

$$\log \lambda_k = \log \theta - b \log t \quad (7.94)$$

Since the $\log \lambda_k$ against $\log t$ plots as a straight line, this plot can be used to estimate values for θ and b. The slope of the line yields the estimate for b. At $t = 1$ on the plot, the value of α is equal to the corresponding cumulative failure rate.

SOFTWARE RELIABILITY

Computer applications have been following an increasing trend. In today's environment the money spent to develop computer software is much greater than the money spent to develop their hardware. For example, according to one estimate the amount of annual expenditure on software will be almost four times greater than the hardware.[10] Because computer software has become very complex, the emphasis has been placed on developing software with certain reliability. In the last few years many mathematical models and procedures have been developed to ensure software reliability. (Literature on software reliability may be found in Dhillon.)

This section presents one mathematical model to predict software reliability.[11] The following assumptions are associated with the model:

1. The hazard rate is proportional to the number of residual errors.
2. Testing does not introduce any new errors.
3. The total number of machine language instructions in the software program remains constant.
4. The number of residual errors is given by the difference between the initial errors and the cumulative errors corrected.
5. At the beginning of integration testing, the number of errors is constant. In addition, as errors are corrected that number decreases directly.

The symbols associated with the model are:

t is the system operating time

m_i is the total number of machine language instructions

z is the debugging time since the beginning of systems integration

I_e is the number of initial errors

θ is the proportionality constant

$\beta_c(z)$ is the cumulative number of errors corrected by time z

$\beta_r(z)$ is the residual errors in program at time z

The residual errors in the program at time z are given by:

$$\beta_r(z) = \frac{I_e}{m_i} - \beta_c(z) \tag{7.95}$$

Thus, the hazard rate, $\lambda(t)$, of the model is defined by:

$$\lambda(t) = \theta\, \beta_r(z) \tag{7.96}$$

Substituting equation (7.96) in equation (7.1) and integrating leads to the following reliability function:

$$R(t;z) = e^{-\theta \int_0^t \beta_r(z)\,dx} = e^{-[\theta \beta_r(z)]\, t} \tag{7.97}$$

Thus, substituting equation (7.97) in equation (7.2) and integrating results in the following mean time to failure (MTTF) formula:

$$\mathrm{MTTF} = \int_0^\infty R(t;z)\,dt$$

$$= \{\theta \beta_r(z)\}^{-1}$$

$$= \theta^{-1}\left\{\left(\frac{I_e}{m_i}\right) - \beta_c(z)\right\}^{-1} \tag{7.98}$$

Amster and Shooman give the moment matching method to estimate values for I_e and θ.[10]

SUMMARY

This chapter is concerned with system reliability evaluation in time-dependent situations. The following topics are covered: (1) Time dependent analysis of reliability networks. The reliability evaluation of series, parallel, series-parallel, parallel-series, partially redundant, and standby networks is presented. Networks mean time to failure and variance of the time-to-failure (in some cases) formulas are developed. (2) System reliability evaluation by using the joint-density-function approach. (3) Confidence limits for mean time between failures (MTBF). (4) Reliability growth modeling, and (5) software reliability.

EXERCISES

7.1. A system's constant failure rate is 0.00025 failures/day. Find the system's reliability for a 50-day mission and its mean time to failure. Assume that the system starts operating at time $t=0$.

7.2. A series system consists of k number of independent components. Each component's failure time is described by the Weibull distribution. Prove that the system's mean time to failure is given by

$$\text{MTTF} = \left[\Gamma\left(\frac{1}{\beta}\right)\right] \beta^{-1} \left\{\sum_{i=1}^{k} \frac{1}{a_i}\right\}^{-1/\beta}$$

where

β is the distribution shape parameter

a_i is the ith component's distribution scale parameter

7.3. A series-parallel network is composed of identical components, however for nonidentical components the network reliability is given by equation (7.68). Obtain an expression for the system's variance of the time to failure. Assume that the system's components are identical.

7.4. A parallel-series network contains two independent and identical subsystems. Each subsystem consists of two identical components. Each component's constant failure rate is 0.002 failures/day. Find the network's reliability for a 40-day mission and its mean time to failure. Assume that the system started operating at time $t=0$.

7.5. Discuss and compare the standby and k-out-of-n unit redundancy.

7.6. With the aid of the Markov technique, prove that a k identical unit standby system's reliability is given by equation (7.76).

7.7. Twenty-five items were put on test at time $t=0$, and testing was terminated when the twelfth failure occurred. This failure occurred at the 120th hour of testing. Assume that the failure distribution involved is an exponential distribution. Calculate the items' mean times between failures (mean life) and mean life upper and lower confidence limits with 95% confidence level. Finally, when an item failure occurred, it was repaired back to its good as new state.

7.8. A reliability network is shown in Figure 7.4. The network is composed of eight independent and nonidentical components. Each component's failure time is exponentially distributed. Develop an expression for the network's mean time to failure.

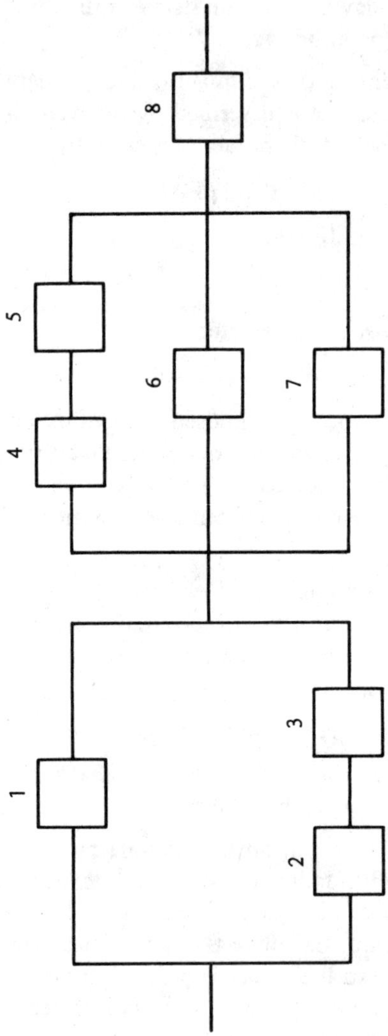

Figure 7.4 Reliability network

NOTES

1. M.L. Shooman, *Probabilistic Reliability: An Engineering Approach* (New York: McGraw-Hill, 1968), pp. 198, 243-247.
2. A.E. Green and A.J. Bourne, *Reliability Technology* New York: John Wiley & Sons, 1977).
3. R.F. Drenick, "The Failure Law of Complex Equipment," *Journal of Society of Industrial Applied Mathematics*, vol. 8 (1960): pp. 680-690.
4. G.H. Sandler, *System Reliability Engineering* (Englewood Cliffs, N.J.: Prentice-Hall, 1963), pp. 98.
5. W.H. Von Alven, *Reliability Engineering* Englewood Cliffs, N.J.: Prentice-Hall, 1964), pp. 173-179.
6. J.M. Clarke, "No-Growth Growth Curve," *Proceeding of the Annual Reliability and Maintainability Symposium*, (1979): 407-12.
7. P.H. Mead, "Reliability Growth of Electronics Equipment," *Microelectronics and Reliability*, vol. 14 (1975): 439-43.
8. J.T. Duane, "Learning Curve Approach to Reliability Monitoring," *IEEE Transactions on Aerospace* (1964): 563-66.
9. B.S. Dhillon, "Software Reliability-Bibliography," *Microelectronics and Reliability*, vol. 22 (1982): 625-40.
10. S.J. Amster and M.L. Shooman, "Software Reliability: An Overview," *Reliability and Fault Tree Analysis: Theoretical and Applied Aspects of System Reliability and Safety Assessment.* (Philadelphia: Society of Industrial Applied Mathematics (SIAM), 1975): 655-85.
11. M.L. Shooman, "Software Reliability: Measurement and Models," *Proceedings of the Annual Reliability and Maintainability Symposium* (1975): 485-91.

8

Management and Value Engineering

A reliability engineer has certain duties which may directly or indirectly deal with managerial aspects. Furthermore, once he or she is in the supervisory position, the engineer may spend a large portion of time performing management functions. This chapter, therefore, discusses the topics of management and value engineering in order to familiarize the reliability engineer with the important areas of management and value engineering, not to make him or her an expert on the subjects.

The subject of management grew out of the U.S. industrial revolution. The father of scientific management, F.W. Taylor, synthesized ideas developed and practiced earlier by others. Because he organized them into a formal framework, these ideas became widely known, and since then several other researchers have contributed to the field of management.

In the late 1940s the idea of value engineering was conceived at the General Electric Company. Lawrence D. Miles of the same company originated the basic value analysis approach in 1947.[1] The Navy Bureau of Ships recognized the merits of value analysis and established a value engineering organization. The Electronics Industries Association formed a subcommittee on value engineering in 1958, which in turn organized a conference on the subject in 1959 in Philadelphia at the University of Pennsylvania. In the same year the Society of American Value Engineers was formed. In 1962 the first value engineering journal was published. Currently, courses on value engineering are given at a number of universities and colleges.

MANAGEMENT

Matrix Organization

Functionally organized companies have advantages and disadvantages. Two common problems associated with functionally organized companies are (1) inefficiency in resolving cross-functional conflicts and (2) in large developmental projects many problems arise.

To overcome these problems the matrix organizational structure plays an important role. With the addition of matrix structure in the functional-oriented organization, project managers are fully responsible for each project. With the matrix organizational approach a horizontal layer of responsibility is introduced to the functional organization of vertical structure.

In the matrix organization, for a given project the total cross-functional authority and responsibility is vested in the project manager. With the project manager's consent, persons are assigned to the project by the functional managers. The functional managers and program manager are responsible for administrative and program matters, respectively, concerning these personnel.

Some advantages and disadvantages of matrix (engineering) management are as follows:

Advantages

Faster decision making

Better control

Defined responsibility

Increased middle-management involvement

Defined authority

Good summary review for top management

Effective use of schedule, performance, and cost data

Disadvantages

Indiscriminate use of matrix organization approach to projects

Shortage of projects may generate surplus skills[12]

Graphic Management Techniques

This section presents a number of useful graphic management techniques.[3] Engineers are more inclined towards plotting the given data, possibly due to the nature of their basic training. Important graphical techniques which are useful in making sound management decisions are as follows:

Program Evaluation Review Technique (PERT)

Gantt charts

Break-even charts

These techniques are briefly discussed below.

♦ **PROGRAM EVALUATION REVIEW TECHNIQUE (PERT)** PERT and the critical path method (CPM) were both developed in 1958. Both methods evolved from the Gantt charts and are concerned with determining at a given point in time the status of a project and with spotting trouble areas. Both PERT and CPM are used to determine the critical path of the network of a project, which, in turn, is used to determine the longest period of time required to accomplish the project in question. Each activity of the critical path has to be completed on time if the end completion date of the project is not to be delayed.

Basically, PERT and CPM are the same. The only difference is that PERT requires three estimates (i, e., most likely, optimistic, and pessimistic) for the duration time of an activity to estimate a single expected time. CPM requires only one estimate for the activity duration time and is therefore used where the activity's duration data are fairly accurate.

The following are the main advantages and disadvantages of PERT:

Advantages

Can be computerized.

Helps to improve communication.

Helps spot the critical points.

Helps understanding.

Interrelationship in work flow is clearly shown.

Duplications and omissions are avoided.

Better utilization of resources which in turn helps in time and cost savings.

Disadvantages

Costly.

Less accurate time estimates.

More complex as compared to Gantt charts.

Tendency to use pessimistic time.

♦ **GANTT CHARTS** These charts were developed by H.L. Gantt during the First World War. The old version of Gantt charts plotted a series of activity bars against time. For a certain portion of a complete job in question, the bars denote the starting, duration, and finish times. Gantt charts may be classified into the following three categories: load chart, planning chart, and chart for time (reserved) planning. Finally, it may be said that for planning and scheduling Gantt charts are used frequently.

♦ **BREAK-EVEN CHARTS** Break-even charts were developed about 72 years ago. Basically, they show (fixed and variable) costs and revenue relationship to the number of units sold. These relationships are plotted on a graph for the decision maker's convenience. The break-even point is where the plotted revenue line and the plotted total cost line intersect.

New Product Development Decision Techniques

This section offers techniques to assist in deciding whether to develop a new product or not. These techniques will be helpful in making go, no-go decisions to produce a product. If careful analysis is not carried out before the product development stage, the go decision may be detrimental to the well-being of the company because the end product may not sell in the market. The indices and formulas discussed below are useful in evaluating new-products development projects:

♦ **MOTTLEY-NEWTON METHOD** This index is used basically to evaluate a project to make go, no-go decisions for its development in relation to the other projects under consideration. Mottley and Newton present this index in detail; the authors believe that the factors that concern the selection of a product development project are as follows:

Completion time

Cost

Success promise

Gain in the market

From the market standpoint the need for successful research[4]

The future profits of a company will be indirectly affected by these five factors. A score from one to three is assigned to each factor; then the scores are multiplied to obtain the final score for a project. Finally, the new projects are ranked according to their total scores (i.e., from highest score to lowest score). The criteria for assigning scores to the five factors are given in Mottley and Newton. These same authors also offer numerical examples, as do Murdick and Karger.

♦ **PROFITABILITY INDEX** This is a quantitative method used to select new projects. Seiler defines the profitability index, α, by[6]

$$\alpha = \left(\prod_{i=1}^{5} A_i \right) / B \tag{8.1}$$

where

A_1 is the probability of commercial success

A_2 is the yearly sales in units (average)

A_3 is the sales price of a unit

A_4 is the probability of technical success

A_5 is static market life

B is the total cost of the project

This index is subject to the constant demand assumption.

♦ **SOBELMAN METHOD** Sobelman developed this index to take into consideration the time value of money. If a project is to be undertaken, the index must be positive. The index, λ, is defined by

$$\lambda = \sum_{i=1}^{g} \alpha(1+k)^{-i} - A \tag{8.2}$$

where

$$A \equiv \sum_{i=1}^{b} \theta(1+k)^{-i} \tag{8.3}$$

$$g \equiv \mu + \Upsilon(1 - c/s) \tag{8.4}$$

$$b \equiv c + s(1 - \mu/\Upsilon) \tag{8.5}$$

The symbols used in equations (8.2) through (8.5) are defined as follows:

θ is the yearly mean development cost

k is the annual interest rate

α is the yearly mean net profit

c is the time when the development is completed (years)

μ is the product's useful life (years)

Υ is the products group mean useful life (it is assummed that the product under consideration is a member of this group)

s is the product's group mean development time (it is assumed that the product under consideration is a member of this group)

Example 8.1

For the following data, find the value λ of a project:

$k = 0.15,\ c = 2$ years, $\mu = 10$ years; $\alpha = \$50{,}000$

$\theta = \$15{,}000;\ \Upsilon = 8$ years, $s = 1.5$ years

By substituting the given data in equations (8.4) and (8.5), respectively, we get:

$$g \equiv 10 + 8(1 - 2/1.5) = 7.33 \text{ years}$$

$$b \equiv 2 + 1.5(1 - 10/8) = 1.625 \text{ years}$$

Now substituting the above calculated values for g and b and the given data in equations (8.2) and (8.3), we get:

$$\lambda = \sum_{i=1}^{7.33} 50{,}000(1.15)^{-i} - A$$

$$A = \sum_{i=1}^{1.625} 15{,}000(1.15)^{-i}$$

Therefore,

$$\lambda = 213{,}669.32 - 20{,}316$$
$$= \$193{,}353.32$$

♦ **RELATIVE WORTH METHOD** This index, α, is defined as

$$\alpha = [P_1 P_2 + P_3 \{M - G\}]/k \tag{8.6}$$

where

$$M \equiv \sum_{j=0}^{m} N_j (1+i)^{-j} \tag{8.7}$$

$$G \equiv \sum_{j=0}^{m} c_j (1+i)^{-j} \tag{8.8}$$

The symbols used in equations (8.6) through (8.8) are defined as follows:

- i is the annual interest rate
- k is the new product research and development cost
- m is the product's market life
- P_i is the ith probability of success: $i = 1$ (technical success), $i = 2$ (commercial success), $i = 3$ (success due to economic factors)
- N_j is the jth year's net income
- c_j is the jth year's capital investment

For detailed information on this method, consult Murdick and Karger.

♦ **CALCULATED-RISK INDEX** The index, I, is given by

$$I=\left(\prod_{i=1}^{2} \mu_i\right)/\beta \tag{8.9}$$

where

μ_1 is the risk factor

μ_2 is the total of all yearly net incomes

β is the cost of total investment (for example, the costs of product and market development and assets)

We should note that the index, I, yields return on investment which is useful for comparison with a predetermined minimum rate. For further reading, consult Seiler's book.

♦ **MANLEY METHOD** This method is used to determine net profit-to-sales ratio. This ratio can be used to estimate the maximum research cost which will yield an acceptable profit. The net profit-to-sales ratio, R_{ps}, is defined by

$$R_{ps} = \left(a+b+\frac{c}{2}\right)/df \tag{8.10}$$

where

f is yearly sales

d is the number of years for break-even (in other words, to recover total expenditures)

a is the plant investment

b is the amount of working capital needed

c is the cost of research (before taxes)

For further reading, consult the Manley article.

♦ **DEAN-SENGUPTA INDEX** This index was developed by Dean and Sengupta.[8] The indices of two projects can be compared to measure their relative performance. The index, θ, is defined as

$$\theta = F/G \tag{8.11}$$

where

$$F \equiv P_1 \cdot P_2 \sum_{i=1}^{m} M_i(1+j)^{-i} \tag{8.12}$$

$$G \equiv \sum_{i=0}^{m} I_i(1+j)^{-i} \tag{8.13}$$

The symbols in equations (8.11) through (8.13) are defined as follows:

P_1 is the technical success probability of the project

P_2 is the probability of marketing the product if the project is successful technically

m is the project's useful life, in years

M_i is the ith year's return from the product under consideration (assume that the product was technical and successfully marketed)

j is the annual interest rate (the money time value)

I_i is the ith year's investment

VALUE ENGINEERING

The simple and straightforward definition of value engineering is that it is a systematic, creative technique used to accomplish a necessary function at the minimum cost.[1] Another way to describe value engineering is as follows:

Value engineering identifies a product function.

For the function under consideration it establishes its value.

It provides the function in question at the minimum cost.

Value Engineering Job Plan

The job plan is a systematic procedure of applying value engineering techniques.[9] Figure 8.1 shows the job plan phases, and a brief summary of each phase is given below:

♦ **GENERAL PHASE** This phase is concerned with applying the techniques of subsequent phases of the job plan effectively. The factors, such as good human relations, teamwork, good business judgment, and so on, are to be practiced seriously throughout the entire job plan.

♦ **INFORMATION PHASE** This phase is concerned with securing the correct facts, determining costs, and establishing relationships between important factors such as costs and requirements.

♦ **FUNCTION PHASE** Defining the function and determining its relationships are the two important elements of this phase.

♦ **CREATIVE PHASE** As the name suggests, this phase is concerned with creativeness. There are two basic approaches: developing creative ideas and establishing positive thinking by creating the necessary environment. The creative and the judicial are the two mental processes involved in this phase.

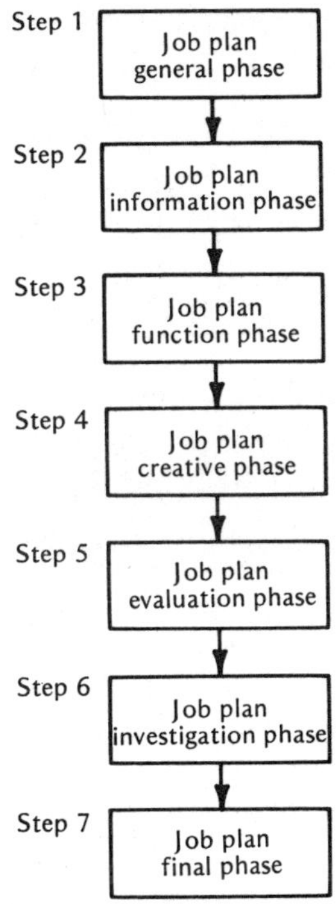

Figure 8.1 Phases of the job plan

♦ **EVALUATION PHASE** The evaluation phase refines and combines ideas, estimates the cost of ideas, develops functional alternatives, and compares the end results.

♦ **INVESTIGATION PHASE** This phase deals with further refinement of the selected ideas so that they can be put into practice, thus providing techniques to perform required functions at a minimum cost and so on.

♦ **FINAL PHASE** This is essentially the conclusion phase which establishes and presents the final recommendations.

Techniques Of Value Engineering

Below are the value engineering techniques which are related to the various phases of the job plan.

1. Define the primary and secondary functions, and perform cost analysis.
2. Use creativeness and function evaluation.

3. Challenge needs: blast, create, and then refine.
4. Make use of standards and available resources.
5. Determine the important facts and make use of information available from the best and reliable sources.
6. Acquire new information and utilize one's own judgment.
7. Put effort on specifics and take advantage of good human relations.
8. Use the company's money and resources as if they were one's own.[10]

Heller elaborates further on these techniques.

SUMMARY

This chapter introduces management and value engineering. The historical aspect of management, and the advantages and disadvantages of the matrix engineering management are presented. Graphic management techniques and various project selection methods are covered. The value engineering job plan as well as value engineering techniques conclude the chapter.

EXERCISES

8.1. Discuss briefly the history of the management field.

8.2. Compare the functional and the matrix organization management structures.

8.3. Describe briefly at least four graphic management techniques.

8.4. List the advantages and disadvantages of PERT.

8.5. Discuss at least three project selection techniques.

8.6. Discuss the history of value engineering and the value engineering job plan.

NOTES

1. *Engineering Design Handbook, Value Engineering,* (Springfield, VA: U.S. Army Material Command, AMCP 706-104, July 1971), pp. 1.2–1.3.
2. H.E. Pywell, "Engineering Management in a Multiple- (Second- and Third-Level) Matrix Organization," *IEEE Transactions on Engineering Management,* vol. Em-26 (1979): 51–55.
3. V.G. Reuter, "Using Graphic Management Tools," *Journal of Systems Management,* vol. 30 (1979): 6–17.

4. C.M. Mottley and R.D. Newton, "The Selection of Projects for Industrial Research," *Operations Research* (1959): 740–51.
5. R.G. Murdick and D.W. Karger, "The Shoestring Approach to Rating New Products," *Machine Design* (1973): 86–89.
6. R.E. Seiler, *Improving the Effectiveness of Research and Development,* (New York: McGraw-Hill, 1965), pp. 50.
7. R. Manley, "Can You Rate Your Research?" *Chemical Week* (May 1959):
8. B.V. Dean and S.S. Sengupta, "Research Budgeting and Project Selection," *IEEE Transactions on Engineering Management* (1962): 158–69.
9. A.E. Mudge, *Value Engineering: A Systematic Approach* (New York: McGraw-Hill 1971), pp. 30–34.
10. E.D. Heller, *Value Management: Value Engineering and Cost Reduction,* (Reading: Addison-Wesley, 1971), pp. 62–75.

9

Managerial Reliability and Maintainability

The history of the reliability field goes back to the Second World War. However, the history of positive thinking on reliability management started in the early 1950s. Later in that decade an ad hoc group was formed to study parts specification management for reliability (PSMR). This group was set up by the U.S. Department of Defense whose report was published in 1960. The subject of reliability management was also emphasized by the ad hoc committee for guided missile reliability which was also established in the late 1950s.

Some of the areas related to reliability and maintainability management are presented in subsequent sections.

PRODUCT ASSURANCE GROUP

Generally, reliability-conscious companies have a product assurance organization which is generally responsible to top-level management. The activities of the group are either directly or indirectly related to product reliability, from the early design stage to the final acceptance stage. Figure 9.1 shows the functions of the product assurance group. The functions are described as follows:

1. *Reliability:* Functions such as product reliability prediction, reliability design review, reliability modeling, reliability demonstration, reliability program plan preparation, and so on are performed by members of the reliability subgroup.

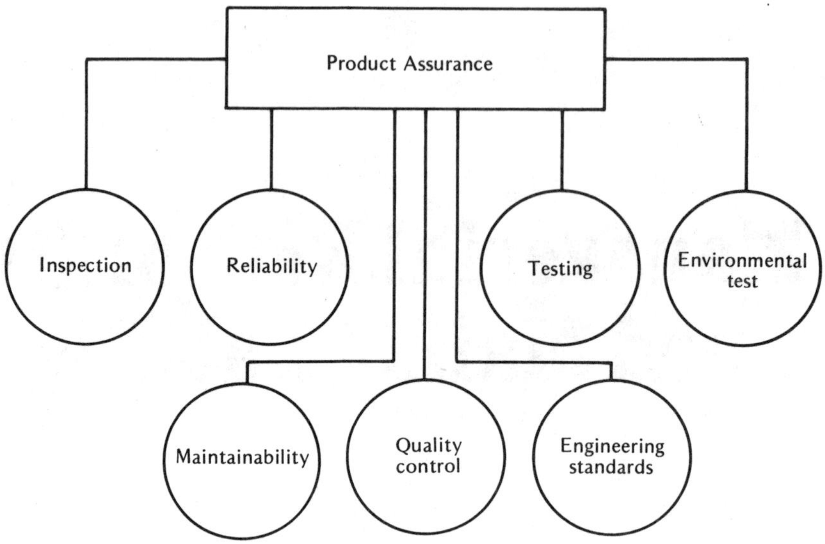

Figure 9.1 Functions of the product assurance group

2. *Maintainability:* Members of this subgroup perform the tasks of design review from the maintainability standpoint, maintainability demonstration, program plan preparation, and projections of logistics.
3. *Engineering standards:* This mainly concerns design standards, specifications for parts procurement, lists of qualified parts, and so on.
4. *Quality Control:* This function includes tasks such as quality auditing, quality control program plan preparation, statistical quality control techniques applications, supplier quality auditing and control, product design review participation, and so on.
5. *Inspection:* The inspection subgroup or department is responsible for incoming and outgoing inspection, shipping control, inspection of in-process assembly, and so on.
6. *Environmental test:* The members of this subgroup look after tasks such as preparation of environmental test plans, acceptance testing from the environmental standpoint, qualification testing (design), and so on.
7. *Test:* This function includes tasks such as final acceptance testing, in-process acceptance testing, controlling and servicing test equipment, and so on.

We should note here that the tasks performed within these seven functions may have some overlap; in addition, some of the tasks may be the responsibility of a group other than the one listed here. This depends on the type and size of the company, management policies, nature of the product manufactured, and so on. To perform these seven functions of product assurance some companies may have separate departments for each function. Other companies may have all seven functions lumped into one or two departments.

PRODUCT RELIABILITY PREDICTION

Product reliability prediction is one of the most important tasks performed by the reliability department. Great care must be taken when predicting the reliability of a product because it will indirectly reflect on the company's profitability. Optimistically predicted reliability not actually in the products means dissatisfied customers, less number of products sold in the market, and so on. On the other hand, the pessimistically predicted reliability means the company spends more money to improve the reliability of the product in order to meet the specified reliability. This will lead to a decrease in company profit.

Product reliability prediction is not a one-time job. It begins at the conceptual design stage of the product when rough estimates of reliability are made. These estimates are revised and refined as the product's design matures. In the product reliability prediction, the following must be considered:

Failure rate calculations based on field data

Expected failure modes

Failures criticalities and the circuit configuration

Environmental conditions

Parts quantities

Types of parts

SELECTION OF PARTS SUPPLIERS

This is one of the most important functions of product assurance management: they must make sure that reliable, capable, and well-experienced parts suppliers are selected. These suppliers should only be selected after evaluating their manufacturing capability as well as comparing their product with similar products of other suppliers. Furthermore, the products of selected suppliers should be monitored on a continuous basis. Rosenthal lists the following items to be considered as measures of performance of suppliers:

Facilities for environmental tests

Inspection equipment

Failure reporting procedures

Failure correction procedures

Quality control procedures

Control of production processes

Responsibility for the financial aspect[2]

MATHEMATICAL MODELS FOR RELIABILITY AND MAINTAINABILITY MANAGERS

Model I

This section presents a mathematical model which will be useful for both reliability and maintainability managers in making sound manpower planning decisions, especially when basic functions of the reliability and maintainability departments are paper study oriented.[3] This type of situation occurs especially in research organizations.

The following assumptions are associated with the model:

1. In one year there are 240 working days.
2. Each person involved reads αR number of reliability reports per year, where R is the number of reports written (turned out) per year and α is the fraction of total reports given to an average professional employed by the department.

The following are the definitions of symbols used to develop the model:

- k is the number of professional persons employed by the department
- d_m is the mean number of days to read a report completely
- R is the number of reports written annually
- α is the fraction of total reports given to an average professional employed by the department
- d_a is the mean number of days to accomplish one report (this time should include from the investigation and analysis phase to the write-up phase)

The number of days, d_c, needed by an average employee to carry out creative work is given by:

$$d_c = 240 - R\,\alpha\,d_m \qquad (9.1)$$

The mean number of reports, β, an employee can turn out is obtained by dividing equation (9.1) by d_a as follows:

$$\beta = \{240 - R\,\alpha\,d_m\}\,/d_a \qquad (9.2)$$

The reports turned out by the department are obtained by multiplying equation (9.2) with k as follows:

$$R = \{240k - R\,\alpha d_m k\} / d_a \tag{9.3}$$

By rearranging equation (9.3) explicitly in terms of R, we get

$$R = 240k/A \tag{9.4}$$

where

$$A \equiv d_a + \alpha\, k\, d_m \tag{9.5}$$

The measure of the department's efficiency, θ, is defined by

$$\theta = R/R_0 \tag{9.6}$$

where R_0 denotes the actual number of reports produced by the department if the total number of work days (240 days) were spent on reporting by everyone in the department.

Substituting equation (9.4) in equation (9.6) leads to:

$$\theta = \{240k/(d_a + \alpha\, k\, d_m)\} / R_0 \tag{9.7}$$

R_0 is given by

$$R_0 = (240k)/d_a \tag{9.8}$$

By utilizing equation (9.8) in equation (9.7) we get:

$$\theta = \frac{\cancel{240k}}{d_a + \alpha\, k\, d_m} \cdot \frac{d_a}{\cancel{(240k)}}$$

$$= \frac{d_a}{d_a + \alpha\, k\, d_m} \tag{9.9}$$

We should note here that θ denotes the fraction of total time spent in preparing department reports.

The following conclusions[3] may be drawn from this analysis:

1. It can be seen from equation (9.9) that for the very large value of k, the efficiency factor, θ, is inversely proportional to k and approaches towards the zero value.

2. From equation (9.4) it can be observed that for the very large value of k, equation (9.4) reduces to

$$R_\ell = 240/\alpha\, d_m \tag{9.10}$$

3. If no person reads any of the circulated reports, then the number of reports produced by the organization from equation (9.8) is:

$$R_0 = 240k/d_a \tag{9.11}$$

However, if each employee reads and writes reports, so then the upper limiting number of reports to be produced by the organization from equation (9.10) is:

$$R = 240/\alpha\, d_m \tag{9.12}$$

If no employee reads any report, then the number of employees required to produce reports R_ℓ can be found by equating expressions (9.11) and (9.12) as follows:

$$\frac{240k}{d_a} = \frac{240}{\alpha\, d_m} \tag{9.13}$$

Thus, solving equation (9.13) for k yields:

$$k = d_a/\alpha\, d_m \tag{9.14}$$

Example 9.1

A reliability and maintainability department has a very large number of professional employees. The average time required to read one report is 1/8 days and $\alpha = 1/5$. Find the maximum number of reports that will be turned out annually by the reliability department.

Substituting the given data in equation (9.10) leads to:

$$R = \frac{240}{\frac{1}{5} \cdot \frac{1}{8}} = 240(5) \cdot (8)$$

$$= 9{,}600 \text{ reports/year}$$

♦ **MODEL II** This model is actually a modified version of model I. The model includes the additional factor that the reading or studying of reports produced by other persons helps to increase overall efficiency and productivity. This is due to the assumption that reading others' reports will increase the knowledge of the employee, which in turn will help to reduce the writing time required to complete a report. Therefore, assume that the report writing time, d_a, is defined by

$$d_a = d_{a0}\,\{g + (1-g)e^{-\lambda\alpha R}\} \tag{9.15}$$

where

d_{a0}	is the report writing time without reading any report
g	is the fraction which is chosen in such a way so that the product of g and d_{a0} denotes the minimum preparation time (this preparation time cannot be reduced any further)
$d_{a0}(1-g)$	is the maximum preparation time reduction which is possible through reading
λ	is the reading effectiveness constant

By substituting equation (9.15) in equation (9.11), we get:

$$R = 240k/[d_{a0}\{g + (1-g)e^{-\lambda\alpha R}\} + \alpha k\, d_m] \tag{9.16}$$

As for model I, for large k, the above expression reduces to

$$R = 240/\alpha\, d_m \tag{9.17}$$

Again, the value of R_0 is given by:

$$R_0 = \frac{240k}{d_{a0}} \tag{9.18}$$

Thus, substituting equations (9.16) and (9.18) in equation (9.6) leads to the following efficiency factor:

$$\theta = \frac{d_{a0}}{[d_{a0}\{g + (1-g)e^{-\lambda\alpha R}\} + \alpha\, k\, d_m]} \tag{9.19}$$

Example 9.2

For the following data from a reliability department, find the number of reports produced annually by the department:

$$k = 50,\ d_{a0} = 20 \text{ days},\ d_m = \frac{1}{8} \text{ days},$$

$$\alpha = 0.2,\ g = 0.5,\ \lambda = \frac{1}{50}$$

By substituting the given data in equation (9.16) we get:

$$R = 240(50)/[20\{0.5 + 0.5\, e^{-(0.2)(0.02)R}\} + (0.2)(50)(0.125)] \tag{9.20}$$

Rewriting equation (9.20) leads to:

$$R = 12000/[10 + 10\, e^{-0.004R} + 1.25]$$

$$= 12000/(11.25 + 10\, e^{-0.004R}) \tag{9.21}$$

Rearranging equation (9.21) results in:

$$R(11.25 + 10\, e^{-0.004R}) - 12000 = 0 \tag{9.22}$$

From this equation the approximate value of R is:

$$R \simeq 1{,}053 \text{ reports/year}$$

If no person reads any report, the number of reports turned out annually by the department from equation (9.18) is:

$$R_0 = \frac{240k}{d_{a0}} = \frac{240(50)}{20}$$

$$= 600 \text{ reports/year}$$

Now we can easily come to the conclusion that more reports are produced when professional employees read reports and the value of k is small.

RELIABILITY MANUAL

Any engineering company functioning in a competitive environment generally has manuals on the organizational structure of the company, design engineering practices, quality control procedures, manufacturing procedures, and so on. The manuals are useful because they help to identify functional relationships between departments, divisions and groups, outline authorities, define responsibilities, outline design procedures to be followed systematically, outline the quality control practices, and so on.

Similarly, the reliability manual should include the following items:

1. Useful reliability techniques, models, and so on
2. Companywide reliability policy
3. Reliability demonstration and test procedures
4. Organizational structure and responsibilities
5. Product design phase procedures from the standpoint of reliability
6. Failure data collection and analysis procedures to be followed
7. Relationship with customers and suppliers

SUMMARY

This chapter briefly discusses the functions of the product assurance group. These functions include quality control, reliability, maintainability, engineering standards, inspection, environmental testing, and so on. Such important reliability engineering department tasks as reliability prediction and selection of part suppliers are also discussed. Useful mathematical models to plan and organize research-oriented reliability manpower are presented, along with the reliability manual.

EXERCISES

9.1. List and describe briefly the important tasks of a reliability department.

9.2. Suppose you are a product assurance director. What departments will be under your direct control?

9.3. Discuss briefly the departments from question 9.2.

9.4. A reliability department which basically concentrates on research has over 300 professional employees; this is considered to be a fairly large department. If $\alpha = 1/5$ and on the average 0.25 days are required to read a report, then calculate the maximum number of reports to be produced by the department professionals in one year. α is defined in the chapter.

NOTES

1. B.S. Dhillon, et al, "Reliability and Maintainability Management," in *Management and Office Information Systems*, edited by S.K. Chang (New York: Plenum Press, in Press).
2. S.A. Rosenthal, "Implementing an Effective Product Assurance Program for High-Reliability Equipment," *IEEE Transactions on Engineering Management*, vol. 13 (1966): 143–54.
3. F.P. Alder, "Relationships Between Organization Size and Efficiency," *Management Science*, vol. 7 (1960): 80–84.

10

Engineering System Economics

In today's environment many new engineering systems are being designed and the old ones discarded. Economics is one of the most important factors, if not the only one, in making the decision to build a new system or to scrap the old one. Furthermore, economic factors are seriously considered at the actual design stage of the system; in fact, the success of engineering projects is often stated in terms of financial efficiency. This may be due to our capitalistic economy. The technical aspect of an engineering project is best understood by engineers; in many cases they end up carrying out combined technical and financial detail studies which provide input to final decisions. Therefore, this chapter presents material which directly or indirectly is concerned with the economics of a system.

In the case of a reliability and maintainability engineer, he or she gets involved in many studies which require considerable knowledge of engineering system economics, for example, such projects as life cycle costing, redundant system reliability optimization subject to cost, weight constraints, and so on.

FORMULAS TO CALCULATE TIME VALUE OF MONEY

This section offers simple formulas to calculate the time value of money. These formulas are described on the following page.

Single Sum Money Formula

The formula for this model is

$$M_f = M_p(1+j)^m \tag{10.1}$$

where

M_p is the present worth of the money

M_f is the future worth of money after m years

m is the number of years

j is the yearly compound interest rate

The present worth of money from equation (10.1) is:

$$M_p = M_f(1+j)^{-m} \tag{10.2}$$

Present Worth of Series of Cash Flows Formula

The formula is defined as follows:[1]

$$M_p = \sum_{i=1}^{m} S_i(1+j)^{-i} \tag{10.3}$$

where S_i represents the ith sum of money (cash flow) at the end of year i. The S_i sum of money could be the amount which is received or paid at the end of year i; this depends on the project under consideration.

Example 10.1

A reliability study project is to be carried out in company A, to which the cost of the project, \$50,000, will be paid by the customer after one year. Simultaneously, company A has subcontracted the entire project to company B to which it will pay \$45,000 after two years. Find the present worth of the profit to company A if the annual compound interest rate is 10%.

By substituting the given data in equation (10.3) we get:

$$\begin{aligned} M_p &= \sum_{i=1}^{2} S_i(1+j)^{-i} \\ &= S_1(1+j)^{-1} + S_2(1+j)^{-2} \\ &= 50{,}000(1+0.1)^{-1} + 45{,}000(1+0.1)^{-2} \end{aligned} \tag{10.4}$$

Since the money has to be paid out to the subcontractor, the second right-hand term of equation (10.4) becomes negative; therefore equation (10.4) is rewritten to the following form:

$$M_p = 50{,}000(1.1)^{-1} - 45{,}000(1.1)^{-2}$$
$$= 45{,}454.55 - 37{,}190.08$$
$$= 8{,}264.46 \text{ dollars}$$

Therefore the present worth of the profit to company A is \$8,264.46.

Future Worth of Series of Cash Flows Formula

The future worth formula is defined as follows:[1]

$$M_f = \sum_{i=1}^{m} S_i(1+j)^{m-i} \tag{10.5}$$

DEPRECIATION METHODS

The basis for depreciation is that with use and time, the value of most property decreases. There are many methods used to calculate the depreciated value of a product or a property over time. Some of the frequently used methods of depreciation are discussed below.

The Straight-Line Technique

This is the most commonly used and simplest method because it is based on the uniform write-off of a property or a product over its useful life. In other words, the yearly depreciation of the product is the same. The annual depreciation charge, d_c, is given by

$$d_c = (C - \theta)/k \tag{10.6}$$

where

- C is the product purchasing cost
- θ is the product salvage value (value of the product at the end of its useful life period)
- k is the product's useful life years

The book or undepreciated value, U_v, of the product at the end of year m is given by:

$$U_v = C - \{C - \theta\}\, m/k \tag{10.7}$$

Example 10.2

A piece of mechanical equipment has been purchased for \$80,000. Its expected useful life is 10 years. After the 10-year period the salvage value of the equipment will be \$10,000. At the end of each year the equipment's value depreciates by the same amount. Calculate the book value of the equipment at the end of the fifth year.

By utilizing the given data in equation (10.6), the annual depreciation charge is:

$$d_c = (80{,}000 - 10{,}000)/10$$
$$= \$7{,}000 \text{ per year}$$

Again, by utilizing the above data in equation (10.7) we get the equipment's book value at the end of the fifth year:

$$U_v = 80{,}000 - 7{,}000(5)$$
$$= \$35{,}000$$

Declining-Balance Technique

This method is concerned with the accelerated write-off of the product's value in the initial years of its useful life and the lesser write-off toward the end of its useful years.[2]

The technique requires that the salvage value of the product be positive. The product's depreciation rate, d_r, is defined by:

$$d_r = 1 - \left(\frac{\theta}{C}\right)^{1/k} \tag{10.8}$$

The book value, U_v, of the product in question at the end of m years is given by:

$$U_v = C\left(\frac{\theta}{C}\right)^{m/k}$$
$$= \theta^{m/k} \cdot C^{1-\frac{m}{k}} \tag{10.9}$$

Example 10.3

Assume in Example 10.2 that the mechanical equipment depreciates according to the declining-balance criteria. Find the book value of the mechanical equipment at the end of the fifth year.

By utilizing the given data in examples 4.2 and 4.3 and equation (10.9), we get:

$$U_v = C\left(\frac{\theta}{C}\right)^{m/k}$$
$$= 80{,}000\left(\frac{10{,}000}{80{,}000}\right)^{5/10}$$
$$= \$28{,}284.27$$

Sum-of-Digits Technique

The name of this technique comes from the calculation procedure used to compute product depreciation.[2] Just like in the declining-balance technique, the product's value depreciates higher in its initial years of useful life and lower in the remaining years of useful life.

The yearly depreciation charge, d_c, is defined by

$$d_c = \frac{(k-m+1)}{(1+2+3+4+\ldots+k)} \cdot (C-\theta) \tag{10.10}$$

where

$(k-m+1)$	is the product's remaining useful life
$(1+2+3+4+\ldots+k)$	is the sum of the digits for the product's useful life
$(C-\theta)$	is the difference between the item's acquisition cost and its salvage value

The sum of the series is:

$$(1+2+3+4+\ldots+k) = \frac{k(k+1)}{2} \tag{10.11}$$

Therefore, the result of substituting relationship (10.11) in equation (10.10) is:

$$d_c = (k-m+1)(C-\theta)2/k(k+1) \tag{10.12}$$

The book value, U_v, after m years is given by:

$$U_v = \theta + (C-\theta)\,2\,\{1+2+3+\ldots+(k-m)\}/(k+1)k \tag{10.13}$$

Example 10.4

Assume in Example 10.2 that the product under consideration depreciates according to the sum-of-digits criteria. Find the book value of the item at the end of the fifth year.

By substituting the known data in equation (10.13), we get:

$$U_v = 10{,}000 + (80{,}000 - 10{,}000)\,2\,\{1+2+3+\ldots+(10-5)\}/(10+1)10$$

$$= 10{,}000 + 140{,}000\,\{15\}/110$$

$$= \$29{,}090.91$$

Units of Production Depreciation Technique

The previously discussed methods make use of the time factor to allocate depreciation and do not take into consideration usage of the product. The units of production depreciation technique is opposite to these earlier ones because it allocates depreciation on the basis of product usage, not on time. The depreciation, d_m, at the end of year m is given by

$$d_m = (C - \theta)\beta_m / \beta_t \tag{10.14}$$

where

- β_m is the number of units manufactured for the year m
- β_t is the total expected number of units to be manufactured during the useful life of the product

PROCEDURE FOR COST-EFFECTIVENESS ANALYSIS

When engineering projects cannot be evaluated in monetary terms, the cost-effectiveness analysis procedure becomes quite useful. In the past the cost-effectiveness procedure has been practiced most when selecting the defense and space systems for certain goals.[1]

According to Kazanowski, in order to perform cost-effectiveness analysis the following three conditions must be satisfied:

1. Identifiability and attainability of common goals.
2. Necessity of reasonable constraints to bound the problem.
3. To meet goals there must be alternatives.[4]

Figure 10.1 outlines the steps which constitute the cost-effectiveness procedure. The detailed description of these 10 steps may be found in Kazanowski.

OPERATION COST ESTIMATION TECHNIQUE

There are various methods and means practiced in industry to estimate operation cost. This section presents only one method frequently used to estimate such cost. Ostwald uses the formula[5]

$$K_0 = A_1 A_2 r_j \tag{10.15}$$

where

$$A_1 \equiv \left(\frac{H_j}{q} + t_{sj}\right) \tag{10.16}$$

$$A_2 \equiv (1 + R_0) \tag{10.17}$$

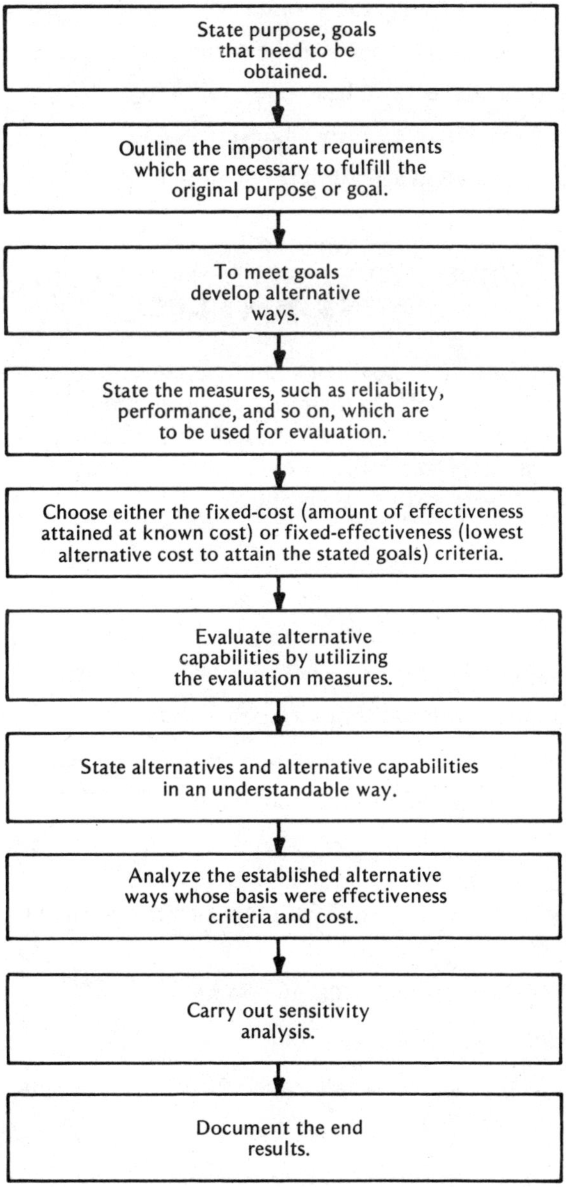

Figure 10.1 Cost-effectiveness steps

Its symbols are defined as follows:

q is the number of units to be produced

H_j denotes the jth operation's set-up time (time is in standard hours)

R_0 is the work center's overhead rate

r_j is the jth operation's hourly labor rate in dollars

t_{sj} is the jth operation's per unit standard time

CORRECTIVE MAINTENANCE COST ESTIMATION MODEL

Engineering systems, units, or items fail, and corrective maintenance is performed to repair them back to their prefailed condition. This cycle continues until the equipment is taken out of service. This section presents a model to estimate the annual corrective maintenance cost of equipment. The yearly corrective maintenance cost, K, is given by[5]

$$K=\left(\frac{\text{MTTR}}{\text{MTBF}}\right)\cdot h\,k_\ell \tag{10.18}$$

where

MTBF is equipment mean time between failures (hours)

MTTR is equipment mean time to repair (hours)

h is the scheduled operating hours of the equipment

k_ℓ is the hourly maintenance labor cost.

Example 10.5

The following data are concerned with the corrective maintenance performed on a minicomputer:

MTBF = 1,000 hours, MTTR = 100 hours

$h = 6{,}000$ hours/year, $k_\ell = \$10$/hour

Calculate the corrective maintenance cost, K, per year. Utilizing the given data in equation (10.18), we get:

$$K=\left(\frac{100}{1{,}000}\right)\cdot(6000)(10)$$

$$= 6{,}000 \text{ dollars/year}$$

A MODEL TO OPTIMIZE REPAIR EFFORT

This mathematical model, taken from Morse's book,[6] was developed to optimize the average duration of repair of a single piece of engineering equipment with a one-crew repair facility. It is assumed in the model that as soon as the equipment fails, repair begins immediately, and as soon as the equipment is repaired, it is put back into service again.

From earlier chapters, equipment steady-state availability, A, and unavailability, UA, are given by

$$A = t_0/(t_0 + t_r) \tag{10.19}$$

where

t_0 is equipment mean time between failures

t_r is equipment mean time to failure

and

$$UA = t_r/(t_0 + t_r) \tag{10.20}$$

The assumption is that the machine crew and its equipment cost is proportional to the repair leads to the maintenance cost expression

$$Kt_r^{-1} \tag{10.21}$$

where K denotes a constant whose value is dependent on the equipment type.

If the equipment or machine operates full time successfully, then it will generate income of amount, I; therefore, to maximize the income from the machine, we write:

$$\frac{d}{dt_r}\left(\frac{It_0}{t_0 + t_r} - \frac{k}{t_r}\right) = 0 \tag{10.22}$$

The above will yield the optimum mean duration of repair. After differentiation, equation (10.22) becomes

$$\frac{k}{t_r^2} - \frac{IA}{T_0 + T_r} = 0 \tag{10.23}$$

where

$$A \equiv t_0/(t_0 + t_r) \tag{10.24}$$

Solving equation (10.23) leads to

$$t_r^* = t_0/(\sqrt{B} - 1) \tag{10.25}$$

where

$$B \equiv I t_0 / k \tag{10.26}$$

In the case of high repair cost, that is, $(k/t_0) > I$, there will be no maximum. This indicates that there is room to purchase better equipment. For more detail on this model, consult Morse.

EQUIPMENT REPLACEMENT MODEL I

This model is taken from Kaufmann.[7] It takes into consideration the replacement of equipment, a system, or a unit whose value depreciates with time.

Equipment cost, $C(t)$, at time t is defined by

$$C(t) = P + C_m(t) - PR(t) \tag{10.27}$$

where

- P is equipment acquisition price
- $PR(t)$ is the reselling price of the equipment at time t (function $R(t)$ decreases monotonically)
- $C_m(t)$ is equipment cumulative maintenance cost (function increases monotonically)

at $t=0, R(0)=1$, and $C_m(0)=0$.

The utilization average cost, $U(t)$, is obtained by dividing equation (10.27) with t as follows:

$$U(t) = \{P + C_m(t) - PR(t)\} / t \tag{10.28}$$

To find the minimum of utilization mean cost, differentiate equation (10.28) with respect to t and set the resulting expression equal to zero as follows:

$$C_m(t) - \frac{t\, dC_m(t)}{dt} + P\left\{1 - R(t) + t\frac{dR(t)}{dt}\right\} = 0 \tag{10.29}$$

For defined $C_m(t)$ and $R(t)$ functions, we can find the minimum value of the utilization mean cost by utilizing equation (10.29). Solved examples may be found in Kaufman.

EQUIPMENT REPLACEMENT MODEL II

The value of equipment after m years is defined by

$$\theta = \text{revenues} - \text{purchase price} - \text{maintenance cost} + \text{salvage value} \tag{10.30}$$

Mathematically, the above equation (10.30) is rewritten to the form:

$$\theta(m) = \int_0^m e(t) \cdot e^{-jt}\, dt - C - \int_0^m r(t) \cdot e^{-jt}\, dt + \alpha(m)\, e^{-jm} \tag{10.31}$$

where

m	is equipment useful life
j	is interest rate
C	is equipment purchase price (initial cost)
$\theta(m)$	is present worth of the equipment at time m
e^{-jt}	is the discounting factor
$\int_0^m e(t) \cdot e^{-jt}\, dt$	is the present worth of revenues
$\int_0^m r(t) \cdot e^{-jt}\, dt$	is the present worth of repair costs
$\alpha(m)\, e^{-jm}$	is salvage or scrap value present worth [$\alpha(m)$ denotes equipment salvage value at time m]
$\int_0^m e(t) \cdot dt$	is total revenues [$e(t)$ is the revenue at time t]
$\int_0^m r(t) \cdot dt$	is total maintenance costs ($r(t)$ is maintenance cost at time t)

Note in this model that the functions $r(t)$ and $\alpha(m)$ are the increasing and decreasing functions, respectively.

In order to maximize the function $\alpha(m)$, differentiate function (10.31) with respect to m and set the resulting expression equal to zero as follows:

$$\frac{d\theta}{dm} = e(m) \cdot e^{-jm} - 0 - r(m) \cdot e^{-jm} + \frac{d\,\alpha(m)}{dm} e^{-jm} - j\,\alpha(m)\, e^{-jm} \tag{10.32}$$

The above equation (10.32) is rewritten to the following form:

$$e(m) - j\,\alpha(m) - r(m) + \frac{d\,\alpha(m)}{dm} = 0 \tag{10.33}$$

The above equation can be solved to find the optimum value for m.

Example 10.6

The functions and data are given as

$$r(t) = a + b\,t$$

where

$$a = 500, \quad b = 100$$

$$\alpha(t) = 4{,}000\, e^{-0.2t}, \quad \frac{d\,\alpha(t)}{dt} = -800\, e^{-0.2t}$$

$$e(t) = 2{,}500 - 25t, \quad C = \$4{,}000, \quad j = 15\%$$

Utilize the above data in equation (10.33) to find the optimum value for m:

$$(2{,}500 - 25m) - (0.15)(4{,}000)e^{-0.2m} - (500) - 100m - 800\, e^{-0.2m} = 0 \tag{10.34}$$

The above equation is simplified to the following form:

$$2{,}000 - 125m - 1{,}400\, e^{-0.2m} = 0 \tag{10.35}$$

The value of m which satisfies equation (10.35) is

$$m^* = 15.5$$

where m^* denotes the optimum value.

The book by Howell and Teichroew is a good source for further information on this model.

LIFE CYCLE COSTING

This concept is not new. In industry it has been practiced over the years in one form or another, although somewhat less systematically. In recent years, due to worsening economic conditions, inflationary trends, and so on, more emphasis is being placed on the subject of life cycle costing.

In today's environment when purchasing or developing a new product, especially for defense uses, special consideration is given to the life cycle cost of the product. The phases generally considered in the life cycle cost applications are as follows:

1. Product concept and definition
2. Product design and development
3. Product manufacturing and installation
4. Product operation and maintenance

Various organizations break down the product life cycle cost phases according to their needs and requirements. For example, the United States Army material command breaks down the product life cycle cost into (1) cost of research and development, (2) cost of investment, and (3) cost of operation and support.

The primary uses of the life cycle cost are as follows:

1. Comparing similar projects
2. Deciding equipment replacement
3. Controlling the project in the pipe line
4. Budgeting and planning

5. Comparing the logistics procedures
6. Choosing competing manufacturers, suppliers, contractors, and so on

These six applications are described further in Seldon.

SUMMARY

The following topics are briefly presented in this chapter: formulas to calculate time value of money, depreciation techniques, cost effectiveness analysis approach, cost estimation techniques, optimizing repair efforts, equipment replacement models, and life cycle costing.

EXERCISES

10.1. If a man invests $5,000 today at the compound interest rate of 15% per annum, find the future worth of the money at the end of 10 years.

10.2. Calculate the present worth of $2,000 invested annually (at the end of each year) for 6 years. The yearly compound interest rate is 15%. The first investment is made at the end of the first year.

10.3. The purchase price of some electronic equipment is $50,000. The scrap value of the equipment is $5,000. In addition, the product has a useful life of 5 years; in other words, the equipment is scrapped at the end of the fifth year. At the end of each year the equipment's value depreciates at a constant value. Calculate the book value of the product at the end of the second year.

10.4. Discuss the cost effectiveness method and the applications of life cycle costing.

10.5. For a piece of mechanical equipment the following data and functions are given:

$$C = \$3{,}000, \quad j = 10\%, \quad e(t) = 1{,}500 - 20t,$$
$$r(t) = 400 + 90t, \quad \alpha(t) = 3{,}000e^{-0.15t}$$

where

C is equipment purchase price

j is interest rate

$e(t)$ is equipment revenue at time t

$r(t)$ is equipment maintenance cost at time t

$\alpha(t)$ is equipment salvage value at time t

Find the optimum value for m (the equipment's useful life) by utilizing equation (10.33).

NOTES

1. J.A. White, M.H. Agee, and K.E. Case, *Principles of Engineering Economic Analysis* (New York: John Wiley & Sons, 1977), pp. 60, 279-280.
2. J.L. Riggs, *Economic Decision Models for Engineers and Managers* (New York: McGraw-Hill, 1968), pp. 199-200.
3. A.M. Wellington, *The Economic Theory of Railway Location* (New York: John Wiley & Sons, 1887), pp. 40.
4. A.D. Kazanowski, "A Standardized Approach to Cost-Effectiveness Evaluations," in *Cost Effectiveness,* edited by J. Morley English (New York: John Wiley & Sons, 1968), pp. 300.
5. P.F. Ostwald, *Cost Estimating for Engineering and Management* (Englewood Cliffs, N.J.: Prentice-Hall, 1974), pp. 281-282, 298.
6. P.M. Morse, *Queues, Inventories and Maintenance* (New York: John Wiley & Sons, 1958), pp. 159-160.
7. A. Kaufmann, *Methods and Models of Operations Research* (Englewood Cliffs, N.J.: Prentice-Hall, 1963), pp. 428-436.
8. J.E. Howell and D. Teichroew, *Mathematical Analysis for Business Decisions* (Homewood, Ill.: Richard D. Irwin, 1971), pp. 260-264.
9. M. Robert Seldon, *Life Cycle Costing: A Better Method of Government Procurement* (Boulder, CO: Westview Press, 1979), pp. 1-12.

11

Reliability and Maintainability Contracting

To procure engineering systems the contracts are usually signed between main contractors and the customer, main contractors and subcontractors, and so on. A contract contains the customer's and the manufacturer's committed requirements which have to be fulfilled at the expiry of the contract; otherwise, either party could be faced with court proceedings. Usually in an engineering system contract, the manufacturer agrees to meet specification requirements of the equipment, delivery date, financial aspects, and so on; then the contract is signed. The system or equipment specification includes such requirements as performance, reliability, maintainability, maintenance, and so on.

In the engineering industry there are many different types of contracts which are signed by the supplier and the purchaser. These depend on the nature of the project, delivery date, financial aspect, and so on. The types of contracts are discussed in the next section.

This chapter is devoted to various aspects of contracting for engineering systems with reference to equipment reliability and maintainability.

TYPES OF CONTRACTS

As mentioned earlier there are various types of contracts which are signed between the equipment manufacturer and the purchaser. Figure 11.1 shows the most common contracts used. Hayes and Romig describe these contracts in detail in their book. Below is a brief summary of each type:

1. *Letter contract:* used as a preliminary contract document when the project has to be started as soon as possible because there is not much time to negotiate a formal contract.
2. *Fixed price:* as the name suggests, the customer pays the mutually agreed price upon the satisfactory delivery of the product.
3. *Fixed price with incentives:* designed to provide incentives to the supplier if he or she manages to produce the specified product at higher efficiency and lower cost.
4. *Fixed-price with escalation:* a fixed-price contract with added escalation clauses. For example, these clauses may cover price fluctuation of material used in the manufacture of the equipment; if the material cost increases, the supplier raises the contract price.
5. *Fixed price, redeterminable:* used in cases where the labor and material costs cannot be estimated accurately, design specifications are less accurate, and so on. At a point in the project when more accurate data is available, the contract price is either raised or lowered.
6. *Firm targets:* at the early stage of the negotiations between the supplier and the customer, the firm ceiling on the price, target price on cost, and the profit are set. In the case of lower or higher project cost or profit, the amount in question is shared between the supplier and the customer according to a mutually agreed formula.

FACTORS TO DETERMINE TYPES OF CONTRACTS

When a customer is determining the type of contract to be negotiated with the equipment supplier or others, many factors will influence his or her final decision. However, according to Hajek, the following factors are essential to consider:

Supplier's past performance

Requirement urgency

Accounting procedures practiced by the suppliers

Existing competition

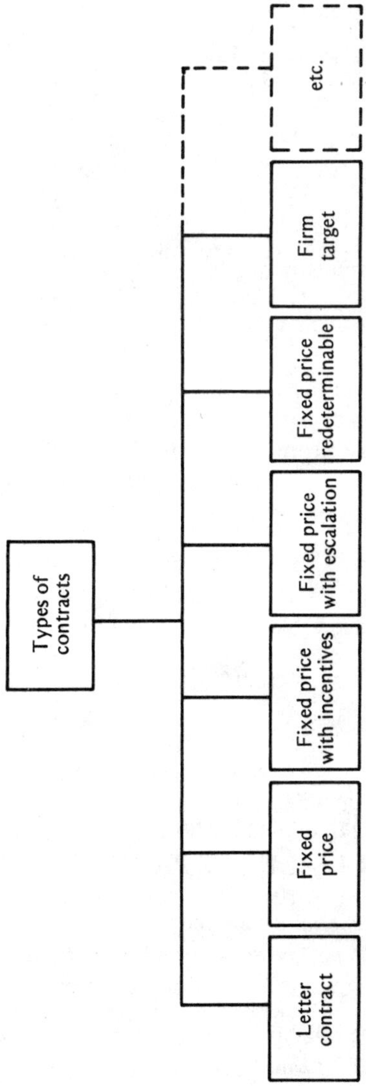

Figure 11.1 List of contract types

Amount of risk to the supplier

Equipment type

Equipment design complexity

Equipment procurement contract life

Administrative costs

Inclination of the supplier towards certain contract types

Availability of necessary data[2]

ATTRIBUTES OF THE CONTRACT NEGOTIATOR

In order to be awarded a contract in the competing environment, the function of the contract negotiator is very important. The success of the contract negotiation largely depends upon the way the negotiation is conducted, the personality of the negotiator, his or her verbal skills, and so on. We should note that even a company with superior product and past reputation may not be awarded a contract because of a poor negotiator. According to Hajek, a negotiator should possess the following qualities:

1. Verbal communication, the ability to express oneself effectively and to be able to present information (technical, financial, etc.) effectively and clearly in an understandable and simplified form.
2. Ability to think quickly and clearly.
3. Objectivity.
4. Patience.[2]

MANAGING AND MONITORING A RELIABILITY PROGRAM

To produce or procure reliable equipment, the contractor and the customer have to work in a cooperative environment. In order to implement and monitor an effective reliability program, the following steps must be followed:

1. State the equipment reliability requirements: the customer must specify the equipment reliability needs in the design specification.
2. Develop the equipment reliability reporting and monitoring schedules: these schedules should be developed by the customer and should cover project evaluation, test plans, reliability reports evaluation, and so on.
3. Preparation of proposal request: this document—prepared by the customer—should include a request for the reliability coverage stated in the proposal.

4. Preparation of proposal: this document is produced by the prospective supplier or manufacturer and presents information on various aspects of reliability and maintainability.
5. Proposals evaluation: in this phase proposals submitted by the prospective manufacturers or contractors are evaluated by the customer.
6. Contractual documents evaluation: prior to contract negotiations, these documents should be evaluated by the customer.
7. Reliability requirements implementation in the design and development of the equipment: these requirements are jointly implemented and monitored by the customer and the manufacturer.
8. Reliability program implementation in the equipment production phase.[3]

RELIABILITY DOCUMENTS

This section briefly describes the documents which are generally applicable to a reliability program. These documents become useful especially when writing reliability requirements in the design specification of equipment. Instead of writing a complete set of requirements in the design specification, these documents are simply referred so that the manufacturer follows the reliability requirements according to the referenced documents. The most commonly referred to documents in the system design specification are those produced by the United States Armed Forces. Aerospace and defense contractors are well aware of these documents. Furthermore, the documents are widely accepted by both aerospace and defense contractors and procurement agencies or customers. The list of documents presented below were applied to the United States Army reliability program.

1. Requirements for reliability program (for systems and equipments): MIL-STD-785*
2. Definition of effectiveness terms for reliability, maintainability, human factors and safety: MIL-STD-721B
3. Reliability tests, exponential distribution: MIL-STD-781A
4. Reliability prediction: MIL-STD-756A
5. Reliability assurance program for electronic parts specification: MIL-STD-790A
6. Failure rate sampling plans and procedures: MIL-STD-690A
7. Reliability stress and failure rate data for electronic equipment: MIL-HDBK-217C
8. Sampling procedures and tables for inspection by attributes: MIL-STD-105D

9. Sampling procedures and tables for continuous inspection by attributes: MIL-STD-1235[3]

Other documents which were utilized by the United States Army may be found in the *Quality Assurance, Reliability Handbook.*

WARRANTIES

Warranties are generally given to customers to assure them that the fielded equipment will perform according to their expectation. Otherwise, the manufacturer will be responsible to improve the equipment according to each customer's requirements as specified in the warranty clauses. The duration period of the warranty is mutually agreed upon between the customer and the purchaser.

According to Balaban and Retterer, in procurements of avionics equipment the warranty period is three to five years and the warranty cost is usually 4% to 10% of the initial purchase price of the equipment.[4] In addition, the authors feel that the factors shown in Figure 11.2 should be considered when choosing a system or some equipment for the warranty coverage.

Reliability Improvement Warranty Risks To Contractor

According to Balaban and Meth, the main contractor reliability improvement warranty risks are as follows:

1. Less precision in the determination of product failure frequency.
2. Less precision in the determination of equipment repair cost.
3. Less precision in knowing the product's rate of usage. (Increase in product use usually leads to a higher number of equipment failures).
4. Required equipment data may not be supplied to supplier or contractor according to the agreement.
5. Poor maintenance in the field which may be beyond the manufacturer's control.
6. Unexpected increase in inflation rate.
7. Due to competition, the asking price to manufacture certain equipment is too low.
8. Unforeseen product usage stresses which may be the cause for the increase in equipment failures.
9. Covering high technology equipment with reliability improvement warranty.[5]

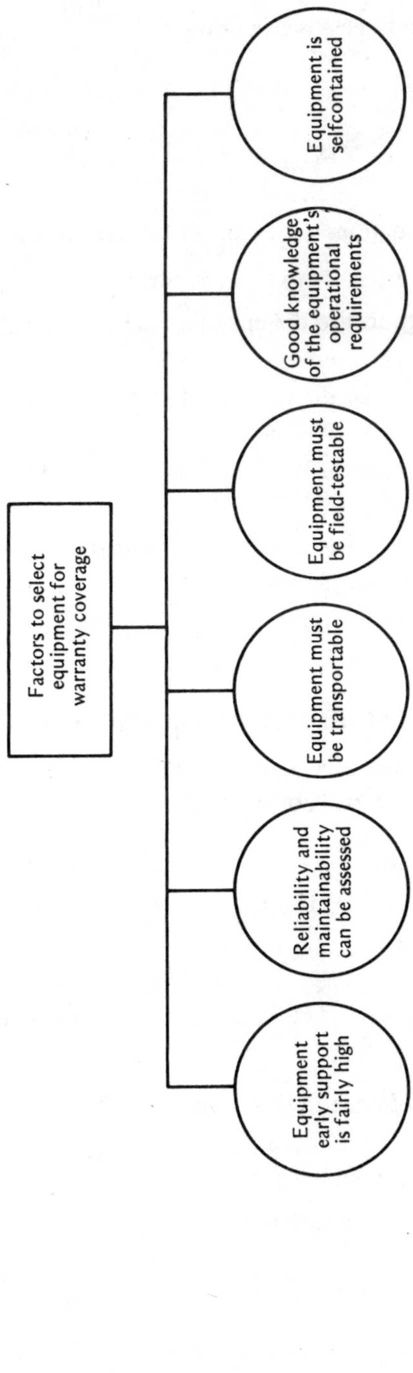

Figure 11.2 Factors to be used to select equipment for the warranty coverage

Equipment Warranty Cost Model

This model is used to calculate manufacturer, supplier, or contractor warranty cost.[5] The warranty cost is given by

$$K_w = k_f + X \tag{11.1}$$

where

$$X \equiv K_r \cdot T \cdot \lambda \tag{11.2}$$

The symbols used in equations (11.1) and (11.2) are defined as follows:

K_f is fixed cost of warranty to manufacturer

K_w is total warranty cost to the manufacturer over the mutually agreed time period

K_r is mean cost to repair the equipment sent to the manufacturing facility because of warranty agreement

λ is mean failure rate per hour of all warranteed equipment during the warranty coverage period

T is total time of operation in hours of all warranteed equipment during the warranty coverage period

The assumptions associated with the model are given in the work of Balaban and Meth.

Equipment Life Cycle Cost Model With Warranty

This model can be used to estimate the life cycle cost of equipment with warranty.[4] The life cycle cost, θ, of the equipment is given by

$$\theta = A + B \tag{11.3}$$

$$A \equiv K \cdot P \cdot F_a + (C_{\ell m} + C_{wr}) R(t)\ (1 + F_c) \tag{11.4}$$

$$B \equiv C_{mc} + C_{rc} \cdot t \tag{11.5}$$

The symbols used in equations (11.3) through (11.5) are defined as follows:

t is time in months

K is the number of units to be bought

F_a is the factor of amortization over the time interval $(0, t)$ (given by t/useful life of the equipment)

P is the equipment acquisition price

$C_{\ell m}$ is the reliability modification expected amortized cost

C_{wr} is the direct cost of warranty repairs

F_c is the contractor's fee

C_{mc} is the direct maintenance cost to the user

C_{rc} is the recurring support cost per month

$R(t)$ is the risk factor for the warranty duration of t months which will be applied by the equipment supplier to costs (given by $(1+i)^{t/12}$ for $0<i<1$)

The model is described in detail in Balaban and Retterer.

SUMMARY

This chapter discusses various types of contracts and the factors used to determine the types of contracts to be negotiated. In addition, the attributes of the contract negotiator are briefly discussed.

The steps required to manage and monitor a reliability program and the commonly utilized reliability documents in the equipment design specification are also presented. The last section is concerned with warranties, their risks (from the contractor's standpoint), and warranty cost models.

EXERCISES

1. List and describe briefly the types of contracts which can be signed when procuring engineering equipment.
2. What factors should a customer consider when determining the type of contract to be signed when purchasing an engineering system?
3. List and briefly describe the attributes of a contract negotiator.
4. Describe the reliability improvement warranty risks to a contractor.

NOTES

1. G.E. Hayes and H.G. Romig, *Modern Quality Control* (Encino, CA: Bruce: a division of Benziger Bruce & Glencoe, 1977), pp. 542–545.
2. V.G. Hajek, *Management of Engineering Projects* (New York: McGraw-Hill, 1977), pp. 75.

3. *Quality Assurance, Reliability Handbook,* AMCP 702-3 (Washington, D.C.: United States Army Material Command, 1968), pp. 2.11-2.14.
4. H. Balaban and B. Retterer, "The Use of Warranties for Defense Avionics Procurement," *Proceedings of the Annual Reliability and Maintainability Symposium* (1974): 363-68.
5. H.S. Balaban and M.A. Meth, "Contractor Risk Associated with Reliability Improvement Warranty," *Proceedings of the Annual Reliability and Maintainability Symposium* (1978): 123-29.

12

Configuration Management

Every year there are many new engineering systems which are designed and put into service. In the development of a complex engineering system many engineering changes may occur; these changes may be associated with product appearance, weight, performance, size, and so on. Therefore, how can the customer and the manufacturer be assured that in the end the product will be the same as what they originally agreed to build? Configuration management is the discipline which attempts to provide such assurance to both parties.[1]

Feller describes configuration management as the management of engineering requirements which defines the engineering product as well as changes thereto.[2]

CONFIGURATION MANAGEMENT HISTORY

In the past, the self-imposed disciplines practiced by equipment manufacturers were quite shallow in regard to documentation uniformity of configuration control and accounting. In the 1950s the people involved with the missile launch program became aware of this shortcoming. They found that when the prototype units were in orbit there was no adequate documentation of changes made to the unit, of part number identification records, and so on.[3]

After extensive research and management consultation, in June 1962 the United States Air Force published a document entitled *Configuration Management During the Development and Acquisition Phases,* AFSCM 375-1. The document was revised in June 1964. In the same year NASA produced a similar document entitled *Appolo Configuration Management,* NPC 500-1.

Another document on configuration management, AMCR 11-26, was issued by the United States Army Material Command in June 1965. Between 1965 and 1967 the United States Navy issued configuration management documents ASWSPO 5200.4, NAVMAT INSTR 5000.6, and NAVMAT INSTR 4130.1. Since then a number of other United States military documents have appeared on the subject; among them are:

MIL-STD-482 in 1970, *Configuration Status Accounting Data Elements and Related Features*

MIL-STD-483 (USAF) in 1970, *Configuration Management Practices for Systems, Equipment, Munitions and Computer Programs*

MIL-STD-1456 in 1972, *Contractor Configuration Management Plans*

MIL-STD-481 A in 1972, *Configuration Control-Engineering Changes, Deviations and Waivers* (short form)

Directive 5010.19 in 1979, Department of Defense Directive, *Configuration Management*

CHANGES TO PRODUCT

When changes to the engineering product occur, one objective of configuration management is to ensure that such changes are systematically documented in the product's support documents. However, the objective of this section is to discuss the types of changes and the reasons for them.

Broadly speaking there are three basic types of changes

Type I: changes due to which a significant product life cycle cost saving will occur

Type II: changes which are necessary to correct deficiencies in the product

Type III: changes which will be useful in improving a product's logistic support or its operational use[5]

According to Harris, these three types of changes usually occur when the product has already been received by the customer.[5]

However, the reasons for the changes during the product's design and production phases are:

1. Availability of better components due to advancement in the state of the art.
2. Deficiencies discovered in the proposed design of the product which may be the result of testing or analysis.

3. New discoveries made by the equipment designer to fulfill the same objective but more efficiently.
4. Substitution of parts, materials, and so on, by the production department in order to reduce cost.
5. The production department found a way to improve the performance of the product (usually this is a rare case).
6. Difficulties experienced by the production personnel to produce the product on time according to the original design.

Therefore, in order to produce the desired quantity of a product on time, changes may have to be made. We should note that the changes which occur during the design phase of the product are those which occur *after* the product design is found to be acceptable.

GOALS OF CONFIGURATION MANAGEMENT

Configuration management strives to ensure that the manufactured equipment is functionally and physically according to contract specifications. To satisfy this objective, the goals of configuration management are as follows:

1. *Identification:* the comprehensive identification of the equipment from final assembly to component level.
2. *Traceability:* ability to trace resultant equipment and its components to their descriptions.
3. *Definition:* establishing a definition of the total documentation regarding equipment design, assembly, and testing.
4. *Description:* the approved equipment configuration descriptions, for example, equipment operating manuals, test procedures, drawings, list of parts, and so on.[6]

According to Hajek, the following are the symptoms of when configuration management is practiced ineffectively:

1. Unclear objectives.
2. Changes cost too much: The configuration management plan requires cost trade-off analysis. If the cost of the change is more than gains, the proposed change idea may not be accepted. In the absence of the cost trade-off analysis, the cost of changes may be excessive.
3. Decisions regarding changes associated with the product are delayed, irrespective of the decision outcome (i.e., yes or no). Usually delay on such decisions have adverse effects. The configuration management plan calls for efficiency here.

4. Inconsistent documentation: Changes made to the product are not consistent with the existing drawings and literature. Configuration management calls for a systematic procedure to be followed to document the product or changes; according to the configuration management plan, the modified product has to be supported on time with the necessary documentation.[7]

LIFE CYCLE PHASES OF A PRODUCT

According to Hajek, the life cycle phases of a product are as shown in Figure 12.1. As can be seen, there are three baselines in the life cycle of a product. A baseline simply denotes a check point before starting the new phase. In other words, the new phase cannot be initiated until all the problems with the present phase are resolved.

In the figure baseline I is known as the characteristic baseline; it ends the conceptual phase. Baseline II denotes the functional baseline which ends the definition phase of the product. Similarly, baseline III, known as the operational baseline, terminates the acquisition phase of the product. There is usually a subbaseline in the acquisition phase which ends the development subphase of the acquisition phase. From these points the manufacturing (production) subphase of the acquisition phase begins. More clearly, the acquisition phase of the

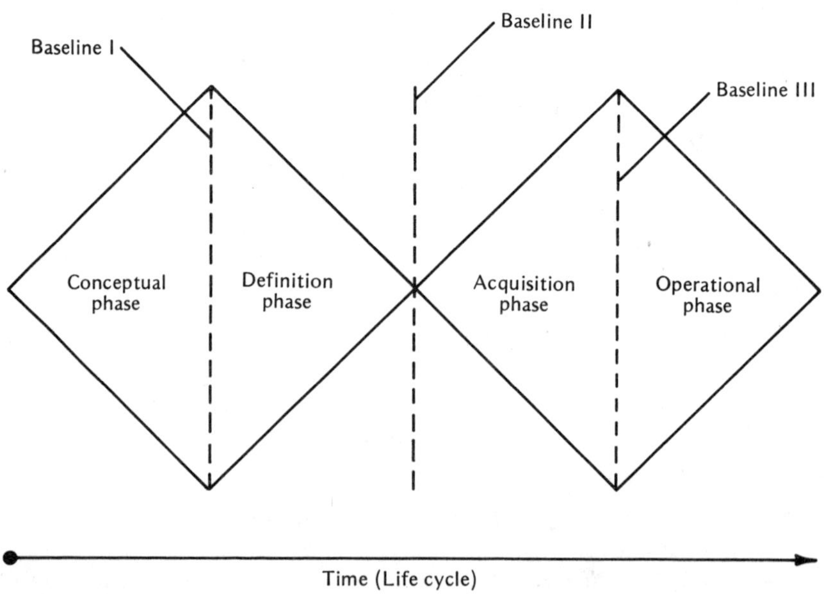

Figure 12.1 Life cycle phases and baselines associated with a product

product is usually subdivided into development and production subphases; this is not shown in Figure 12.1, however. Since the product's conceptual, definition, acquisition, and operational phases are self-explanatory, they will not be discussed here. However, for more information on these phases, consult the works of Samaras and Czerwinski, and of Hajek.

TECHNIQUES OF CONFIGURATION MANAGEMENT

There are three basic procedures used to practice configuration management systematically: identification, control, and accounting and auditing.

Identification

Identification is concerned with the current, complete, and accurate descriptions of the equipment during each phase. Configuration identification needs systematic control of the specifications, parts, assignment of serial numbers, data list numbers, and so on.

Finally, the objective of configuration identification is that the configuration item's hardware and support documentation are compatible throughout its life cycle.

Control

Control is an on-going function. It begins at the initial stage of the equipment's development project and terminates at the retirement of the equipment. In short, configuration control ensures that all actions performed in a certain phase of the product are properly authorized or approved and that they are taken into consideration in the baseline documentation completely and accurately.

Accounting and Auditing

Through accounting records are established which will be useful in providing systematic logistic support. In other words, accounting deals with establishing a systematic procedure to document product descriptions and revisions. This way the required equipment data can be retrieved easily and with accuracy.

The process of auditing provides a systematic check because it reviews the status of changes periodically.

IMPORTANT CHARACTERISTICS OF CONFIGURATION MANAGEMENT

Successful configuration management is the one which fulfils its expected objectives at a minimum cost.[6] The key features of successful configuration management are given in Figure 12.2.

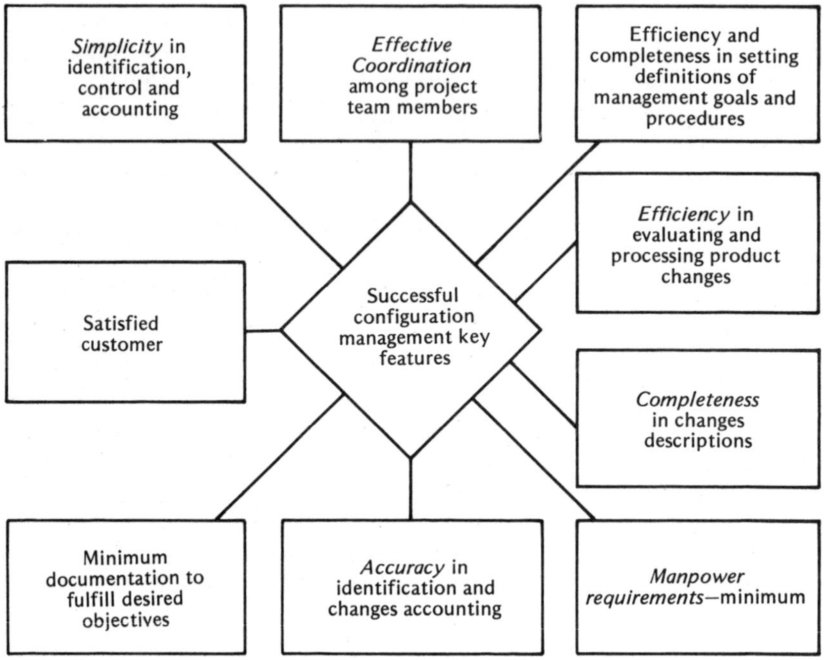

Figure 12.2 Features of successful configuration management

ATTRIBUTES OF A CONFIGURATION MANAGER

According to Samaras and Czerwinski, the configuration manager should have the following attributes:

Technical knowledge about reliability, quality control, testing, manufacturing, design, and so on

Ability to organize

Administration capability

Tactfulness and diplomacy

Knowledge of the entire organization or company

Documentation skills

Knowledge of the product

Be approachable[6]

SUMMARY

This chapter discusses the historical aspect of configuration management and the reasons for changes in the production and design phases of the product. In addition, the goals of configuration management and the life cycle phases of a product are presented. Techniques of the configuration management are briefly discussed along with the qualities of a configuration manager.

EXERCISES

12.1. Describe the process of configuration management.

12.2. Briefly discuss the history of configuration management.

12.3. What are the reasons for the changes which occur during the product design and production phases?

12.4. Describe briefly, with the aid of a diagram, the phases and baselines associated with product life cycle.

NOTES

1. M.J. Laine and E.C. Spevak, "Configuration Management," *Space/Aeronautics*, (November 1966): 74–81.
2. M. Feller, "Configuration Management," *IEEE Transactions on Engineering Management*, vol. 16 (1969): 64–66.
3. E.G. Hantz and A.E. Lager, "Configuration Management: Its Role in the Aerospace Industry," *Proceedings of Product Assurance Conference* (1968): 295–300.
4. E.H. Bersoff, V.D. Henderson and S.G. Siefel, *Software Configuration Management: An Investment in Productivity Integrity* (Englewood Cliffs, N.J.: Prentice-Hall, 1980), pp. 352–362.
5. A.P. Harris, "Introduction to Configuration Management," presented at Society of Reliability Engineers Symposium, (Ottawa: A.P. Harris, 1981), pp. 5–6.
6. T.T. Samaras and F.L. Czerwinski, *Fundamentals of Configuration Management* (New York: John Wiley & Sons, 1971), pp. 7–9.
7. V.G. Hajek, *Management of Engineering Projects* (New York: McGraw-Hill, 1977), pp. 158, 159–162.

13

Maintainability Principles

Maintainability deals with the operational readiness of equipment. As a discipline it is not even 25 years old.[1] However, the concern to maintain equipment in the field in operable condition has been there for a long time.

In modern times, the history of maintainability goes back to the early 1950s.[1] Attention was given to maintainability features in the equipment design stage in the late 1950s. In 1959 the United States Air Force published the MIL-M-26512 document concerning maintainability. Since then a number of military documents on maintainability have resulted:

MIL-STD-778: concerned with maintainability terminology

MIL-STD-470, 1966: *Maintainability Program Requirements* (for systems and equipments)

MIL-STD-471, 1966: *Maintainability Demonstration*

MIL-HDBK-472, 1966: *Maintainability Prediction*

AMCP 706-134, 1972: *Maintainability Guide for Design*

MIL-STD-721B, 1966: *Definition of Effectiveness Terms for Reliability, Maintainability, Human Factors and Safety*

In addition, there are many articles and books which have been written on the subject.

DEFINITIONS USED IN MAINTAINABILITY ENGINEERING

The following definitions are either directly or indirectly concerned with the maintainability discipline:

Maintainability: the probability that an inoperable item (i.e., failed equipment) is restored to a working state within a defined downtime period.

Availability: the probability that at time *t* the system is functioning normally when used under specified conditions, where administrative time, logistic time, and operating time are the components of the total time.

Repairability: the probability that the equipment in its failed state will be repaired back to its operable state within a stated active repair period.

Down time: the total time during which the equipment is in an unsatisfactory operable state.

Operating time: the time during which the equipment is operating satisfactorily, as expected by the operator, although the equipment's unacceptable operation is sometimes due to the maintenance person's assessment.

Active repair time: the equipment's downtime in which one or more maintenance people are performing their duty in order to effect an equipment repair.

Preventive maintenance: maintenance which is carried out to retain equipment in an acceptable operating state by providing orderly detection and inspection in addition to prevention of incipient failures.[3]

Corrective maintenance: maintenance which is carried out to restore failed equipment to an acceptable operable condition.[3]

Other terms associated with maintainability engineering may be found defined in the literature.[1,3,4]

MAINTAINABILITY MANAGEMENT

The functions and tasks carried out by the maintainability department or organization are shown in Figure 13.1. Each function is described below.

Analysis

A notable amount of time is spent on maintainability analysis. The following tasks are the components of such analysis:

1. Preparation of maintainability demonstration documentation.

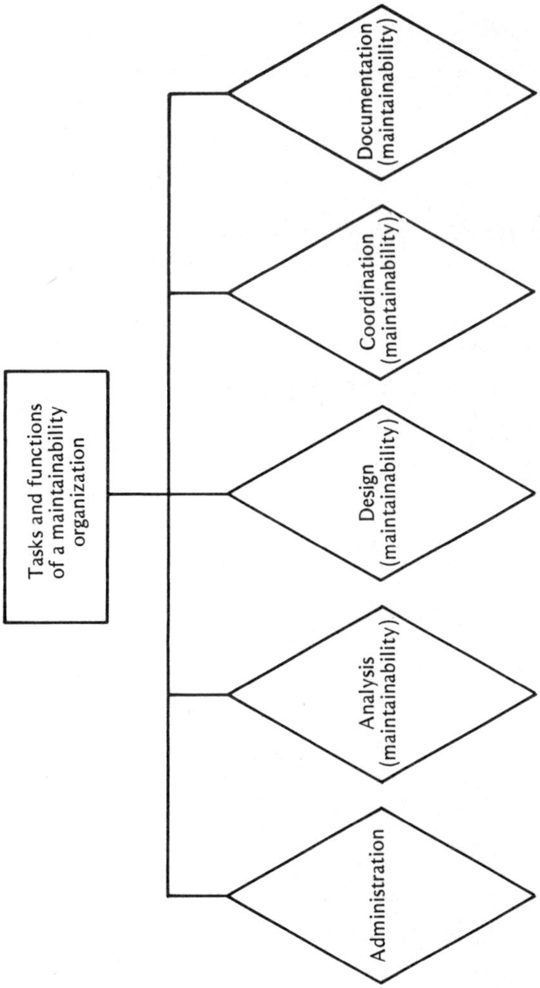

Figure 13.1 Maintainability organization functions

2. Analysis of maintainability trade-offs
3. Allocations of maintainability
4. Reviewing of such documents as proposals, specifications, operational and system requirements
5. Predictions about maintainability
6. Participation in engineering maintenance analysis
7. Participation in system analysis[1]

Design

Maintainability design looks into those equipment characteristics from the design standpoint which will help to reduce the need for logistic support. The main activities here are:

Preparing design reports

Taking part in product design reviews

Monitoring item designs

Approving product design drawings

Consulting services

Taking part in the preparation of maintainability documents for internal use

Administration

The tasks involved with the administration of maintainability are as follows:

Organizing

Staffing

Preparing a maintainability program plan

Preparing budgets, schedules, and so on.

Assigning responsibilities

Developing and executing procedures and policies

Participating in design reviews

Coordination and Documentation

These are two important functions of maintainability management. Documentation involves documenting maintainability management information, design review results, data, and so on.

Coordination is concerned with the interfaces with subcontractors, customers, system engineering, and so on.

SYSTEM EFFECTIVENESS MODEL

System effectiveness is defined as the probability that an item is able to meet an operational requirement within a specified period when used under stated conditions.[2] The model used to calculate system effectiveness probability is:

$$P_{st} = p_r \cdot R_m \cdot p_d \tag{13.1}$$

where

P_{st} is the system's effectiveness probability

R_m is the mission's reliability

p_r is the probability of operational readiness

p_d is the probability of design adequacy

Since this model is taken from von Alven, more information may be found in his book.

As we can easily see, system effectiveness probability is given by the product of three independent probabilities.

Example 13.1

Calculate the system effectiveness probability for $p_d = 0.85$, $p_r = 0.99$, and $R_m = 0.93$. By substituting this data in equation (13.1) we get:

$$P_{st} = p_r \cdot R_m \cdot p_d = (0.99)(0.93)(0.85)$$
$$= 0.7826$$

SYSTEM OPERATIONAL READINESS MODELS

This model can be defined as the probability that an item or a system is operating in an acceptable manner or is in a satisfactory operational readiness state at any point in time on demand when utilized under specified conditions. Some of the operational readiness mathematical models are discussed below.

Model I

Operational readiness, p_r, is expressed as

$$p_r = A\,q_1 + \alpha p_1 \tag{13.2}$$

where

A is the system's availability

α is the system's probability that it will not fail when it is in a non-active mode (i.e., in storage or not being used)

p_1	is the system's probability at any point in time that it is not being utilized, given that the system was functioning normally when it was used or stored last time
$(1-p_1)=q_1$	is the system's probability that at any point in time the system is either functioning normally or maintenance is being performed on the system
p_r	is operational readiness probability

System availability, A, is given by

$$A = \frac{T_0}{T_0 + \beta T_d} \tag{13.3}$$

where

T_0	is total system operating time
T_d	is total system downtime
β	is free time exists if the value of the β is between zero and unity (if β is equal to unity, then there is no free time)

Model II

According to Bazovsky, system operational readiness, p_r, is expressed as[5]

$$p_r = p_s(t) + Q_s(t) \cdot F(t_1 < t_2) \tag{13.4}$$

where

t	is the mission's duration time
$Q_s(t)$	is the probability that in the preceding mission there was one or more failures
$p_s(t)$	is the probability that in the preceding mission there were no failures

The term $F(t_1 < t_2)$ in equation (13.4) is equal to

$$F(t_1 < t_2) = \int_{t_1=0}^{\infty} g(t_1) \cdot A \cdot dt_1 \tag{13.5}$$

where

$$A \equiv \int_{t_2=t_1}^{\infty} f(t_2) \cdot dt_2 \tag{13.6}$$

The terms in expressions (13.5) and (13.6) are defined as follows:

$g(t_1)$ is the maintenance time probability density function

$f(t_2)$ is the time to the arrival of the next demand call for operation counted from the time the system arrived from the previous (preceding) mission in such a state which required a repair probability density function

The following assumptions are associated with the model:

1. If the preceding mission of duration t was failure-free, then the system is ready for the next operation on demand.
2. If the preceding mission of duration t was not failure-free, then the system will only be ready for the next operation if its maintenance time, t_1, is less than the time, t_2, at which the immediate new call for its use arrives.
3. Each mission's duration time is the same.

Suppose that $g(t_1)$ and $f(t_2)$ are defined by

$$g(t_1) = \frac{1}{\mu} e^{-\frac{1}{\mu} t_1} \tag{13.7}$$

$$f(t_2) = \frac{1}{\beta} e^{-\frac{1}{\beta} t_2} \tag{13.8}$$

where

μ is the average maintenance time

β is the average time until the next demand call for system use

Substituting probability density function (13.8) in expression (13.6) results in:

$$A \equiv \int_{t_1}^{\infty} \frac{1}{\beta} e^{-\frac{1}{\beta} t_2} dt_2$$

$$= e^{-\frac{1}{\beta} t_1} \tag{13.9}$$

Thus, by substituting equations (13.7) and (13.9) in expression (13.5), we get:

$$F(t_1 < t_2) = \frac{1}{\mu} \int_0^{\infty} e^{-\left(\frac{1}{\beta} + \frac{1}{\mu}\right) t_1} dt_1 \tag{13.10}$$

$$= \beta/(\beta + \mu) \tag{13.11}$$

By utilizing relationship (13.11) in equation (13.4) for the exponential case, the operational readiness is given by:

$$p_r = p_s(t) + Q_s(t) \cdot \beta(\beta + \mu)^{-1} \tag{13.12}$$

Example 13.2

An aircraft is used for a mission whose duration is one day. The remaining data associated with the mission are as follows:

$$p_s(1)=0.85, \quad Q_s(1)=0.15, \quad \mu=2 \text{ days}, \quad \beta=4 \text{ days}$$

Utilize equation (13.12) to calculate the operational availability probability. Thus:

$$p_r=0.85+(0.15)(4)(4+2)^{-1}$$
$$=0.95$$

Model III

This model is the result of further development on model I.[5] System operational readiness probability is defined as

$$p_r=\int_0^\infty p_s(t)\cdot q_s(t)\,dt+A_1 \tag{13.13}$$

where

$$A_1\equiv\{F(t_1<t_2)\}\int_0^\infty Q_s(t)\cdot q_s(t)\cdot dt \tag{13.14}$$

In equations (13.13) and (13.14) $q_s(t)$ denotes the system's mission duration time probability density function, which means that each mission's duration time is not the same as it was for model II.

SYSTEM AVAILABILITY MODELS

In reliability and maintainability work the terms instantaneous availability, mission availability, and steady-state availability are commonly used. This section will discuss these three terms.

System Instantaneous Availability

This is defined simply as the probability that at time t the system will be available for mission. The single system instantaneous availability, $AV(t)$, at time t is given by

$$AV(t)=\frac{\gamma}{D}+\frac{\lambda}{D}e^{-Dt} \tag{13.15}$$

where

$$D\equiv\gamma+\lambda \tag{13.16}$$

In equation (13.15) the symbols λ and γ denote system constant failure rate and constant repair rate, respectively. Equation (13.15) can be developed by applying the Markov technique of chapter 7. However, the complete derivation of equation (13.15) may be found in Shooman.

System Mission Availability

According to Arsenault and Roberts, system mission availability $AV_m(t)$, at time t is defined by[7]

$$AV_m(t) = (t_b - t_a)^{-1} \int_{t_a}^{t_b} AV(t) \cdot dt \tag{13.17}$$

where

t_a is the mission's time beginning

t_b is the mission's time end

If we assume $t_a = 0$ and $t_b = t$ in equation (13.17), then substituting expression (13.15) in that equation yields:

$$AV_m(t) = \int_0^t t^{-1} \left\{ \frac{\gamma}{D} + \frac{\lambda}{D} e^{-Dt} \right\} dt \tag{13.18}$$

After integration, the above equation becomes:

$$AV_m(t) = \frac{\gamma}{D} + \frac{\lambda}{D^2 t} \{1 - e^{-Dt}\} \tag{13.19}$$

System Steady-State Availability

System steady-state availability is defined as follows:

$$AV_s(\infty) = \lim_{t \to \infty} \frac{1}{t} \int_0^t AV(t) \cdot dt \tag{13.20}$$

This availability is useful only in finding the long-term availability (i.e., when time t is very large) of a system.

Example 13.3

For expressions (13.15) and (13.19), find the steady-state availabilities by utilizing equation (13.20).

By substitituting equation (13.15) in expression (13.20) we get:

$$AV_s(\infty) = \lim_{t \to \infty} \frac{1}{t} \int_0^t \left\{ \frac{\gamma}{D} + \frac{\lambda}{D} e^{-Dt} \right\} dt$$

$$= \frac{\lambda}{D} \tag{13.21}$$

Similarly, utilizing equation (13.19) in equation (13.20) leads to:

$$A\,V_s(\infty) = \lim_{t\to\infty} \frac{1}{t} \int_0^t \left[\frac{\gamma}{D} + \frac{\lambda}{D^2 t} \;\{1 - e^{-Dt}\}\right] dt$$

$$A\,V_s(\infty) = \frac{\gamma}{D} \tag{13.22}$$

We may conclude from equations (13.21) and (13.22) that for the large value of t, the single system instantaneous availability and the mission availability reduce to the same value when system failure and repair rates are constant.

Redundant Unit System Availability Models

This section presents expressions for series and for parallel system steady-state availabilities.

♦ SERIES SYSTEM MODEL This model represents an independent k repairable unit series system. In such a case, if any unit of the series fails, the entire system fails. The steady-state availability, $A\,V_{ss}$, of that system is given by:

$$A\,V_{ss} = \prod_{i=1}^{k} \gamma_i / D_i \tag{13.23}$$

The above expression is for m non-identical units.

♦ PARALLEL SYSTEM MODEL This model represents an independent n repairable unit parallel system. It is assumed in this model that the system's units are active. In addition, at least one unit of the system is required for system success. The parallel system's steady-state unavailability, UA_{ps}, is given by:

$$UA_{ps} = \prod_{i=1}^{n} \left(1 - \frac{\gamma_i}{D_i}\right) \tag{13.24}$$

The above expression is for n non-identical units. Subtracting both sides of equation (13.24) from unity yields the parallel system steady-state availability, $A\,V_{ps}$, as follows:

$$A\,V_{ps} = 1 - UA_{ps} = 1 - \prod_{i=1}^{n} \left(1 - \frac{\gamma_i}{D_i}\right) \tag{13.25}$$

MAINTAINABILITY FUNCTIONS

This section covers the maintainability functions of selected probability distributions. The maintainability function, $L(t)$, is defined as

$$L(t) = \int_0^t f(y) \cdot dy \tag{13.26}$$

where

t is the variable repair time

$f(t)$ is the probability density function of the duration of repair times

The maintainability function $L(t)$ denotes the probability that when the repair begins at $t = 0$ it will be accomplished within time t.

The following maintainability functions are obtained from relationship (13.26) when the repair times follow exponential and log-normal probability density functions, respectively:

$$L(t) = \int_0^t \mu e^{-\mu y} \, dy = 1 - e^{-\mu t} \tag{13.27}$$

where

μ is the constant repair rate and is equal to 1/MTTR

MTTR is mean time to repair

And

$$L(t) = \int_0^\infty t f(t) \cdot dt = \frac{1}{\sigma\sqrt{2\pi}} \int_0^\infty e^{-z} \, dt \tag{13.28}$$

$$z \equiv \left(\frac{\ell n\, t - \mu}{\sigma}\right)^2 / 2 \tag{13.29}$$

where μ and σ are the $\ell n\, t$ mean and standard deviations, respectively.

We should note here that the log-normal probability density function is quite frequently used in maintainability engineering because it fits well, especially to electronic systems repair times.[7]

Repair Rate Function

This function is expressed as

$$\mu_m(t) = f(t) / \{1 - L(t)\} \tag{13.30}$$

where $\mu_m(t)$ is the time-dependent repair rate function.

Example 13.4

An air traffic control system's repair times are described by the probability density function

$$f(t) = \frac{1}{\alpha} e^{-\frac{1}{\alpha} t} \tag{13.31}$$

where α is the mean time to repair.

Find the repair rate of the air traffic control system. By substituting probability density equation (13.31) in relationship (13.26) and integrating, we get:

$$L(t) = 1 - e^{-\frac{1}{\alpha}t} \tag{13.32}$$

Now, substituting equations (13.31) and (13.32) in equation (13.30) leads to:

$$\mu_m(t) = \frac{\alpha^{-1} e^{-\alpha^{-1} t}}{1 - \{1 - e^{-\alpha^{-1} t}\}} = \alpha^{-1} \tag{13.33}$$

Finally, we should note here that the repair rate of the control system is constant and is given by α^{-1}.

Example 13.5

A military vehicle's repair times are represented by the probability density function

$$f(t) = \frac{b}{\theta^b} t^{b-1} e^{-(t\,\theta^{-1})^b} \tag{13.34}$$

where θ is the scale parameter and b is the shape parameter.

Find the time-dependent repair rate of the vehicle. Similarly, as for example 13.4, utilizing equation (13.34) in equation (13.26) and integrating leads to

$$L(t) = 1 - e^{-(t\,\theta^{-1})^b} \tag{13.35}$$

The following expression for the time-dependent repair rate is obtained by substituting equations (13.34) and (13.35) in equation (13.30):

$$\begin{aligned} \mu_m(t) &= \{b\,\theta^{-b} t^{b-1} e^{-(t\,\theta^{-1})^b}\} \,/\, \{1 - (1 - e^{-(t\,\theta^{-1})^b})\} \\ &= b\,\theta^{-b}\, t^{b-1} \end{aligned} \tag{13.36}$$

Mean Repair Time

In this function the mean repair time, T_m, is given by:

$$T_m = \int_0^\infty \{1 - L(t)\}\, dt \tag{13.37}$$

Example 13.6

Find the air traffic control system's mean repair time with the aid of equation (13.32). Thus, by substituting equation (13.32) in equation (13.37) and integrating, the resulting mean repair time is:

$$T_m = \alpha \tag{13.38}$$

Example 13.7

Find the military vehicle's mean repair time by utilizing equation (13.35).

As in example 13.6, substituting equation (13.35) in equation (13.37) and integrating leads to the following mean repair time equation:

$$T_m = \int_0^\infty [1 - \{1 - e^{-(t\,\theta^{-1})^b}\}]\, dt$$
$$= \theta\Gamma(1 + b^{-1}) \qquad (13.39)$$

Time to Repair Probability Density Function

The probability density function, $f(t)$, is given by

$$f(t) = \mu_m(t)\,\{1 - L(t)\} \qquad (13.40)$$

Example 13.8

In Example 13.5 the military vehicle's maintainability function and time-dependent repair rate are defined by equations (13.35) and (13.36), respectively. Obtain the vehicle's repair time probability density function.

Utilizing relationships (13.35) and (13.36) in equation (13.40) results in the following probability density function:

$$f(t) = b\,\theta^{-b} t^{b-1} \cdot e^{-(t\,\theta^{-1})^b} \qquad (13.41)$$

SUMMARY

This chapter covered the history of maintainability engineering. In addition, the following topics were discussed: important terms used in maintainability engineering, maintainability management, system effectiveness, system operational readiness models, system availability models, and maintainability functions.

EXERCISES

13.1. Relate the history of maintainability engineering.

13.2. Define the following terms used in maintainability engineering:

a) maintainability

b) operational readiness

c) corrective maintenance

d) preventive maintenance

e) availability

f) mean time to repair

g) mission time

h) active repair time

13.3. Discuss briefly the functions of a maintainability department.

13.4. A two failure mode system's instantaneous availability is given by

$$AV(t) = \frac{\gamma_1 \gamma_2}{c_1 c_2} + B_1 - B_2$$

where

$$B_1 \equiv \left\{ \frac{(c_1 + \gamma_1)(c_1 + \gamma_2)}{c_1(c_1 - c_2)} \right\} e^{c_1 t}$$

$$B_2 \equiv \left\{ \frac{(c_2 + \gamma_1)(c_2 + \gamma_2)}{c_2(c_1 - c_2)} \right\} e^{c_2 t}$$

$$c_1 c_2 \equiv \gamma_1 \gamma_2 + \lambda_1 \gamma_2 + \lambda_2 \gamma_1$$

$$c_1 + c_2 \equiv -(\gamma_1 + \gamma_2 + \lambda_1 + \lambda_2)$$

λ_1 is the constant failure rate of the system (mode I)

λ_2 is the constant failure rate of the system (mode II)

γ_1 is the constant repair rate of the system from failure mode I

γ_2 is the constant repair rate of the system from failure mode II

Find the system's steady-state availability.

13.5. A series system is composed of four repairable, independent, and identical units. Each unit has the constant falure rate λ, and the constant repair rate μ, as follows:

$\lambda = 0.002$ failures/hour

$\mu = 0.003$ repairs/hour

Calculate the system's steady-state availability.

13.6. An active parallel system is composed of three repairable and independent units. The system's ith unit has the constant failure rate λ_i, and constant repair rate, μ_i, for $i = 1, 2, 3$:

Unit 1: $\lambda_1 = 0.002$ failures/hour, $\mu_1 = 0.004$ repairs/hour

Unit 2: $\lambda_2 = 0.003$ failures/hour, $\mu_2 = 0.005$ repairs/hour

Unit 3: $\lambda_3 = 0.001$ failures/hour, $\mu_3 = 0.002$ repairs/hour

Compute the system's steady-state availability.

NOTES

1. "Maintainability Engineering Theory and Practice," in *Engineering Design Handbook,* AMCP 706-133 (Alexandria, VA:), pp. 31-32.
2. W.H. Von Alven, *Reliability Engineering* (Englewood Cliffs, N.J.: Prentice-Hall, 1964), pp. 398–400.
3. A.S. Goldman and T.B. Slattery, *Maintainability: A Major Element of System Effectiveness* (New York: John Wiley & Sons, 1967), pp. 25–31.
4. MIL-STD-721B, Definitions of Effectiveness Terms for Reliability, Maintainability, Human Factors and Safety, (Washington, D.C.: Department of Defense, 1966), pp. 1-10.
5. I. Bazovsky, "Weapon Systems Operational Readiness," *Proceedings of the Annual Reliability and Maintainability Symposium* (1975): 174–78.
6. M.L. Shooman, *Probabilistic Reliability: An Engineering Approach* (New York: McGraw-Hill, 1968).
7. J.E. Arsenault and J.A. Roberts, eds., *Reliability and Maintainability of Electronics Systems* (Potamic, MD: Computer Science Press, 1980), pp. 408–409.

14

Equipment Maintenance and Replacement Policies

Once engineering equipment has been put into service, it has to be maintained according to specified conditions in order to optimize its reliability and availability. Equipment preventive maintenance and replacement decisions have to be made in the field so that its ownership cost is at the minimum. For example, if preventive maintenance on the equipment is performed more frequently than needed, it may be too costly. On the other hand, if preventive maintenance is performed less frequently than required, the equipment may break down often, which will also be too costly. Similar reasoning is applied to equipment replacement, that is, if equipment is salvaged earlier than its useful life the decision will be costly, or if it continues to be used after its useful life, the maintenance cost could be too high.

We should note here that equipment preventive maintenance and replacement decisions are taken not only on the history of breakdown and the number of years in service but also other factors such as performance, maintenance facility, fuel consumption, and so on.

This chapter, then, discusses various areas associated with equipment maintenance and replacement.

FORMULAS TO CALCULATE MAINTENANCE PARAMETERS

This section presents formulas which can be used to compute the values of various maintenance parameters.

Formula I

Formula I is used to compute mean preventive maintenance time, T_{pmd}. The formula is expressed as

$$T_{pmd} = \left(\sum_{i=1}^{k} t_{pmdi} \right) / k \tag{14.1}$$

where

t_{pmdi} is the ith preventive maintenance (PM) task active (maintenance) down time

k is the total (simulated) tasks of PM

Formula II

The expression to calculate the average corrective maintenance downtime, T_{cmd}, is

$$T_{cmd} = A/m \tag{14.2}$$

where

$$A \equiv \sum_{i=1}^{m} t_{cmdi} \tag{14.3}$$

t_{cmdi} is the ith corrective maintenance (CM) task active (maintenance) downtime

m is the total (simulated) tasks of CM

Formula III

This formula is concerned with calculating mean downtime, T_{md}, which is given by

$$T_{md} = (T_{pmd} f_{pm} + T_{cmd} f_{cm}) / F \tag{14.4}$$

where

$$F \equiv f_{pm} + f_{cm} \tag{14.5}$$

f_{pm} is the expected PM tasks

f_{cm} is the expected CM tasks

The tasks data for f_{pm} and f_{cm} are to be obtained within the equipment's operating time duration. According to von Alven, the operating time duration for ground equipment should be at least 5,000 hours.[2]

Formula IV

This formula is used to compute the maximum corrective maintenance downtime, T_{cmax}. The value of log T_{cmax} is given by

$$\log T_{cmax} \cong \alpha_1 + 1 \cdot 645 \left(\frac{\alpha_2 - \alpha_3/m}{m-1}\right)^{1/2} \tag{14.6}$$

where

$$\alpha_1 \equiv \text{average of } \log t_{cmdi} = \frac{\sum_{i=1}^{m} \log t_{cmdi}}{m} \tag{14.7}$$

$$\alpha_2 \equiv \sum_{i=1}^{m} (\log t_{cmdi})^2 \tag{14.8}$$

$$\alpha_3 \equiv \left(\sum_{i=1}^{m} \log t_{cmdi}\right)^2 \tag{14.9}$$

AVAILABILITY FORMULAS

There are a number of formulas by which to calculate various types of availabilities of a system. We will look at three here. (Item instantaneous, mission, and steady-state availabilities are discussed in chapter 13.)

System Operational Availability

This availability is defined as

$$AV_{0p} = \frac{t_1}{t_1 + t_2} \tag{14.10}$$

where

- AV_{0p} item's operational availability
- t_1 item's average time between maintenance
- t_2 item's average downtime

System Achieved Availability

System achieved availability, AV_{ch}, is defined as

$$AV_{ch} = t_3 / \sum_{i=3}^{5} t_i \tag{14.11}$$

where

t_3 is the equipment's operating time

t_i is the ith total time per stated period;
$i = 4$ means corrective maintenance time (unscheduled)
$i = 5$ means preventive maintenance time (scheduled)

The achieved availability factor is generally utilized during equipment development testing and early production testing.[3]

Availability of a Parallel Redundant System with Repair

This mathematical model represents a system composed of m repairable, independent, and identical units.[4] These units form an active parallel configuration. In addition, the system consists of only one repair facility, and at least g units must be functioning normally for system success. Each unit's failure and repair rates are constant.

The following notations are associated with the model:

$P_j(t)$ is the jth state probability of the system at time t: $j = 0$ (all units operating normally), $j = 1$ (one units failed), $j = 2$ (two units failed), $j = 3$ (three units failed), . . . , $j = m$ (all units failed)

i is the number of failed system units, for $i = 1, 2, 3, \ldots, (m - 1)$

λ is the constant failure rate of the unit

α is the constant repair rate of the unit

m is the total number of units in the system

By utilizing the Markov model,[4] the following equations are developed for the model:

$$\frac{dP_0(t)}{dt} + m\lambda P_0(t) = \alpha P_1(t) \tag{14.12}$$

$$\frac{dP_i(t)}{dt} + \{(m-i)\lambda + \alpha\} P_i(t) = (m-i+1)\lambda P_{i-1}(t) + \alpha P_{i+1}(t)$$
$$\text{for } 1 \leqslant i \leqslant m-1 \tag{14.13}$$

$$\frac{dP_m(t)}{dt} + \mu P_m(t) = \lambda P_{m-1}(t) \tag{14.14}$$

at $t = 0, P_0(0) = 1$, and $P_i(0) = 0$ for $i = 1, 2, 3, \ldots, m$.

To find steady-state solutions, set derivative of equations (14.12) through (14.14) equal to zero as follows:

$$m\lambda P_0 - \alpha P_1 = 0 \tag{14.15}$$

$$\{(m-i)\lambda+\alpha\}P_i-(m-i+1)\lambda P_{i-1}-\alpha P_{i+1}=0 \quad \text{for } 1\leqslant i\leqslant m-1 \tag{14.16}$$

$$\mu P_m-\lambda P_{m-1}=0 \tag{14.17}$$

In order to solve equations (14.15) through (14.17), we must use the following relationship:

$$\sum_{i=0}^{m} P_i=1 \tag{14.18}$$

The following recursion formula is obtained from the above equations:

$$P_{i+1}=P_i\{(m-i)\lambda/\alpha\} \tag{14.19}$$

Similarly, we obtain

$$P_i=(\lambda/\alpha)^i P_0\cdot(m)_i \tag{14.20}$$

where

$$\begin{aligned}(m)_i &\equiv m(m-1)(m-2)\ldots(m-i+1)\\ &\equiv m!/(m-i)!\end{aligned} \tag{14.21}$$

and

$$P_0=1/\left[\sum_{i=0}^{m}(m)_i(\lambda/a)^i\right] \tag{14.22}$$

The system's steady-state operational readiness probability, AV_0, is given by:

$$AV_0=\sum_{i=0}^{(m-g)}P_i \tag{14.23}$$

EQUIPMENT MAINTENANCE AND REPLACEMENT DECISION MODELS

Various models are implemented in connection with equipment maintenance and replacement. Let's look at four of them.

Model I

This model is concerned with finding the optimum component replacement period when the failure distribution is defined.[2] The model, developed by W.E. Weissbaum in 1960,[2,5] uses the following equation to obtain mean hourly cost, C_{mh}:

$$C_{mh}(x)=\{c_t-(c_t-c_{sr})g(x)\}/P \tag{14.24}$$

where

$$P=\int_0^x g(t)\,dt \tag{14.25}$$

where

- $g(x)$ is the new component's probability that the component will be useful for at least x units of time without a failure
- x is the time to component replacement (counted from the last replacement)
- c_t is the in-service failure total cost
- c_{sr} is the scheduled replacement component's total cost

In this model the ratio of c_t to c_{sr} ($c = c_t/c_{sr}$) plays an important role in determining the optimum replacement period. As can be seen by plotting $C_{mh}(x)$ against x for fixed c, as the value of c increases the minimum value of $C_{mh}(x)$ is realized. Therefore, the following two conclusions can be drawn:

1. For $c = 1$, the scheduled component replacement does not have any advantage.
2. For $c > 1$, the scheduled component replacement practice is advantageous

Further discussion on the model may be found in both von Alven and Weissbaum.

Model II

This model minimizes a single item's costs, for example[6]

$$\text{minimize } \theta(\lambda) + \phi(\alpha) \tag{14.26}$$

subject to the constraint:

$$\beta = \frac{\lambda}{\alpha} = (1 - AV)/AV \tag{14.27}$$

The symbols used above are defined as follows:

- λ is the item's constant failure rate
- α is the item's constant repair rate
- AV is the item's steady-state availability
- $\theta(\lambda)$ are the costs associated with the item's reliability
- $\phi(\alpha)$ are the costs associated with the item's maintainability

We should note here that relationship (14.27) is developed from the equation

$$AV = \frac{\alpha}{\lambda + \alpha} \tag{14.28}$$

where AV is the steady-state availability of the item.

By dividing the top and bottom of the right-hand side of equation (14.28) by α and letting $\beta = \lambda/\alpha$, we get:

$$AV = \frac{1}{1+\beta} \tag{14.29}$$

Rearranging the above expression yields:

$$\beta = \frac{\lambda}{a} = \frac{1-AV}{AV} \tag{14.30}$$

Thus, equation (14.30) is same as equation (14.27).

Taking advantage of the Lagrange technique and utilizing relationships (14.26) and (14.27) leads to

$$L = \theta(\lambda) + \phi(\alpha) + \mu\left(\frac{\lambda}{\alpha} - \frac{1-AV}{AV}\right) \tag{14.31}$$

where μ is the Lagrange multiplier.

Taking the partial derivatives of equation (14.31) with respect to λ, α, and μ yields

$$\frac{\partial L}{\partial \lambda} = \frac{\partial \theta(\lambda)}{\partial \lambda} + \frac{\mu}{\alpha} \tag{14.32}$$

$$\frac{\partial L}{\partial \alpha} = \frac{\partial \phi(\alpha)}{\partial \alpha} - \frac{\mu\lambda}{\alpha^2} \tag{14.33}$$

$$\frac{\partial L}{\partial \mu} = \{\lambda AV - \alpha(1-AV)\}/\alpha AV \tag{14.34}$$

By setting the partial derivatives of equations (14.32) through (14.34) equal to zero, we get:

$$\frac{\partial \theta(\lambda)}{\partial \lambda} + \frac{\mu}{\alpha} = 0 \tag{14.35}$$

$$\frac{\partial \phi(\alpha)}{\partial \alpha} - \frac{\mu\lambda}{\alpha^2} = 0 \tag{14.36}$$

$$\lambda \cdot AV - \alpha(1-AV) = 0 \tag{14.37}$$

Solving equations (14.35) through (14.37) for λ and a leads to the resulting solutions which are labeled as $\lambda_1(AV)$ and $\alpha_1(AV)$, respectively.

Thus, substituting $\lambda_1(AV)$ and $\alpha_1(AV)$ for λ and a, respectively, in relationship (14.24) leads to

$$L_1(AV) = \theta\{\lambda_1(AV)\} + \phi\{\alpha_1(AV)\} \tag{14.38}$$

where $L_1(AV)$ is the minimum cost. This cost is a function of item availability.

Model III

This model is used to determine equipment optimal inspection frequency which will maximize the per unit time profit.[7]

When equipment is under repair there is no production output which in turn reduces profit. Equipment is inspected periodically in order to reduce equipment breakdowns and, thus, production output loss. When equipment is inspected the minor defects (if any) are rectified. However, if inspected too frequently, then there is danger that it may cost more due to loss of production output, cost of materials, wages, and so on, than production loss due to equipment breakdown. Therefore, this model is concerned with finding the optimum inspection frequency which will maximize profit over a large time duration.

The following were assumed in order to develop this mathematical model:

1. Equipment failure rate and repair rate are constant
2. k inspections are performed per unit of time
3. A negative exponential function with mean time $1/\theta$ represents the distribution of inspection times
4. For no downtime losses, b denotes the profit value
5. The equipment failure rate, λ, depends upon k—it is a function of k

The following symbols are used to develop this model:

λ is the equipment's constant failure rate

α is the equipment's constant repair rate

c_i is mean inspection cost per uninterrupted unit of time

c_r is mean repair cost per uninterrupted unit of time

Profit, D_p, per unit of time is given by

$$D_p = b\left\{1 - \frac{k}{\theta} - \frac{\lambda(k)}{\alpha}\right\} - \frac{k}{\theta}c_i - \frac{c_r\,\lambda(k)}{\alpha} \tag{14.39}$$

where

$\frac{bk}{\theta}$ is the production output value loss per unit of time because of inspection

$\frac{k\,c_i}{\theta}$ is the inspection cost per unit of time

$\frac{c_r\,\lambda(k)}{\alpha}$ is the repair cost per unit of time

$\frac{b\lambda(k)}{\alpha}$ is the production output value loss per unit of time because of repairs

Differentiating equation (14.39) with respect to k yields:

$$\frac{dD_p}{dk} = -\frac{b}{\theta} - \frac{b}{\alpha} \cdot \frac{d\lambda(k)}{\partial k} - \frac{c_i}{\theta} - \frac{c_r}{\alpha} \cdot \frac{d\lambda(k)}{dk} \tag{14.40}$$

In order to find the maximum value of k, we set the left-hand side of equation (14.40) equal to zero as follows:

$$b\left\{-\frac{1}{\theta} - \frac{1}{\alpha} \cdot \frac{d\lambda(k)}{dk}\right\} - \frac{c_i}{\theta} - \frac{c_r}{\alpha}\frac{d\lambda(k)}{dk} = 0 \tag{14.41}$$

Solving equation (14.41) in terms of $d\lambda(k)/dk$, we get:

$$\frac{d\lambda(k)}{dk} = -\frac{1}{\theta}(b + c_i)/\left(\frac{b}{\alpha} + \frac{c_r}{\alpha}\right) \tag{14.42}$$

The optimum value of k is that value which makes the left and right sides of equation (14.42) equal.

Example 14.1

Suppose a piece of equipment, $\lambda(k)$, is defined by

$$\lambda(k) = m\, e^{-k} \tag{14.43}$$

where m is the equipment constant failure rate (at $k = 0$). Develop an expresson for the optimum value of k by utilizing equation (14.42).

Differentiating equation (14.43) with respect to k, we get:

$$\frac{d\lambda(k)}{dk} = -m\, e^{-k} \tag{14.44}$$

Thus, substituting equation (14.44) in equation (14.42) yields:

$$-m\, e^{-k} = -\frac{1}{\theta}(b + c_i)/\left(\frac{b}{\alpha} + \frac{c_r}{\alpha}\right) \tag{14.45}$$

By rearranging equation (14.45), the following expression is obtained for the optimum value of k:

$$k^* = 1n\left\{\frac{m\theta\,(b + c_r)}{\alpha\,(b + c_i)}\right\} \tag{14.46}$$

Example 14.2

The following data is given for a piece of equipment:

$$\frac{1}{\alpha} = 0.05 \text{ month}$$

$$\frac{1}{\theta} = 0.01 \text{ month}$$

$$\begin{aligned} \lambda(0) = m &= 2 \text{ failures/month} \\ b &= \$20{,}000\text{/month} \\ c_r &= \$300\text{/month} \\ c_i &= \$100\text{/month} \end{aligned}$$

Find the optimum value of k by utilizing equation (14.46);

By substituting the given data in equation (14.46), we get:

$$k^* = 1n\left\{\frac{2(0.01)^{-1}(20{,}000 + 300)}{(0.05)^{-1}(20{,}000 + 100)}\right\}$$

$$= 2.3125 \text{ inspections/month}$$

Model IV

This model enables us to determine optimum inspection frequency in order to minimize the per unit of time downtime of equipment.[7] Equipment (per unit time) total downtime is dependent on inspection frequency, k. More clearly, it is a function of k as

$$T(k) = \sum_{i=1}^{2} A_i \tag{14.47}$$

where

$T(k)$	is the equipment's total downtime per unit of time
$A_1 = \dfrac{\lambda(k)}{\alpha}$	is the equipment's downtime because of per unit of time repairs
$A_2 = k/\theta$	is the equipment's downtime because of per unit of time inspection

Now, differentiating equation (14.47) with respect to k leads to:

$$\frac{d\,T(k)}{dk} = \frac{d\lambda(k)}{dk} \cdot \alpha^{-1} + \theta^{-1} \tag{14.48}$$

In order to find the optimum value of k, set the left-hand side of equation (14.48) equal to zero as follows:

$$\frac{d\lambda(k)}{dk} \cdot \alpha^{-1} + \theta^{-1} = 0 \tag{14.49}$$

Rearranging equation (14.49) results in:

$$\frac{d\lambda(k)}{dk} = -\frac{\alpha}{\theta} \tag{14.50}$$

That value of k is the optimum which makes the left-hand and right-hand sides of equation (14.50) equal. The optimum value of k will yield equipment minimum total downtime per unit of time.

Example 14.3

Suppose, as in Example 14.1, a piece of equipment, $\lambda(k)$, is given by:

$$\lambda(k) = m\,e^{-k} \tag{14.51}$$

Develop an expression for the optimum value of k. Thus differentiating equation (14.51), with respect to k, yields:

$$\frac{d\lambda(k)}{dk} = m\,e^{-k} \tag{14.52}$$

Hence, utilizing the above relationship in equation (14.50) leads to:

$$-m\,e^{-k} = -\frac{\alpha}{\theta} \tag{14.53}$$

Therefore,

$$k^* = 1n \left[\frac{\theta m}{\alpha}\right] \tag{14.54}$$

where k^* is the optimum inspection frequency.

Example 14.4

For the given values of θ, m, and α in Example 14.2, determine the optimum value of k by utilizing equation (14.54). In addition, find the equipment's minimum tool monthly downtime.

The result of substituting the defined values of θ, m, and α from Example 14.2 in equation (14.54) is:

$$k^* = \ln\left[\frac{(0.01)^{-1} \cdot 2}{(0.05)^{-1}}\right]$$

$$= 2.3026 \text{ inspections/month}$$

In order to find the equipment's minimum total monthly downtime, we substitute for $\lambda(k)$ from equation (14.51) in equation (14.47) to get:

$$T(k) = \frac{m\,e^{-k}}{\alpha} + \frac{k}{\theta} \tag{14.55}$$

Thus, for the optimum value of k equation (14.55) is rewritten to the following form:

$$T(k^*) = \frac{m\,e^{-k^*}}{\alpha} + \frac{k^*}{\theta} \tag{14.56}$$

The numerical optimum value of k is rounded off to 2. Therefore, substituting the given data into equation (14.56) yields:

$$T(2) = \frac{2\,e^{-2}}{(0.05)^{-1}} + \frac{2}{(0.01)^{-1}}$$

$$= 0.0335 \text{ month}$$

SUMMARY

This chapter deals with equipment maintenance and replacement in the field. The chapter begins with formulas to calculate maintenance parameters. These formulas are used to compute mean preventive maintenance time, mean corrective maintenance time, mean downtime, and maximum corrective maintenance downtime. The chapter also gives formulas to calculate system operational availability, achieved availability, and steady-state availability. The last section consists of four mathematical models which are concerned with equipment maintenance and replacement.

EXERCISES

14.1. A repairable system is composed of three independent and identical units in parallel. In addition, the active system contains one repair facility. The system's Markov state-space diagram is shown in Figure 14.1. Each unit's failure rate, λ, and repair rate, μ are constant. Calculate the sys-

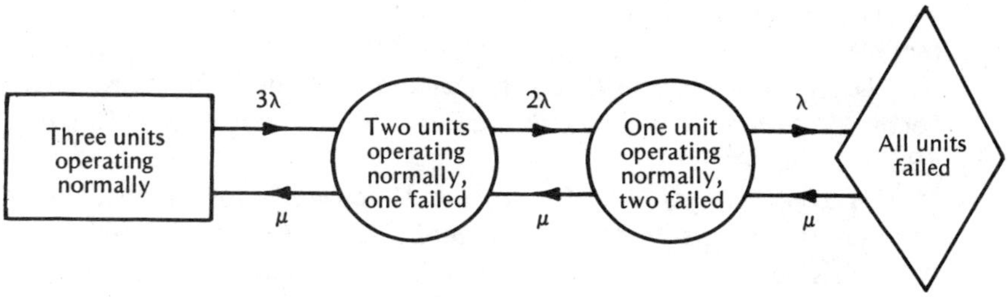

Figure 14.1 System transition diagram

tem's steady-state unavailability for $\lambda = 0.008$ failures/hour and $\mu = 0.009$ repairs/hour.

14.2. Suppose we have the same system as given in exercise 14.1, but with one exception–it contains two units instead of three units. Develop an expression for the system's availability and calculate the system's unavailability.

14.3. Assume that a piece of equipment, $\lambda(k)$ is given by

$$\lambda(k) = \frac{m}{k} \tag{14.57}$$

where m is the equipment's constant failure rate (at $k = 1$). Utilize equation (14.42) to develop an expression for the optimum value of k.

14.4. Prove that a piece of equipment's steady-state availability, AV, is given by

$$AV = \frac{1}{1+\rho} \tag{14.58}$$

where

ρ equals β/α

β is the equipment's constant failure rate

α is the equipment's constant repair rate

NOTES

1. "Maintainability Prediction," in *Military Standardization Handbook*, MIL-HDBK-472 (Washington, D.C.: Department of Defense, 1966), pp. 2.1-4.18.
2. W.H. Von Alven, ed., Reliability Engineering (Englewood Cliffs, N.J.: Prentice-Hall, 1964), pp. 388.

3. J.C. Conlon, W.A. Lilius and P.H. Tubbesing, *Test and Evaluation of System Reliability, Availability and Maintainability,* DOD 3235.1-H (Washington, D.C.: Office of the Director, Defense Test and Evaluation, Under Secretary of Defense for Research and Engineering, Department of Defense, 1982), pp. 4.2–4.5.
4. M.A. Wilson, "Effects of Maintenance and Support Factors on Availability of Systems," *Annals of Reliability and Maintainability* (1967): 562–72.
5. W.E. Weissbaum, "Probability–Theoretic Solution of Some Maintenance Problems," *Fourth Signal Maintenance Symposium* 1960: pp. 1-10.
6. A.S. Goldman and T.B. Slattery, *Maintainability: A Major Element of System Effectiveness* (New York: John Wiley & Sons, 1967), pp. 40–42.
7. A.K.S. Jardine, *Maintenance, Replacement and Reliability* (London, Pitman Publishing, 1973), pp. 103-107, 108-109.

15

Queueing Theory Applications in Maintainability

Queues are part of everyone's day to day life, for example, in a bank, a doctor's office, etc. As its name suggests, queueing theory studies waiting lines, whether they are formed in a bank, in a maintenance shop, or somewhere else.

The history of queueing theory goes back to the 1920s when Erlang, a Danish citizen, published a paper on telephone traffic theory. His paper was originally published in Danish, but was later translated into other languages. T.C. Fry, E.C. Molina, and G.F. O'Dell are among those who have carried out extensive work on queueing theory.

In the field of maintainability engineering, queueing theory plays an important role, especially in equipment repair tasks, for example, to determine the size of a repair facility, the size of a repair crew, and so on. Therefore, this chapter presents the basics of queueing theory with an emphasis on its application to equipment maintainability problems.

EXAMPLES OF WAITING LINES

As mentioned earlier, there are many examples of queueing theory problems. Here we will discuss only two: equipment maintenance and a bank.

Figure 15.1 shows an equipment repair waiting line situation. The failed pieces are the repair arrivals or the elements of the system which require ser-

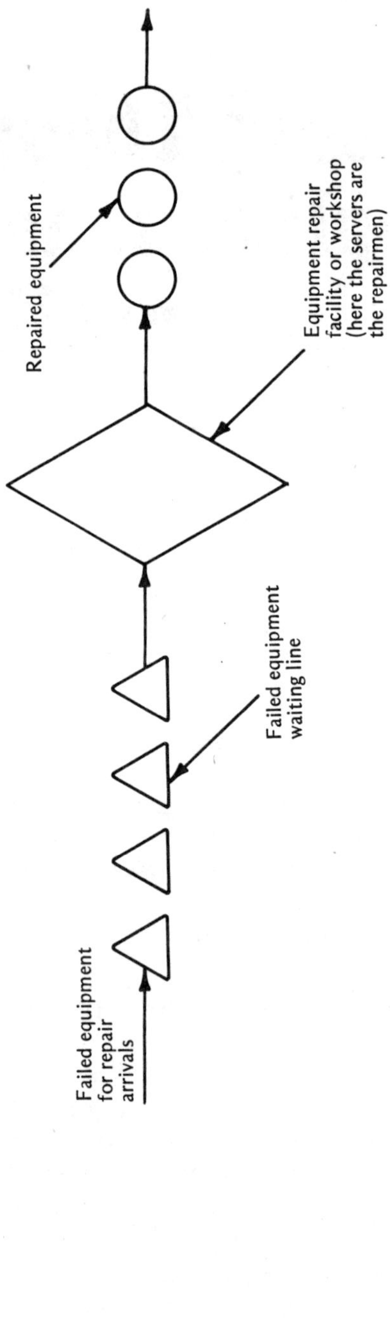

Figure 15.1 Equipment repair queueing system

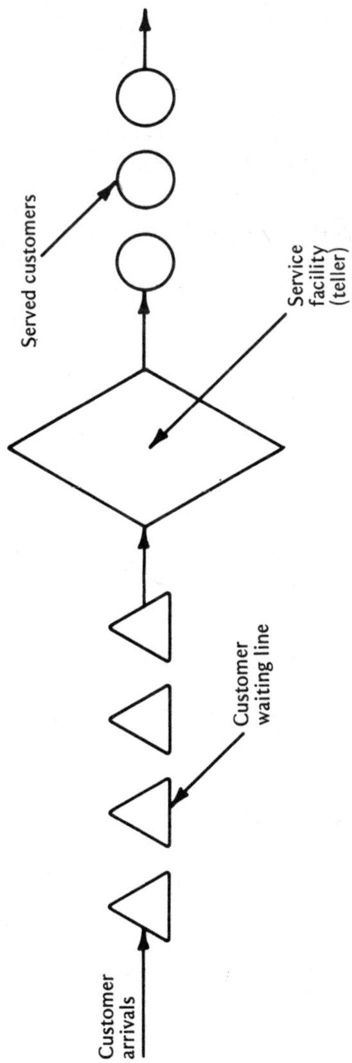

Figure 15.2 Queueing system representing a waiting line situation in a bank.

vice or repair. When a failed equipment cannot be immediately serviced or repaired, then a queue begins to form, as illustrated. The place where the repair is performed is called the repair shop, workshop, or the service facility. In the service facility the equipment is serviced or repaired by one or more people. Once the equipment is repaired, it goes out of the repair facility.

Another typical example of the queueing system may be found in a bank, as illustrated in Figure 15.2. As we can see, this queueing system is identical to the one in Figure 15.1.

POISSON MODEL

This section will develop the Poisson probability density function from the first principle.[6] The derivation of this function is presented here because many queueing theory mathematical models make the assumption of Poisson arrivals.

In order to develop the Poisson function, we assume that there are k pieces of equipment, but only one at a time. Figure 15.3 shows the Markov system diagram. Note that we are only interested with the operational states of the system.

The following symbols are associated with the model:

- m is the number of pieces of equipment that failed
- λ is the equipment's constant failure rate
- $P_m(t)$ is the probability that the system is in state m at time t, for $m = 0, 1, 2, \ldots$.
- s is the Laplace transform variable

The following system of differential equations are associated with Figure 15.3:

$$\frac{dP_0(t)}{dt} + \lambda P_0(t) = 0 \tag{15.1}$$

$$\frac{dP_1(t)}{dt} + \lambda P_1(t) = P_0(t) \cdot \lambda \tag{15.2}$$

$$\frac{dP_2(t)}{dt} + \lambda P_2(t) = P_1(t) \cdot \lambda \tag{15.3}$$

$$\vdots \qquad \vdots$$

$$\frac{dP_m(t)}{dt} + \lambda P_m(t) = P_{m-1}(t) \cdot \lambda \tag{15.4}$$

at time $t = 0, P_0(0) = 1$, and $P_i(0) = 0$ for $i = 1, 2, 3, \ldots, m$.

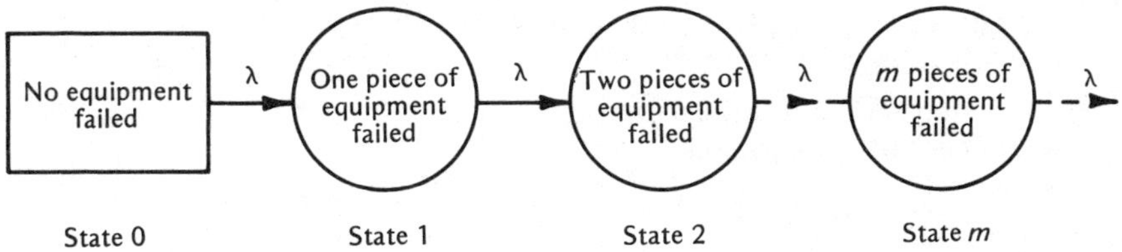

Figure 15.3 System state-space diagram

If we solve equations (15.1) through (15.4) by utilizing the Laplace transforms, we get:

$$sP_0(s) + \lambda P_0(s) = 1 \tag{15.5}$$

Therefore:

$$P_0(s) = (s + \lambda)^{-1} \tag{15.6}$$

Similarly:

$$P_1(s) = \lambda(s + \lambda)^{-2} \tag{15.7}$$

$$P_2(s) = \lambda^2(s + \lambda)^{-3} \tag{15.8}$$

$$\vdots \qquad \vdots$$

$$P_m(s) = \lambda^m (s + \lambda)^{m+1} \tag{15.9}$$

Taking the inverse Laplace transforms of equations (15.6) through (15.9) leads to:

$$P_0(t) = e^{-\lambda t} \tag{15.10}$$

$$P_1(t) = \lambda\, t\, e^{-\lambda t} \tag{15.11}$$

$$P_2(t) = (\lambda t)^2\, e^{-\lambda t}/2! \tag{15.12}$$

$$\vdots \qquad \vdots$$

$$P_m(t) = (\lambda t)^m\, e^{-\lambda t}/m! \tag{15.13}$$

The Poisson distribution function is given by:

$$P(t; m) = e^{-\lambda t} \sum_{j=0}^{m} (\lambda t)^j / j! \tag{15.14}$$

The above function becomes useful when finding the probability, within a defined interval of time, that at least m number of pieces of equipment failed.

MATHEMATICAL MODELS OF WAITING LINES

This section offers simple queueing theory models. In all the models the arrivals are the failed pieces of equipment.

Model I

This is the simplest model of queueing theory and is known as the single-channel, single-phase (SCSP) model.[8,9] A typical example of this model is a single facility equipment repair shop.

The following main assumptions are associated with the model:

1. The waiting line discipline is of a first-come, first served form.
2. The equipment repair rate is greater than the failed equipment arrival rate.
3. Infinite queue.
4. The arrival source population is infinite.
5. Arrivals (failed equipment) are according to Poisson distribution.
6. Service times are exponentially distributed.

The following difference equations are associated with the model:

$$P_0(t+\Delta t)=P_0(t)(1-\lambda\Delta t)+P_1(t)(\beta\Delta t) \tag{15.15}$$

where

λ	is the expected arrival rate of failed equipment
β	is the expected repair rate of failed equipment
Δt	is the time interval
t	is time
P_g	is the probability that g failed pieces of equipment are in the system which require repair, for $g=0,1,2,3,\ldots.$
$P_0(t)$	is the probability of zero (none) failed equipment at time t
$(1-\lambda\Delta t)$	is the probability of no failed equipment arrival
$P_1(t)$	is the probability of one failed equipment at time t
$\beta\Delta t$	is the probability of repair of one failed equipment

$$P_1(t+\Delta t)=P_1(t)(1-\lambda\Delta t)(1-\beta\Delta t)+P_0(t)\circ(\lambda\Delta t)+P_2(t)\cdot\beta\Delta t \tag{15.16}$$

Note that in difference equation (15.16) $(1-\lambda\Delta t)(1-\beta\Delta t)$ is the joint probability of no failed equipment arrival and no repair of failed equipment. By expanding the product of probabilities of no arrival and no departure, we get:

$$(1-\lambda\Delta t)(1-\beta\Delta t)=1-\lambda\Delta t-\beta\Delta t+\lambda\beta(\Delta t)^2 \tag{15.17}$$

Since the last right-hand term of equation (15.17) is very small (i.e., $(\Delta t)^2 \simeq 0$), that term is neglected. Equation (15.17) reduces to:

$$(1-\lambda\Delta t)(1-\beta\Delta t)=1-\lambda\Delta t-\beta\Delta t \tag{15.18}$$

Thus, substituting equation (15.18) in equation (15.16) leads to:

$$P_1(t+\Delta t)=P_1(t)\,\{1-\lambda\Delta t-\beta\Delta t\}+P_0(t)\cdot\lambda\Delta t+P_2(t)\cdot\beta\Delta t \tag{15.19}$$

The above equation is generalized for g failed pieces of equipment in the system as follows:

$$P_g(t+\Delta t)=P_g(t)\,\{1-\lambda\Delta t-\beta\Delta t\}+P_{(g-1)}(t)\,\lambda\Delta t+P_{(g+1)}(t)\,\beta\Delta t$$

$$\text{for } g \geqslant 1 \tag{15.20}$$

Rearranging difference equations (15.15), (15.19), and (15.20) results in the following:

$$\frac{P_0(t+\Delta t)-P_0(t)}{\Delta t}=-\lambda P_0(t)+\beta P_1(t) \tag{15.21}$$

$$\frac{P_1(t+\Delta t)-P_1(t)}{\Delta t}=-(\lambda+\beta)\cdot P_1(t)+\lambda P_0(t)+\beta\cdot P_2(t) \tag{15.22}$$

$$\vdots \qquad \vdots \qquad \vdots$$

$$\frac{P_g(t+\Delta t)-P_g(t)}{\Delta t}=-(\lambda+\beta)\cdot P_g(t)+\lambda\cdot P_{g-1}(t)+\beta P_{g+1}(t) \tag{15.23}$$

Taking the limit of equations (15.21) through (15.23) as $\Delta t \to 0$ yields:

$$\frac{dP_0(t)}{dt}=-\lambda P_0(t)+\beta P_1(t) \tag{15.24}$$

$$\frac{dP_1(t)}{dt}=-(\lambda+\beta)P_1(t)+\lambda P_0(t)+\beta P_2(t) \tag{15.25}$$

$$\vdots \qquad \vdots \qquad \vdots$$

$$\frac{dP_g(t)}{dt}=-(\lambda+\beta)P_g(t)+\lambda P_{g-1}(t)+\beta\cdot P_{g+1}(t) \tag{15.26}$$

Since equation (15.25) is the special case of (15.26) at $g = 1$, that equation is omitted after setting derivatives of equations (15.24) through (15.26) equal to zero in order to obtain steady-state solutions:

$$-\lambda P_0 + \beta P_1 = 0 \tag{15.27}$$

$$-(\lambda + \beta) P_g + \lambda P_{g-1} + \beta P_{g+1} = 0 \tag{15.28}$$

To solve equations (15.27) and (15.28), we have to make use of the following relationship:

$$\sum_{g=0}^{\infty} P_g = 1 \tag{15.29}$$

Solving equations (15.27) and (15.28) leads to

$$P_g = P_0\, \theta^g \tag{15.30}$$

where

$$\theta = \lambda/\beta \tag{15.31}$$

Utilizing equation (15.30) in equation (15.29) and rearranging leads to:

$$P_0 = \sum_{g=0}^{\infty} \theta^{g\ -1} \tag{15.32}$$

It is noted from the above equation that $\sum_{g=0}^{\infty} \theta^g$ is an infinite geometric series whose sum is given by:

$$\sum_{g=0}^{\infty} \theta^g = (1 - \theta)^{-1} \tag{15.33}$$

Thus, substituting relationship (15.33) in equation (15.32) leads to:

$$P_0 = (1 - \theta) \tag{15.34}$$

Utilizing the above equation in equation (15.30) yields:

$$P_g = (1 - \theta)\theta^g \tag{15.35}$$

The probability of m or greater number of failed pieces of equipment in the system is given [8] by:[8]

$$P_{g \geqslant m} = \theta^m \tag{15.36}$$

♦ **AVERAGE NUMBER OF FAILED PIECES OF EQUIPMENT (SYSTEM)** The average number, N_a, of failed pieces of equipment in the system can be calculated from the following relationship:

$$N_a = \sum_{g=0}^{\infty} g \cdot P_g \tag{15.37}$$

By substituting equation (15.35) in the above relationship and carrying out a few steps in between, we get:

$$N_a = \frac{\lambda}{\beta - \lambda} \tag{15.38}$$

♦ **AVERAGE TIME OF FAILED EQUIPMENT IN THE SYSTEM** This is given by

$$T_a = (\beta - \lambda)^{-1} \tag{15.39}$$

where T_a is the average time in the system.

♦ **AVERAGE NUMBER OF FAILED PIECES OF EQUIPMENT (QUEUE)** The average number of failed pieces of equipment, N_{aq}, in the queue is given by:

$$N_{aq} = \theta^2/(1 - \theta) \tag{15.40}$$

♦ **AVERAGE TIME OF FAILED EQUIPMENT IN THE QUEUE** This average time can be otained from:

$$T_{aq} = \theta/(\beta - \lambda) \tag{15.41}$$

Example 15.1

An equipment repair shop has one service facility and one channel for incoming failed equipment. More clearly, it is a single-channel, single-phase system. The failed equipment arrives according to a Poisson distribution with an average rate of 10 failed pieces per day ($\lambda = 10$ equipment/day). The equipment repair times are exponentially distributed. The average repair rate is equal to 20 repairs per day (i.e., $\beta = 20$ repairs/day). Calculate the following for a steady-state situation:

1. Probability of having zero failed pieces of equipment in the system.
2. Average number of failed pieces of equipment in the system
3. Average time of failed equipment in the system
4. Average number of failed pieces in the queue
5. Average time of failed equipment in the queue

By substituting the given data in equation (15.34), the probability of having zero failed pieces of equipment in the system is:

$$P_0 = (1 - \theta) = \left(1 - \frac{\lambda}{\beta}\right) = \left(1 - \frac{10}{20}\right) = 0.5$$

From equation (15.38), the average number of failed pieces of equipment in the system is given by:

$$N_a = \frac{\lambda}{\beta - \lambda} = \frac{10}{20 - 10} = 1 \text{ piece of equipment}$$

Equation (15.39) yields the average time of failed equipment in the system:

$$T_a = (20 - 10)^{-1} = 10^{-1} = 0.1 \text{ day}$$

Average number of failed pieces of equipment in the queue is given by equation (15.40):

$$N_{aq} = \frac{\theta^2}{(1-\theta)} = \frac{(0.5)^2}{(1-0.5)} = 0.05 \text{ equipment}$$

Average time of failed pieces of equipment in the queue from equation (15.41) is:

$$T_{aq} = \frac{\theta}{(\beta - \lambda)} = \frac{0.5}{(20-10)} = \frac{0.5}{10} = 0.05 \text{ day}$$

Model II

This model is the same as model I but with one exception—the queue is finite. Furthermore, the equipment repair rate need not to be greater than the equipment arrival rate.[8] The following steady-state equations are obtained from[8,9]:

$$P_g = \theta^g \cdot (1-\theta)/(1-\theta^{G+1}) \qquad \text{for } g \leqslant G \tag{15.42}$$

where G is the maximum number of failed pieces of equipment in the system.

$$P_0 = \{(1-\theta)/(1-\theta^{G+1})\} \tag{15.43}$$

♦ **AVERAGE NUMBER OF FAILED PIECES OF EQUIPMENT (SYSTEM)** This is given by:

$$N_a = \frac{\theta}{1-\theta} - \frac{(G+1)\theta^{G+1}}{A} \tag{15.44}$$

where

$$A \equiv 1 - \theta^{G+1} \tag{15.45}$$

♦ **AVERAGE TIME OF FAILED EQUIPMENT IN THE SYSTEM** This is given by:

$$T_a = N_a/\lambda(1-P_G) \tag{15.46}$$

♦ **AVERAGE NUMBER OF FAILED PIECES OF EQUIPMENT (QUEUE)** These can be obtained from the following equation:

$$N_{aq} = N_a - \theta(1-P_G) \tag{15.47}$$

◆ **AVERAGE TIME OF FAILED EQUIPMENT IN THE QUEUE** The following formula is used to obtain the average time of failed equipment in the queue:

$$T_{aq} = \frac{N_a}{\lambda(1 - P_G)} - \frac{1}{\beta} \tag{15.48}$$

Example 15.2

Suppose that in Example 15.1 we have, $\lambda = 10$ pieces of equipment/day, $\beta = 30$ repairs/day, and the maximum number of failed pieces of equipment in the system is five. Calculate the steady-state values of P_G, P_0, N_a, T_a, N_{aq}, and T_{aq}.

Utilizing the given data in equation (15.43) yields the probability of having no equipment in the system:

$$P_0 = (1 - 0.333)/\{1 - (0.333)^{5+1}\} = 0.6676$$

since

$$\theta = \frac{\lambda}{\beta} = \frac{10}{30} = 0.3333$$

and

$$G = 5$$

Similarly, by utilizing equation (15.42) we get:

$$P_G = P_5 = (0.333)^5 P_0 = (0.333)^5 \cdot (0.6676)$$
$$= 0.0027$$

The average number of failed pieces of equipment in the system from equation (15.44) is:

$$N_a = \frac{0.333}{1 - 0.333} - \frac{(5 + 1)(0.333)^{5+1}}{A} = 0.4911$$

$$A \equiv 1 - (0.3333)^{5+1}$$

From equation (15.46) the average time of failed equipment in the system is:

$$T_a = N_a/\lambda(1 - P_G)$$
$$= 0.4911/10(1 - 0.0027) = 0.0492 \text{ day}$$

From relationship (15.47) the average number of failed pieces of equipment in the queue is:

$$N_{aq} = N_a - \theta(1 - P_G) = 0.4911 - 0.333(1 - 0.0027)$$
$$= 0.1590$$

The average time of failed equipment in the queue is obtained from equation (15.48) as follows:

$$T_{aq} = \frac{N_a}{\lambda(1-P_G)} - \frac{1}{\beta} = \frac{0.4911}{10(1-0.0027)} - \frac{1}{30}$$
$$= 0.0159 \text{ day}$$

Model III

Again, this model is a modified version of model I. We assume here that the calling population is finite instead of infinite.[8] A typical example of this model is a machine shop containing a finite number of machines which are repaired after they fail. In this case each machine may be within the queueing system or outside the queueing system. When a machine is outside the queueing system, the machine is operating. In contrast, when a machine is within the queueing system, the machine is either in the queue or is being repaired. In this case, the mean time between failures of machines is equal to $1/\lambda$. It is assumed that repair times and the time spent outside the queueing system between breakdowns are exponentially distributed. Therefore, the following steady-state equations are obtained:

$$P_g = \frac{S!}{(S-g)!}\theta^g \left\{ \sum_{g=0}^{S} \frac{S!}{(S-g)!} \cdot \theta^g \right\}^{-1} \tag{15.49}$$

for $g = 1, 2, 3, \ldots, S$, where S denotes the size of the population.

$$P_0 = \left\{ \sum_{g=0}^{S} \frac{S!}{(S-g)!} \cdot \theta^g \right\}^{-1} \tag{15.50}$$

♦ **AVERAGE NUMBER OF MACHINES (SYSTEM)** The average number of machines is

$$N_a = S - \left\{ \left(\frac{\theta+1}{\theta} \right) - 1 \right\} B \tag{15.51}$$

where

$$B \equiv 1 - P_0 \tag{15.52}$$

♦ **AVERAGE TIME MACHINE IS IN THE SYSTEM** This is given by

$$T_a = \frac{1}{\beta} + \frac{1}{(S-N_a)\lambda} \cdot \left\{ S - \frac{(\theta+1)B}{\theta} \right\} \tag{15.53}$$

♦ **AVERAGE NUMBER OF MACHINES (QUEUE)** This is given by the following equation:

$$N_{aq} = S - \frac{B(1+\theta)}{\theta} \tag{15.54}$$

♦ **AVERAGE TIME MACHINE IS IN THE QUEUE** The formula to obtain this average is

$$T_{aq} = \frac{1}{(S - N_a)\lambda} \cdot \left\{ S - \frac{(\theta + 1)B}{\theta} \right\} \tag{15.55}$$

Model IV

This model will calculate a multiple-channel, single-phase queueing system. It is basically the same as model I, but instead of having only one service channel, now we have k number of identical channels.[8,9] Figure 15.4 shows a multiple-channel, single-phase queueing system.

The following assumptions are associated with the model:

1. Infinite source population.
2. Infinite queue.
3. Poisson arrivals, exponential service times.
4. The waiting line discipline is of the form first-come, first-served.
5. The system's mean repair rate, k, is greater than the arrival rate of failed equipment.
6. The repair channels are identical.

The resulting steady-state equations associated with the model are as follows:

$$P_g = \frac{\theta^g}{g!} \left[\left\{ \sum_{g=0}^{k-1} \frac{\theta^g}{g!} \right\} + \left\{ \frac{\theta^k}{k!(1 - k^{-1}\theta)} \right\} \right]^{-1} \quad \text{for } g \leqslant k \tag{15.56}$$

$$P_g = \left\{ \frac{\theta^g}{k!\, s^{g-k}} \right\} \cdot \left[\left\{ \sum_{g=0}^{k-1} \frac{\theta^g}{g!} \right\} + \left\{ \frac{\theta^k}{k!(1 - k^{-1}\theta)} \right\} \right]^{-1} \tag{15.57}$$

$$P_0 = \left[\left\{ \sum_{g=0}^{k-1} \frac{\theta^g}{g!} \right\} + \left\{ \frac{\theta^k}{k!(1 - k^{-1}\theta)} \right\} \right]^{-1} \tag{15.58}$$

♦ **AVERAGE NUMBER OF FAILED PIECES OF EQUIPMENT (SYSTEM)** The mean number of failed equipment is given by:

$$N_a = \theta + \{P_0\, \theta^k\, \lambda/k!k\, \beta(1 - k^{-1}\theta)^2\} \tag{15.59}$$

♦ **AVERAGE TIME EQUIPMENT IS IN THE SYSTEM** The mean time is:

$$T_a = \beta^{-1} + \{P_0\, \theta^k/k!k\, \beta(1 - k^{-1}\theta)^2\} \tag{15.60}$$

♦ **AVERAGE NUMBER OF PIECES OF EQUIPMENT (QUEUE)** These are given by:

$$N_{aq} = \{P_0\, \theta^k\, \lambda/k!k\, \beta(1 - k^{-1}\theta)^2\} \tag{15.61}$$

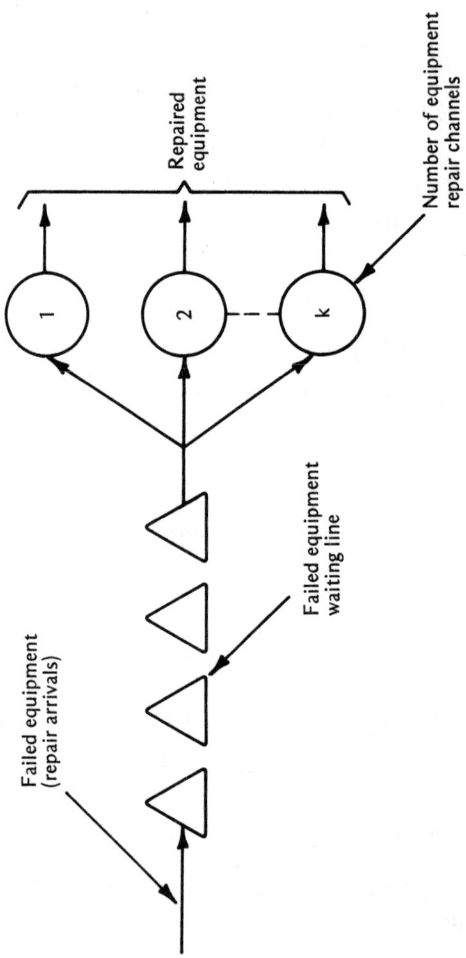

Figure 15.4 Multiple-channel, single-phase queuing system

♦ **AVERAGE TIME EQUIPMENT IS IN THE QUEUE** The formula to obtain this average is:

$$T_{aq} = \{P_0 \, \theta^k / k! \, k \, \beta(1 - k^{-1} \, \theta)^2\} \tag{15.62}$$

Model V

We use this model to find the optimum value of the repair rate of a single repairman which will minimize the total cost (repairman cost and losses due to machine failure) per unit of time.[10] In this case a single repairman looks after a number of machines or pieces of equipment. When the repairman is not busy and a machine fails, then the repairman immediately starts repairing that machine; otherwise it has to wait in the queue.

It is assumed in this model that (1) the failed machines' arrivals are according to Poisson distribution and (2) repair times are exponentially distributed. The following symbols are associated with the model:

- b output value of a single machine (when operating) per unit of time
- λ is the failed machines' arrival rate
- β is the failed machines' repair rate
- $k(\beta)$ cost of a single repairman per unit of time is a function of β

The per unit of time total cost, $K_t(\beta)$, is given by

$$K_t(\beta) = k(\beta) + b\,\theta + b\left\{\frac{\theta^2}{1-\theta}\right\} \tag{15.63}$$

where

- θ equals λ/β
- $b\theta$ is the output value losses when failed machines are under repair
- $b\left\{\frac{\theta^2}{1-\theta}\right\}$ is the output value losses when failed machines are waiting for repair in the waiting line

Rewriting equation (15.63) results in:

$$K_t(\beta) = k(\beta) + \frac{\lambda b}{\beta} + b\,\frac{\lambda^2}{\beta(\beta-\lambda)}$$

$$= k(\beta) + \lambda\, b(\beta - \lambda)^{-1} \tag{15.64}$$

In order to optimize β, we differentiate equation (15.64) with respect to β as follows:

$$\frac{d\,K_t(\beta)}{d\beta} = \frac{d\,k(\beta)}{d\beta} - \lambda b\,(\beta - \lambda)^{-2} \tag{15.65}$$

Thus, setting the left-hand side of equation (15.65) equal to zero and rearranging yields:

$$\frac{dk(\beta)}{d\beta} = \lambda\, b(\beta - \lambda)^{-2} \tag{15.66}$$

When at a specific value of β the left-hand side of equation (15.66) is the same as its right-hand side value, that value of β is the optimum value.

Example 15.3

For the following given functions, develop expressions for the optimum value of β by utilizing equation (15.66):

$$k(\beta) = C\beta \tag{15.67}$$

$$k(\beta) = 1 - e^{-\beta} \tag{15.68}$$

where C is a constant.

Differentiating equations (15.67) and (15.68) with respect to β yields:

$$\frac{dk(\beta)}{d\beta} = C \tag{15.69}$$

$$\frac{d\,k(\beta)}{d\beta} = e^{-\beta} \tag{15.70}$$

Thus, substituting equation (15.69) in equation (15.66) leads to:

$$c = \lambda\, b(\beta - \lambda)^{-2} \tag{15.71}$$

Rearranging the above equation yields an expression for the optimum value of β:

$$\beta^* = \lambda + \left(\frac{\lambda b}{c}\right)^{1/2} \tag{15.72}$$

Similarly, substituting equation (15.70) in equation (15.66) yields:

$$e^{-\beta} = \lambda\, b(\beta - \lambda)^{-2} \tag{15.73}$$

That value of β is the optimum value which makes the left-hand side of equation (15.73) the same as its right-hand side.

Example 15.4

For the following defined function and given data, calculate the optimum value of β by utilizing equation (15.66):

$$k(\beta) = c\,\beta^2 \tag{15.74}$$

where c is a constant and

$c = 200$, $\lambda = 2$ machines/day

$b = \$20{,}000$ per machine/day

By differentiating equation (15.74) with respect to β, we get:

$$\frac{d\,k(\beta)}{d\beta} = c\,2\,\beta \tag{15.75}$$

Substituting equation (15.75) in equation (15.66) yields:

$$c^2\,\beta = \lambda b(\beta - \lambda)^{-2} \tag{15.76}$$

By utilizing the given data in equation (15.76), we get:

$$2(200)\beta = 2(20{,}000)(\beta - 2)^{-2} \tag{15.77}$$

We should note here that the optimum value of β can only be approximated. In fact, from equation (15.77) the value of β is the optimum value which makes the left-hand side of that equation equal to its right-hand side. Therefore, for various values of β, the left-hand side and right-hand side values of equation (15.77) are tabulated in Table 15.1.

It can be seen from the tabulated values that at $\beta = 6.06$ the left and right sides are approximately equal. Therefore, the optimum value of β is 6.06 repairs/day.

Table 15.1. Left and Right Sides Tabulated Values of Equation (15.77)

β	*Left-hand side* $[2(200)\beta]$	*Right-hand side* $2(20{,}000)(\beta - 2)^{-2}$
50	20,000	17.36
20	8,000	123.45
7	2,000	1,600
6.06	2,424	2,427
6	2,400	2,500
5	2,000	4,444
4	1,600	10,000

SUMMARY

The main objective of the chapter is to present commonly known queueing theory models. Therefore, in addition to a brief history of queueing theory, the following topics are discussed: examples of waiting lines, Poisson model, and mathematical models of waiting lines.

Under this last model five mathematical models are presented. The first three models concern single-channel, single-phase (SCSP) queueing systems, whereas the fourth model deals with multiple-channel, single-phase queueing systems. The last model is used to find the optimum value of the repair rate of a single repairman.

EXERCISES

15.1. Discuss the following two items: the history of queueing theory and at least four examples of queues.

15.2. Prove that the mean number of repairable machines in the queueing system is given by

$$M = \lambda/(\mu - \lambda)$$

where

M is the mean number of repairable machines in the queueing system

λ is the failed machines' arrival rate

μ is the failed machines' repair rate

Assume the following:

1. Single-channel, single-phase queueing system
2. First-come, first-served (service)
3. Infinite queue
4. Infinite arrival source population
5. $\mu > \lambda$
6. Poisson arrival, exponential service

15.3. For the following data, calculate the optimum value of the repair rate by utilizing equation (15.67):

$\lambda = 5$ machines/week, $b = \$25{,}000$ per machine/day

15.4. Prove that in a single-channel, single-phase queueing system with finite queue, the steady-state probability of zero failed machines in the system is given by

$$P_0 = \{(1-\rho)/(1-\rho^{L+1})\}$$

where

ρ equals λ/μ (λ is the arrival rate and μ is the repair rate)

L is the maximum number of failed machines in the system

All the assumptions of exercise 15.2 are valid with the exception of number 3.

15.5. The following data are known in the preceding exercise:

$\lambda = 15$ machines/day, $\mu = 20$ repairs/day, $L = 6$

Calculate the steady-state probability of having no failed machines in the system.

NOTES

1. T.L. Saaty, *Elements of Queueing Theory with Applications* (New York: McGraw-Hill, 1961), pp. 20–25.
2. E. Brockmeyer, H.L. Halstrom and A. Jensen, *The Life and Works of A.K. Erland* (Copenhagen: Copenhagen Telephone Company, 1948).
3. T.C. Fry, "The Theory of Probability as Applied to Problems of Congestion," in *Probability and Its Engineering Uses*, edited by (Princeton: D. Van Nostrand Company, 1928).
4. E.C. Molina, "Application of the Theory of Probability to Telephone Trunking Problems," *Bell System Technical*, vol. 6 (1927):461–94.
5. G.F. O'Dell, "Theoretical Principles of the Traffic Capacity of Automatic Switches," *P.O. Electrical Engineers Journal*, vol. 13 (1920):209–23.
6. G.H. Sandler, *System Reliability Engineering*, (Englewood Cliffs, N.J.: Prentice-Hall, 1963), pp. 72–75.
7. D. Gross and C.M. Harris, *Fundamentals of Queueing Theory* (New York: John Wiley & Sons, 1974), pp. 240–253.
8. S.M. Lee, L.J. Moore and B.W. Taylor, *Management Science* (Dubuque, IO: Wm. C. Brown, 1981), pp. 446–447.
9. H.G. Daellenbach and J.A. George, *Introduction to Operations Research Techniques* (Boston: Allyn and Bacon, 1978), pp. 328–331.
10. A.K.S. Jardine, *Maintenance, Replacement and Reliability* (London: Pitman Publishing, 1973), pp. 144–146.

16

Failure Modes and Effects Analysis

In order to evaluate system design from the point of view of reliability, failure modes and effects analysis (FMEA) is a vital tool. The history of FMEA goes back to the early 1950s when the technique was utilized in the design and development of flight control systems.[1,2] Since then the technique has received widespread acceptance in the industry.

The difference between the FMEA and FMECA is that FMEA is a qualitative technique used to evaluate a design, whereas FMECA is another design technique composed of FMEA and critical analysis (CA). Critical analysis is basically a quantitative method which is used to rank critical failure mode effects by taking into consideration their occurrence probability.

Another reliability evaluation technique, which is closely related to FMEA and FMECA, is known as fault tree analysis. This technique was first developed at Bell Laboratories in the early 1960s to evaluate the design of the Minuteman launch control system. The basic difference between FMEA and the fault tree technique is that the former is malfunction-oriented, whereas the latter is event-oriented.[4] Both these techniques are presented in subsequent sections.

FAILURE MODES AND EFFECTS ANALYSIS STEPS

According to Jordan, the following main steps are involved in performing failure modes and effects analysis:

Step 1: *System definition*—this first step is concerned with defining the system and its requirements.

Step 2: *Ground rules*—in order to perform FMEA, the ground rules are established

Step 3: *System hardware description*—the hardware of the system in question is described.

Step 4: *Functional blocks description*—the functional blocks of the system are described.

Step 5: *Failure modes and their effects identification*—failure modes and their effects are identified.

Step 6: *Critical item list*—the list of critical items is compiled.

Step 7: *Documentation*—the analysis is documented.[3]

Figure 16.1 shows in abbreviated form the steps required to perform FMEA. These steps are described in detail below:

♦ **SYSTEM DEFINITION** This first step defines the system. The system definition is concerned with (1) decomposing the system into main blocks and defining their functions, and (2) defining the interface between blocks.

We should note here that to establish a good definition of the system at this stage is not an easy task. However, the FMEA analyst usually has to establish his or her own system definition with the aid of the following items: specifications, system development plans, drawings, and so on.

♦ **GROUND RULES** This next step deals with formulating the ground rules to perform FMEA. In the failure modes and effects analysis, the following are examples of these rules:

1. Limits of environmental stress
2. Primary mission objective statement
3. Secondary mission objective statement
4. Limits of operational stress
5. Mission phases delineation
6. Analysis level statement

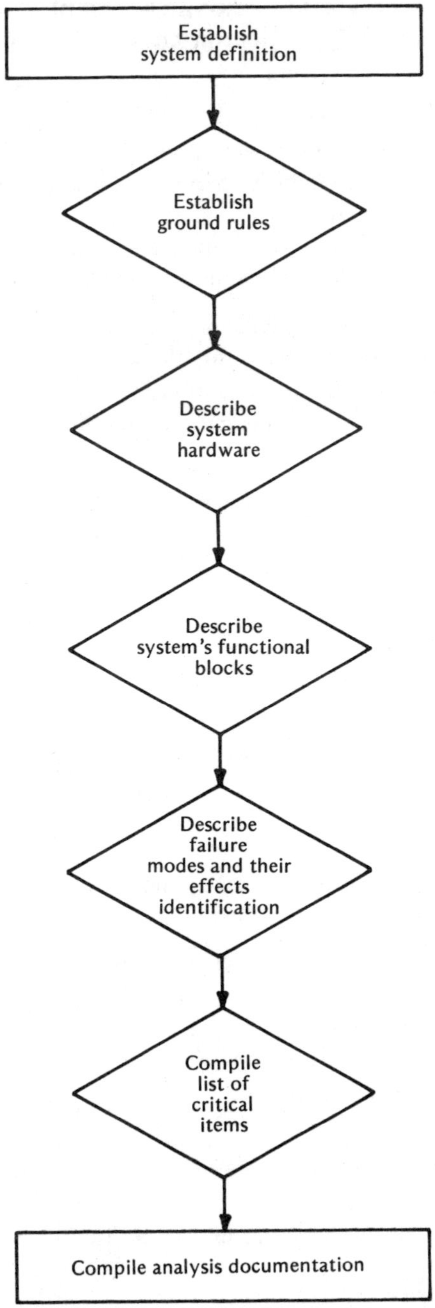

Figure 16.1 Failure modes and effects analysis steps

♦ **SYSTEM HARDWARE AND FUNCTIONAL BLOCK DESCRIPTION** Step 3 prepares the description of the system in question. This description is usually divided into two parts:

1. System block diagram description: This shows graphically the total elements of the system under evaluation, in other words, the elements of the system which are to be analyzed. In addition, the description identifies, among the system's components, the series and parallel relationships. The system's and its components' inputs and outputs are shown on the block diagram graphical description.
2. Functional statement: In addition to system functional statement, each subsystem and element have a functional statement. This is prepared for each operational mode or phase of each item. The description content's detail depends upon item application, function uniqueness, and so on.

♦ **IDENTIFICATION OF FAILURE MODES AND THEIR EFFECTS** This step is concerned with systematically identifying the failure modes and their effects. Figure 16.2 shows a typical worksheet used to perform failure modes and effects analysis.[3] Column (11) is concerned with categorizing the potential effect of failure.

According to Jordan, the potential effect of failure may be classified into the following four categories:

1. Life or lives may be lost due to failure.
2. Mission may be lost due to failure.
3. Activation may be delayed due to failure.
4. The failure has no effect at all.[3]

The remaining columns of Figure 16.2 are not described here because they are considered to be self-explanatory.

♦ **LIST OF CRITICAL ITEMS** In this step the critical items list is compiled to provide useful input to sound management decisions. Figure 16.3 shows a typical critical items list worksheet. The last column is used for the explanation of whether to retain the critical condition or recommend corrective actions. Columns 1-5 are self-explanatory.

♦ **RESULTS DOCUMENTATION** This final step of the failure modes and effects analysis is concerned with the documentation of analysis. The final document consists of failure modes and their effects, ground rules of FMEA, list of critical items, definition of the system, and description of the system.

1	2	3	4	5	6	7	8	9	10	11	12
Identification of item	Function of item	Item failure mode	Phase (operational or mission)	Effects of failure on				Method used for failure detection	Corrective measure	Category of criticality	Remarks
				Subsystem	Total system	Associated personnel	Intended mission				
Failure Mode and Effects Analysis				By : ______ Date : ______ Page : ______				System : ______ Subsystem : ______ Drawing : ______			

Figure 16.2 Typical FMEA worksheet

Critical Items List					
1	2	3	4	5	6
Identification of item	Item failure mode	Loss effect	Classification of criticality	Page no. of FMEA analysis	Retention rationale

Figure 16.3 Typical critical items list worksheet

FAILURE MODES, EFFECTS AND CRITICALITY ANALYSIS

This analysis is being widely practiced by defense, aerospace, and other industries. FMECA is the result of extensions to FMEA. In fact, as mentioned earlier FMECA is composed of FMEA and critical analysis. The objective of critical analysis is to rank the effects of the critical failure mode according to occurrence probability. Critical analysis is discussed in detail in Jordan.

Advantages of FMECA

The following are the many advantages of FMECA:

1. Serves as each possible failure mode occurrence detection technique.
2. All possible failure modes and their effects on mission, personnel, and system are identified.
3. Provides useful input data when performing system safety and maintainability analyses.
4. Uses a systematic approach to classify hardware failures.
5. Provides a useful data base for program planning components.

6. Uses a systematic approach which can be easily understood.
7. Provides input data for test planning.
8. Provides useful input data for maintenance decision making.
9. Is a visibility tool for a manager.
10. For small, large, and complex systems, the analysis is effective and useful.
11. Procedure begins from the detailed level and works upward.
12. Useful for design comparison purposes.
13. Communication among design interface personnel is improved.

FAULT TREES

This technique was developed in the early 1960s at Bell Laboratories to perform analysis of the Minuteman launch control system. The technique was further refined by Boeing Corporation personnel at a latter stage. Most of the published literature on the fault tree technique is listed in the book by Dhillon and Singh.

Fault tree analysis starts by identifying an undesirable event, called top event, associated with a system.[14] Events which could cause the top event are generated and connected by logic operators AND, OR, and EOR. The AND gate provides a TRUE (failed) output if and only if all the inputs are TRUE (failures). The OR gate provides a TRUE (failure) output if and only if one or more inputs are TRUE (failures). The EOR (Exclusive OR) gate provides a TRUE (failure) output if and only if one but not more than one input is true. The fault tree construction proceeds by generation of events in a successive manner until the events need not be developed further. These events are called primary events or primals. The fault tree itself is the logic structure relating the top event to the primals.

There is probably nothing basically new about the principle underlying the generation of fault trees. It consists of successively asking the question "How could this event occur?" The newness lies in the use of logic operators in the organization and graphical representation of the logic structure relating the top event to the primals.

The basic symbols of fault tree technique are given in Figure 16.4. Other fault tree symbols may be found in Dhillon and Singh.[13] The rectangle represents the resultant event which occurs from the combination of failure events through the input of a gate (e.g., an AND, OR, Exclusive OR, etc). The circle denotes a basic fault (failure) event. The failure of a system component is an example of the basic fault event. The basic fault event parameters are failure and repair rates, unavailability and failure probability.

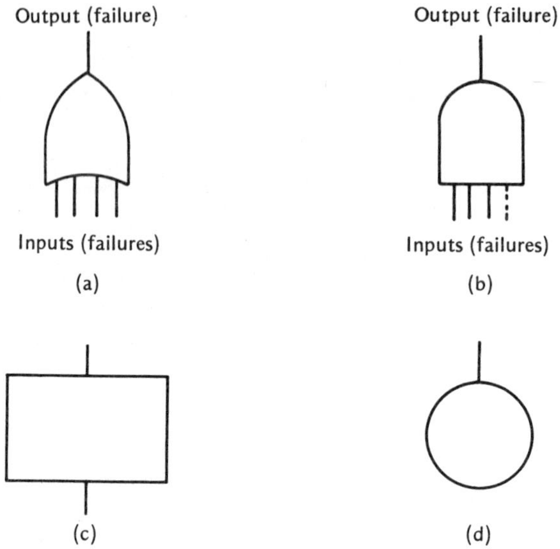

Figure 16.4 Fault tree technique symbols: (a) OR gate, (b) AND gate, (c) resultant event, (d) basic fault event

Some of the useful characteristics associated with fault trees are:

1. *An event at a time:* The fault tree method enables the analyst to focus on one particular undesired event at a time. In general, fault trees are event oriented, whereas reliability block diagrams are usually hardware oriented.
2. *Provides insight into system behavior:* For constructing meaningful fault trees, the analyst has to interact with the designers and operators to understand the system fully. The insight obtained during this process is of major benefit to system design as many weaknesses are spotted and corrected during this period.
3. *Visibility tool:* The graphical representation of the logic structure provides a visibility tool to both engineers and management and is useful for justifying design changes and performing trade-off studies.
4. *Top-down approach:* The fault tree, being in essence top-down failure modes and effect analysis, lends itself to better organization and control than conventional failure modes and effect analysis. Because of the top-down approach, it also offers more flexibility in terms of termination at any hardware level as well as selectively exploring certain critical faults in greater depth.

Like all other methods, fault trees, too, have their drawbacks and some of these are mentioned below:

1. For large and complex systems, fault trees can be time consuming, expensive to produce, and the detail can be overwhelming.
2. It is difficult to handle degraded component states. Fault tree analysis considers the components in working or failed states.
3. Analytical solutions for fault trees having priority AND gates and cold standbys are difficult to obtain in the general case.
4. It requires considerable effort to include all types of common cause failures in the fault tree.

Fault trees can be used to obtain minimum cut sets which define the modes of system failure and identify critical components. If the failure data on primary events is available, the reliability measures for the top event can be obtained.

To obtain OR and AND gates' output probability of failure, the following two formulas, respectively, can be utilized:

$$Q_{OR} = 1 - \prod_{j=1}^{k} (1 - Q_j) \tag{16.1}$$

where

Q_{OR} is the OR gate's output fault event probability

Q_j is the probability of the jth input's fault event

k is the total number of independent input fault events

If the probabilities of the input fault events are very small, then equation (16.1) reduces to

$$Q_{OR} \simeq \sum_{j=1}^{k} Q_j \tag{16.2}$$

and

$$Q_{AND} = \prod_{j=1}^{n} Q_j \tag{16.3}$$

where

Q_{AND} is the AND gate output fault event probability

n is the total number of independent input fault events

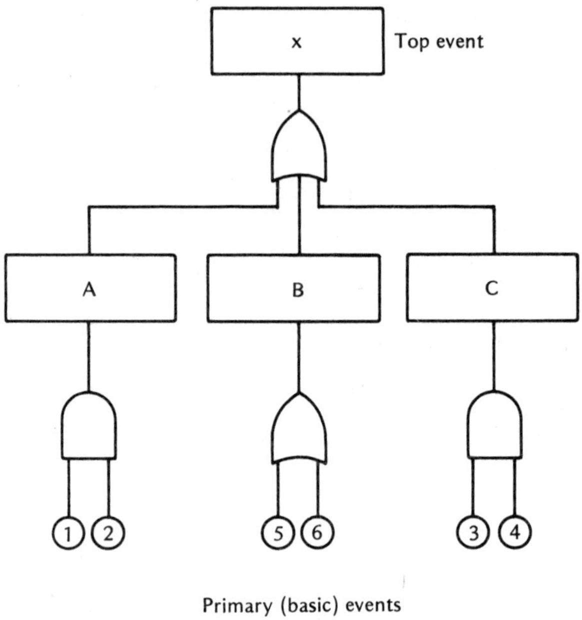

Figure 16.5 Example of a fault tree

Example 16.1

A fault tree with six primary (basic) fault events is shown in Figure 16.5. The probability of fault event i will be denoted by Q_i. The fault tree can be solved either by the process of Boolean reduction or, more generally, by using minimum cut sets.

In Figure 16.5 the probability of the top event's occurrence is obtained by utilizing equations (16.1) through (16.3). By utilizing equation (16.3) the probability of occurrence of the AND gate's top event A is

$$Q_A = Q_1 Q_2 \tag{16.4}$$

where

Q_1 is the probability of fault event 1

Q_2 is the probability of fault event 2

Similarly, with the aid of equation (16.3) the probability of occurrence of the AND gate's top event C is

$$Q_C = Q_3 Q_4 \tag{16.5}$$

where

Q_3 is the probability of fault event 3

Q_4 is the probability of fault event 4

The OR gate's top event B probability of occurrence from equation (16.1) is given by

$$Q_B = Q_5 + Q_6 - Q_5 Q_6 \tag{16.6}$$

where

Q_5 is the probability of fault event 5

Q_6 is the probability of fault event 6

The probability of occurrence of the fault tree's top event X with the aid of equations (16.1) and (16.4) through (16.6) is:

$$Q_X = 1 - (1 - Q_A)(1 - Q_B)(1 - Q_C) \tag{16.7}$$

By substituting Q_A, Q_B, and Q_C from equations (16.4) through (16.6), we get:

$$Q_X = 1 - \{1 - Q_1 Q_2\} \; \{1 - (Q_5 + Q_6 - Q_5 Q_6)\} \; \{1 - Q_3 \cdot Q_4\} \tag{16.8}$$

The reliability block diagram equivalent of the fault tree of this example is shown in Figure 16.6. Here the reliability, R_A, of the left-hand side independent component subsystem is:

$$R_A = 1 - Q_1 Q_2 \tag{16.9}$$

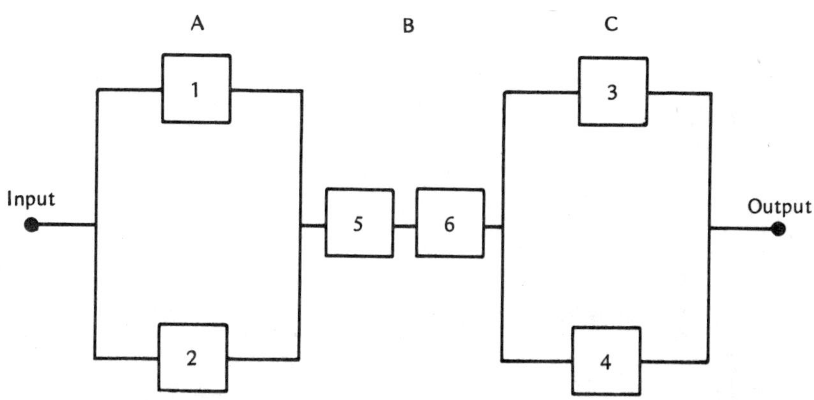

Figure 16.6 Reliability block diagram equivalent of the fault tree in Figure 16.5

Similarly, the reliability, R_C, of the right-hand side of the independent component subsystem is:

$$R_C = 1 - Q_3 \cdot Q_4 \tag{16.10}$$

Reliability of the subsystem composed of independent components 5 and 6 (in Figure 16.6) is:

$$R_B = 1 - Q_5 - Q_6 + Q_5 Q_6 \tag{16.11}$$

By utilizing equations (16.9) through (16.11), in Figure 16.6, system unreliability is:

$$\begin{aligned} Q_X &= 1 - R_A \cdot R_B \cdot R_C \\ &= 1 - (1 - Q_1 Q_2)(1 - Q_5 - Q_6 + Q_5 Q_6)(1 - Q_3 \cdot Q_4) \end{aligned} \tag{16.12}$$

It is concluded that equations (16.8) and (16.12) are exactly the same.

Example 16.2

In Figure 16.5 the basic fault events' probabilities are as follows:

$$Q_1 = 0.03; \quad Q_2 = 0.04$$
$$Q_3 = 0.05; \quad Q_4 = 0.01$$
$$Q_5 = 0.06; \quad Q_6 = 0.07$$

Calculate the top event's probability of occurrence. Thus, by substituting the given data in equation (16.8), we get:

$$\begin{aligned} Q_X &= 1 - \{1 - (0.03)(0.04)\}\ \{1 - (0.06 + 0.07 - (0.06)(0.07))\} \\ &\quad \{1 - (0.05)(0.01)\} \\ &= 1 - \{0.9988\}\ \{0.8742\}\ \{0.9995\} \\ &= 0.1273 \end{aligned}$$

The top event's probability of occurrence is 0.1273.

FMEA AND FAULT TREE ANALYSIS

This section compares FMEA and fault tree analysis. Some of the comparisons are as follows:

1. Fault tree analysis is prepared by a person or persons who understand the system and is a useful systems analysis tool. In contrast, FMEA is performed normally by a designer and is basically a useful design tool.

2. In comparison to FMEA, the fault tree analysis is more narrow because the analysis concentrates on a single fault event.
3. The fault tree analysis is more dramatic than FMEA and succinct because it is a graphic technique.
4. Fault tree analysis makes use of Boolean algebra, therefore it is not regarded as basic as FMEA.
5. Fault tree analysis is restricted to failures whose analysis can be performed economically. In contrast, any conceivable failure is included in FMEA.
6. A designer performs FMEA as a normal engineering activity, whereas fault tree analysis may involve a specialist and other persons.[4]

SUMMARY

The chapter begins with the history of FMEA and fault tree analysis. The steps to perform failure modes and effects analysis are then described in detail. FMECA and its advantages are briefly presented. The last item discussed is the fault tree technique.

EXERCISES

16.1. Discuss briefly the history of failure modes and effects analysis.

16.2. What are the advantages and disadvantages of FMECA?

16.3. Describe the main steps of FMEA.

16.4. Discuss the term critical analysis and its association with FMEA.

16.5. What are the definitions of OR and AND gates?

16.6. Calculate the probability of the top event, *TE*, of the fault tree shown in Figure 16.7.

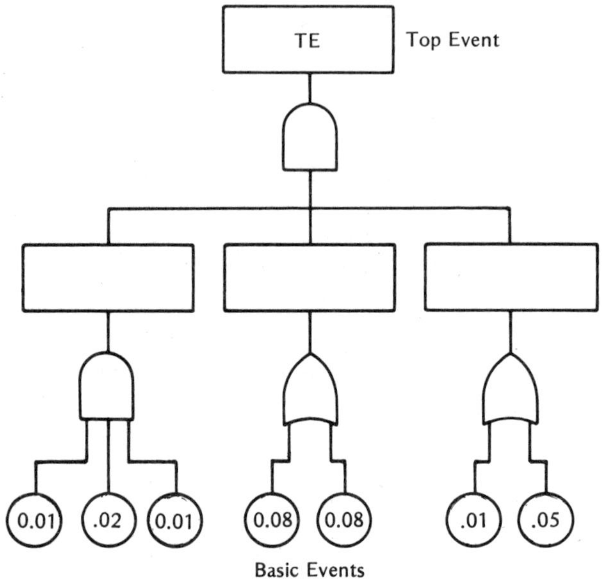

Figure 16.7 Hypothetical fault tree

NOTES

1. H.E. Arnzen, "Failure Mode and Effect Analysis: A Powerful Engineering Tool for Component and System Optimization," Report No. 347.40.00.00-k4-05(c5776) (Corona, CA: GIDEP Operations Center, 1966), pp. 355.
2. J.S. Countinho, "Failure-Effect Analysis," *Transactions of the New York Academy of Sciences*, vol. 26 (1964);564–84.
3. W.E. Jordan, "Failure Modes, Effects and Criticality Analysis," *Proceedings of the Annual Reliability and Maintainability Symposium* (1972):30–37.
4. V.L. Grose, "Status of Failure (Hazard) Mode and Effect Analysis, Fault Tree Analysis and Prediction, Apportionment and Assessment," *Annals of Reliability and Maintainability* (1971):415–23.
5. K.Onodera, M. Miki and K. Nukada, "Reliability Assessment for Heaby Machinery by 'HI-FMECA' Method," *Proceedings of the Annual Reliability and Maintainability Symposium* (1977):346–52.
6. R.R. Erick, "A FMECA's Use—By Whom and How," *Transactions of the American Society for Quality Control* (1978):59–65.

7. G.L. Barbour, "Failure Modes and Effects Analysis by Matrix Method," *Proceedings of the Annual Reliability and Maintainability Symposium* (1971):114–19.
8. H.E. Arnzen, "Failure Mode and Effect Analysis: A Powerful Engineering Tool for Component and System Optimization," *Annals of Reliability and Maintainability* (1966):355–71.
9. H. Ohlef, W. Binroth and R. Haboush, "Statistical Model for a Failure Mode and Effect Analysis and Its Application to Computer Fault Tracing," *IEEE Transactions on Reliability*, vol. R-27 (1978):16–22.
10. J.M. Legg, "Computerized Approach for Matrix-Form FMEA," *IEEE Transactions on Reliability*, vol. R-27 (1978):254–57.
11. K. Greene and T.J. Cunningham, "Failure Mode, Effects and Criticality Analysis," *Annual Symposium on Reliability* (1968):374–84.
12. P.L. Crown, "Design Effective Failure Mode and Effect Analysis," *Annual Symposium on Reliability* (1969):514–21.
13. B.S. Dhillon and C. Singh, Engineering Reliability: New Techniques and Applications (New York: John Wiley & Sons, 1981), pp. 48–52.
14. B.S. Dhillon and C. Singh, "On Fault Trees and Other Reliability Evaluation Methods," *Microelectronics and Reliability*, vol. 19 (1979):57–64.

17

Reliability and Maintainability Allocation

In order to meet the overall specified reliability and maintainability of a system under development, the general procedure is to set reliability and maintainability targets for its subsystems. Similarly, to fulfill the subsystem's reliability and maintainability goal, one has to set reliability and maintainability targets for its components. This way the overall specified reliability and maintainability goal for a system will be achieved automatically. Therefore, this chapter will cover system reliability and maintainability allocation.

RELIABILITY ALLOCATION TECHNIQUE I

This method, known as the ARINC method, is based on component constant failure rate. Assumptions associated with the method are:

1. System components form a series configuration. It means that if any one of the components fails, the series systems fails.
2. Component failures are statistically independent.

Series system reliability, $R_{ss}(t)$, at time t is given by

$$R_{ss}(t) = R_1(t) \cdot R_2(t) \cdot R_3(t) \cdot \ldots \cdot R_k(t) \tag{17.1}$$

where

k is the total number of components in the series system

$R_i(t)$ is the ith component's reliability at time t for $i = 1, 2, 3, \ldots, k$

For constant failure rate, the ith component's reliability, $R_i(t)$, at time t is given by

$$R_i(t) = e^{-\lambda_i t} \tag{17.2}$$

where λ_i is the ith component's constant failure rate.

Thus, substituting equation (17.2) in equation (17.1) leads to:

$$R_{ss}(t) = e^{-\lambda_1 t} \cdot e^{-\lambda_2 t} \cdot e^{-\lambda_3 t} \cdot \ldots \cdot e^{-\lambda_k t} \tag{17.3}$$

For component constant failure rates, series system reliability, $R_{ss}(t)$, at time t is

$$R_{ss}(t) = e^{-\lambda_{ss} t} \tag{17.4}$$

where λ_{ss} is the series system's constant failure rate.

Thus, substituting equation (17.4) in equation (17.3) yields

$$e^{-\lambda_{ss} t} = e^{-\lambda_1 t} \cdot e^{-\lambda_2 t} \cdot e^{-\lambda_3 t} \cdot \ldots \cdot e^{-\lambda_k t} \tag{17.5}$$

and

$$\lambda_{ss} = \sum_{i=1}^{k} \lambda_i \tag{17.6}$$

In terms of system reliability, $R_{ss}(t)$ or λ_{ss}, reliability allocation for an overall requirement can be carried out somewhat by the same procedure. Therefore, two types of allocation approaches are (1) failure rate allocations based on a system failure rate requirement and (2) allocations based on a system reliability requirement.

Failure Rate Allocation Approach

The following steps are associated with this method:

Step 1. Equation (17.6) demonstrates that the system failure rate is given by:

$$\lambda_{ss} = \sum_{i=1}^{k} \lambda_i \tag{17.7}$$

If the system's failure rate requirement is λ_{sr}, then the objective is to allocate component failure rate, $\hat{\lambda}_i$, such that

$$\sum_{i=1}^{k} \hat{\lambda}_i \leqslant \lambda_{sr} \tag{17.8}$$

Step 2. By utilizing field or other data, estimate system component failure rates:

$$\lambda_1, \lambda_2, \lambda_3, \ldots, \lambda_k$$

Step 3. This step is concerned with calculating the *i*th component's relative weight, θ_i. The equation to determine such weight is:

$$\theta_i = \lambda_i / \sum_{i=1}^{k} \lambda_i, \quad \text{for } i = 1, 2, 3, \ldots, k \tag{17.9}$$

Here we should note that

$$\sum_{i=1}^{k} \theta_i = 1 \tag{17.10}$$

because θ_i denotes the *i*th component's relative failure vulnerability.

Step 4. Allocate the *i*th component's failure rate requirement utilizing

$$\hat{\lambda}_i = \theta_i \lambda_{sr}, \quad \text{for } i = 1, 2, 3, \ldots, k \tag{17.11}$$

The above equation is subject to the condition that the equality holds in equation (17.8).

Reliability Allocation Approach

This method is very similar to the above method, however, the difference is that the series system requirement is expressed in terms of its reliability, $R_{sr}(t)$, at time t instead of its failure rate. Thus, we may say that

$$R_{sr}(t) = e^{-\lambda_{sr} t} \tag{17.12}$$

and

$$e^{-\lambda_{sr} t} \leqslant e^{-\sum_{i=1}^{k} \hat{\lambda}_i t} \tag{17.13}$$

After substituting for $\hat{\lambda}_i$ in equation (17.13) from equation (17.8), we get:

$$R_{sr}(t) \leqslant e^{-\left(\sum_{i=1}^{k} \theta_i \lambda_{sr} t\right)} \tag{17.14}$$

This leads to the allocation relationship

$$\hat{R}_i(t) > \{R_{sr}(t)\}^{\theta_i} \tag{17.15}$$

where $\hat{R}_i(t)$ is the *i*th component's estimated reliability at time t.

Since $R_{sr}(T) = e^{-\lambda_{sr} T}$, the formula for λ_{sr} is

$$\lambda_{sr} = -\frac{\ln R_{sr}(T)}{T} \tag{17.16}$$

where T is the time period.

Example 17.1

An aerospace system's specified constant failure rate is 0.05 failures/day. The system is composed of four subsystems in series. The estimated failure rates of subsystems 1, 2, 3, and 4 are $\lambda_1 = 0.01$ failures/day, $\lambda_2 = 0.03$ failures/day, $\lambda_3 = 0.02$ failures/day, and $\lambda_4 = 0.025$ failures/day, respectively. Allocate the required system failure rate to its four subsystems.

By utilizing equation (17.7) and the given data, the total estimated system failure rate is:

$$\lambda_{ss} = \sum_{i=1}^{4} \lambda_i = 0.01 + 0.03 + 0.02 + 0.025$$

$$= 0.085 \text{ failures/day}$$

The relative weight of the ith subsystem from equation (17.9) is

$$\theta_1 = \frac{0.01}{0.085} = 0.1177$$

$$\theta_2 = \frac{0.03}{0.085} = 0.353$$

$$\theta_3 = \frac{0.02}{0.085} = 0.235$$

$$\theta_4 = \frac{0.025}{0.085} = 0.294$$

With the aid of equation (17.11), the subsystems' allocated failure rates are

$$\hat{\lambda}_1 = \theta_1 \cdot \lambda_{sr} = (0.1177)(0.05) = 0.005885 \text{ failures/day}$$

$$\hat{\lambda}_2 = \theta_2 \cdot \lambda_{sr} = (0.353)(0.05) = 0.01765 \text{ failures/day}$$

$$\hat{\lambda}_3 = \theta_3 \cdot \lambda_{sr} = (0.235)(0.05) = 0.01175 \text{ failures/day}$$

$$\hat{\lambda}_4 = \theta_4 \cdot \lambda_{sr} = (0.294)(0.05) = 0.0147 \text{ failures/day}$$

where $\hat{\lambda}_1$, $\hat{\lambda}_2$, $\hat{\lambda}_3$, and $\hat{\lambda}_4$ are the allocated failure rates of subsystems 1, 2, 3, and 4, respectively.

Example 17.2

An electronic system is composed of five subsystems forming a series configuration. The system's specified reliability for a five-day mission is 0.95.

From past failure data subsystems' 1, 2, 3, 4, and 5 estimated failure rates are $\lambda_1 = 0.01$ failures/day, $\lambda_2 = 0.02$ failures/day, $\lambda_3 = 0.03$ failures/day, $\lambda_4 = 0.02$ failures/day, and $\lambda_5 = 0.04$ failures/day, respectively. Allocate the system's specified reliability to each subsystem.

The total failure rate of the series system from equation (17.7) is:

$$\lambda_{ss} = \sum_{i=1}^{5} \lambda_i = 0.01 + 0.02 + 0.03 + 0.02 + 0.04 = 0.12 \text{ failures/day}$$

The relative weight of the ith subsystem from equation (17.9) is:

$$\theta_1 = \frac{0.01}{0.12} = 0.833$$

$$\theta_2 = \frac{0.02}{0.12} = 0.1667$$

$$\theta_3 = \frac{0.03}{0.12} = 0.25$$

$$\theta_4 = \frac{0.02}{0.12} = 0.1667$$

$$\theta_5 = \frac{0.04}{0.12} = 0.3333$$

From relationship (17.15), each subsystem's allocated reliability for a five-day mission is:

$$R_1(5) = (0.95)^{0.0833} = 0.9957$$

$$R_2(5) = (0.95)^{0.1667} = 0.9915$$

$$R_3(5) = (0.95)^{0.25} = 0.9873$$

$$R_4(5) = (0.95)^{0.1667} = 0.9915$$

$$R_5(5) = (0.95)^{0.3333} = 0.9830$$

Therefore, the allocated reliabilities for subsystems 1, 2, 3, 4, and 5 are 0.9957, 0.9915, 0.9873, 0.9915, and 0.9830, respectively.

RELIABILITY ALLOCATION TECHNIQUE II

Assume in this technique that k number of independent subsystems form a series configuration. However, since the technique allocates the same reliability for all subsystems, it is known as the equal apportionment method.[5] A series system's required reliability, R_{re}, is given by

$$R_{re} = R_1 \cdot R_2 \cdot R_3 \cdot R_4 \cdot \ldots \cdot R_k \tag{17.17}$$

where R_j is the jth subsystem's reliability for $i = 1, 2, 3, \ldots, k$.

Therefore, from equation (17.17) for equal subsystems the reliabilities result is:

$$R_j = (R_{re})^{1/k} \tag{17.18}$$

Example 17.3

A series system is composed of 10 subsystems. To develop any one of these subsystems is expensive and costs the same amount of money for each. The series system's specified reliability is 0.99. Allocate reliability to each subsystem in order to meet the required reliability of the series system.

From equation (17.18) and the given data, we get the jth subsystem's reliability:

$$R_j = (0.99)^{1/10} = 0.999$$

Each subsystem's allocated reliability should be 0.999 if the specified reliability of the system is to be achieved.

RELIABILITY ALLOCATION TECHNIQUE III

This method is known as the AGREE (Advisory Group on Reliability of Electronic Equipment) method.[8] It is somewhat more complex than the allocation techniques presented earlier. In comparison to technique I, the AGREE technique is based on the complexity of the subsystem (unit or component) instead of on subsystem failure rate. In addition, AGREE takes the subsystem's importance into consideration. The formula presented in the AGREE report is utilized to determine each subsystem's minimum mean time to failure (mean life) in order to meet the system's specified reliability.

The following assumptions are associated with the technique:

1. The subsystems' failure rates are constant.
2. The subsystems form a series system.
3. The subsystems' failures are statistically independent.

We should note that a subsystem's complexity is defined in terms of modules. A transistor or a magnetic amplifier are examples of a module. In this technique it is assumed that the modules' failure rates are equal. For the system's success, the contribution of each module is the same. The kth subsystem's allocated failure rate, λ_k, is given by[4,8]

$$\lambda_k = \beta_k \{-\ell n\, R_{sr}(T)\} / \beta \gamma_k t_k \tag{17.19}$$

where

- β is the number of modules contained in the system
- γ_k is the kth subsystem's importance factor (This factor is defined in terms of system failure probability for a particular subsystem if that subsystem fails. If the value of the importance factor is equal to unity for a particular subsystem, then it means that subsystems must function normally for system success. However, if the factor is equal to zero, then it means that the failure of the subsystem in question does not affect the operation of the system.)
- β_k is the total number of modules contained in the kth subsystem.
- t_k is the kth subsystem's (required) operation time during system operation time T for $0 < t_k \leqslant T$
- $R_{sr}(T)$ is the specified reliability of the system at time T

Note that in the above formula it is assumed that $e^{-y} \simeq 1 - y$ which is true for very small y.

For the operation time t_k, the kth subsystem's allocated reliability, $R_k(t_k)$, is

$$R_k(t_k) = 1 - \frac{B}{\gamma_k} \tag{17.20}$$

where

$$B \equiv 1 - \{R_{sr}(T)\}^{(\beta_k/\beta)} \tag{17.21}$$

This formula is subject to the condition that the importance factor for each subsystem is close to unity.

Example 17.4

An electrical system is composed of six independent subsystems in series. The overall required reliability of the system is 0.98 for a 15-hour operation. The number of modules contained in each subsystem is given in Table 17.1. Subsystems 1-3 are required to function throughout the operational period of the system. Their importance factor is equal to unity. However, subsystems 4 and 5 are expected to operate for 10 hours during the operational period of the system. Finally, subsystem 6 must function for five hours during the operational period of the system. The importance factors of subsystems 4-6 are 0.94, 0.95, and 0.97, respectively.

Table 17.1 Modules data

Subsystem	*Number of Modules*
1	50
2	40
3	100
4	60
5	80
6	200

With the aid of formulas (17.19) and (17.20), allocate subsystem failure rates and subsystem reliabilities. The total number of modules, β, contained in the system from Table 17.1 is:

$$\beta = 50 + 40 + 100 + 60 + 80 + 100 = 430$$

By utilizing equation (17.19) and the given data, subsystems' 1-6 allocated failure rates are as follows, respectively:

$$\lambda_1 = 50\,\{-\ell n\ 0.98\}\,/(430)(1)(15)$$
$$= 0.001566$$

$$\lambda_2 = 40\,\{-\ell n\ 0.98\}\,/(430)(1)(15)$$
$$= 0.0001253$$

$$\lambda_3 = 100\,\{-\ell n\ 0.98\}\,/(430)(1)(15)$$
$$= 0.003132$$

$$\lambda_4 = 60\,\{-\ell n\ 0.98\}\,/(430)(0.94)(10)$$
$$= 0.0002999$$

$$\lambda_5 = 80\,\{-\ell n\ 0.98\}\,/(430)(0.95)(10)$$
$$= 0.0003956$$

$$\lambda_6 = 200\,\{-\ell n\ 0.98\}\,/(430)(0.97)(5)$$
$$= 0.0019374$$

Similarly, by utilizing formula (17.20) and the given data, the subsystems' 1-6 allocated reliabilities, respectively, are as follows:

$$R_1(15) = 1 - \left[\frac{1 - (0.98)^{50/430}}{1}\right]$$
$$= 0.9976536$$

$$R_2(15) = 1 - \left[\frac{1-(0.98)^{40/430}}{1}\right]$$
$$= 0.998122$$

$$R_3(15) = 1 - \left[\frac{1-(0.98)^{100/430}}{1}\right]$$
$$= 0.9953127$$

$$R_4(10) = 1 - \left[\frac{1-(0.98)^{60/430}}{0.94}\right]$$
$$= 0.9970053$$

$$R_5(10) = 1 - \left[\frac{1-(0.98)^{80/430}}{0.95}\right]$$
$$= 0.996051$$

$$R_6(5) = 1 - \left[\frac{1-(0.98)^{200/430}}{0.97}\right]$$
$$= 0.9903581$$

RELIABILITY ALLOCATION TECHNIQUE IV

This allocation method is known as the similar familiar system technique. The basis for this approach is the experience and objective judgment of the design personnel, in other words, the familiarity of such personnel with similar systems. This technique becomes very useful in the conceptual design stage of the system. The approach assumes that from the reliability angle the earlier design has been adequate and that similar systems are carrying out the same function.

The following items are to be considered when applying the similar familiar system approach:

Similarities of design and manufacturing

Comparison of performance

System or equipment physical comparison[9]

RELIABILITY ALLOCATION TECHNIQUE V

Known as the factors of influence approach, this method is utilized when system field data are not available and the system is new.[10] The procedure is based on the influential factors affecting a system under development. In this method each subsystem of the system is rated with respect to such influential factors as complexity/time, environmental condition, criticality, and state-of-the-art. The rating scale varies from 1 to 10. A 1 is assigned to the subsystem least affected by the factor in question, whereas 10 is assigned to the subsystem most affected by the factor in question. Thus, the reliability targets can be set by utilizing the weight of these numbers for factors in question.[9]

Briefly, the factors are as follows:

Environmental factor: It is concerned with the subsystem's exposure or susceptibility to environmental conditions such as humidity, vibration, and temperature.

Complexity/time: Complexity is associated with the number of subsystem parts, whereas time is concerned with the subsystem's operating time in relation to the total functional period.

Subsystem criticality: This factor is associated with the subsystem's failure criticality effect on the system.

State-of-the-art: Advancement in the state-of-the-art for a subsystem is taken care of in this factor.

RELIABILITY ALLOCATION TECHNIQUE VI

This allocation procedure is known as the combined factors of influence and familiar systems method. As its name suggests, this procedure is the result of combining allocation techniques IV and V. Since the resulting method has the advantages of both those techniques, the tendency is to use the combination approach in allocation problems.

MAINTAINABILITY ALLOCATION METHOD

This section offers a method used to allocate required system maintainability to its subsystems or components.[11] In other words, this allocation technique apportions the required mean time to repair (MTTR) of a system to its subsystems or components. It is assumed that the failure rates are constant and the repair times follow the log normal distribution.

The basis for this method is to make use of a weighting factor when allocating system mean corrective maintenance time. The minimum time is apportioned to subsystems with high failure rates, and maximum time is allocated to subsystems with low failure rates. It is generally accepted that the subsystems or units which are frequently visited for maintenance should consume the least time. The weighting factor takes into consideration complexity, accessibility, fault isolation technique, environment, maintainability characteristics, and so on.

The system weighting factor, w, is defined by

$$w = \left(\sum_{i=1}^{m} \lambda_i w_i\right) / \lambda_s \tag{17.22}$$

$$\lambda_s \equiv \sum_{i=1}^{m} \lambda_i \tag{17.23}$$

where

λ_s is the total failure rate of the system

λ_i is the constant failure rate of the ith subsystem

w_i is the ith subsystem's weighting factor

m is the number of subsystems in a system

Rearranging equation (17.22) leads to:

$$\lambda_s = \left(\sum_{i=1}^{m} \lambda_i w_i\right) / w \tag{17.24}$$

System MTTR is defined by

$$\text{MTTR} = \left(\sum_{i=1}^{m} \lambda_i t_{ai}\right) / \lambda_s \tag{17.25}$$

where t_{ai} denotes the active repair time of the ith subsystem.

Rearranging equation (17.25) results in:

$$\lambda_s = \left(\sum_{i=1}^{m} \lambda_i t_{ai}\right) / \text{MTTR} \tag{17.26}$$

Equating expressions (17.24) and (17.26) leads to:

$$\frac{\left(\sum_{i=1}^{m} \lambda_i w_i\right)}{w} \equiv \frac{\left(\sum_{i=1}^{m} \lambda_i t_{ai}\right)}{\text{MTTR}} \tag{17.27}$$

The above equation is rewritten to the following form:

$$\frac{\lambda_i w_i}{w} + \ldots + \frac{\lambda_n w_m}{w} \equiv \frac{\lambda_i t_{ai}}{\text{MTTR}} + \ldots + \frac{\lambda_n t_{am}}{\text{MTTR}} \tag{17.28}$$

Rearranging equation (17.28) results in:

$$\lambda_i \left(\frac{w_i}{w} - \frac{t_{ai}}{\text{MTTR}}\right) + \ldots + \lambda_n \left(\frac{w_n}{w} - \frac{t_{am}}{\text{MTTR}}\right) = 0 \quad (17.29)$$

Thus, from equation (17.29) we get:

$$\left(\frac{w_i}{w} - \frac{t_{ai}}{\text{MTTR}}\right) = 0 \quad (17.30)$$

Therefore, from equation (17.30) we get:

$$\frac{w_i}{w} = \frac{t_{ai}}{\text{MTTR}} \quad (17.31)$$

Rearranging equation (17.31) yields the ith subsystem's allocated active repair time

$$t_{ai} = \frac{w_i}{w} \cdot \text{MTTR} \quad (17.32)$$

where w_i denotes the weighting factor, which is also known as the unavailability contribution factor of the ith subsystem.

$$w_i \equiv (w_{i1} + w_{i2} + w_{i3} + \ldots + w_{ik})/k \quad (17.33)$$

where k denotes the subsystem's weight factors.

For example, w_{i1} may denote the weighting factor by generic module types; w_{i2} denotes the fault isolation technique weighting factors, w_{i3} denotes the weighting factor by differences in maintainability design characteristics, and so on.

Tables for various factors are given in Arsenault and Roberts.[12]

We should note here again that MTTR denotes the system's MTTR which is to be apportioned. From equation (17.22), the system's weighting factor is given by:

$$w = \left(\sum_{i=1}^{m} \lambda_i w_i\right) / \lambda_s \quad (17.34)$$

Example 17.5

A series system is composed of three subsystems. The system's specified mean time to repair is two hours and the constant failure rates of subsystems 1, 2, and 3 are 0.001 failures/hour, 0.002 failures/hour, and 0.004 failures/hour, respectively. Each subsystem's complexity, environmental, packaging, handling, accessibility, and fault isolation factors are given in Table 17.2.

Table 17. 2 Weighting Factors

	WEIGHTING FACTORS						
	1	2	3	4	5	6	
Subsystem	*Fault isolation technique*	*Com-plexity*	*Environ-mental*	*Packag-ing*	*Han-dling*	*Accessi-bility*	w_i
1	7	3	2	1	3	2	3
2	3	3	1	2	1	4	2.33
3	1	4	3	3	1	1	2.167

Allocate the required system MTTR to its subsystem by utilizing the maintainability allocation technique.

The value of w_i in the last column of the table is calculated by utilizing equation (17.33). In that equation the weighting factors, w_{i1}, w_{i2}, w_{i3}, w_{i4}, w_{i5}, and w_{i6} are for fault isolation technique, complexity, environment, packaging, handling, and accessibility, respectively.

The t_{ai} allocation for each subsystem is given in Table 17.3.

Utilizing the end results of columns 3 and 4 of Table 17.3 in equation (17.34) yields:

$$w = \frac{0.016328}{0.007} = 2.3357$$

From equation (17.32) and the given data, we get:

$$t_{ai} = \frac{w_i}{(2.33257)} \cdot (2) \tag{17.35}$$

Using the data for w_i given in the last column of Table 17.2 in equation (17.35) leads to the following allocated active repair times for subsystems 1, 2, and 3, respectively.

$$t_{a1} = \frac{3(2)}{2.33257} = 2.57227 \text{ hours}$$

$$t_{a2} = \frac{2.33(2)}{2.33257} \simeq 2 \text{ hours}$$

Table 17.3 Allocation analysis

Subsystem	w_i	λ_i	$w_i\lambda_i$	*Allocated* t_{ai}
1	3	0.001	0.003	2.57227
2	2.33	0.002	0.00466	2
3	2.167	0.004	0.008668	1.858
Total		$\sum_{i=1}^{3} \lambda_i = 0.007$	$\sum_{i=1}^{3} w_i\lambda_i = 0.016328$	

$$t_{a3} = \frac{2.167(2)}{2.33257} = 1.8580364 \text{ hours}$$

SUMMARY

This chapter covers reliability and maintainability allocation. Eight reliability and maintainability allocation techniques are presented, among them the AGREE method, ARINC method, similar familiar approach, maintainability allocation approach, and so on.

EXERCISES

17.1. An engineering system consists of five independent subsystems in series. The system's specified constant failure rate is 0.08 failures/month. The estimated constant failure rates of the subsystems are as follows:

Subsystem 1: $\lambda_1 = 0.01$ failures/month

Subsystem 2: $\lambda_2 = 0.02$ failures/month

Subsystem 3: $\lambda_3 = 0.02$ failures/month

Subsystem 4: $\lambda_4 = 0.015$ failures/month

Subsystem 5: $\lambda_5 = 0.03$ failures/month

Apportion the required system failure rates to the five subsystems.

17.2. An aerospace system's required reliability for a 20-hour mission is 0.96. The system is composed of four independent subsystems forming a series configuration. The constant failure rates for subsystems 1, 2, 3, and 4 are $\lambda_1 = 0.002$ failures/hour, $\lambda_2 = 0.004$ failures/hour, $\lambda_3 = 0.005$ failures/hour, and $\lambda_4 = 0.001$ failures/hour, respectively. Allocate the required reliability for the system to its subsystems.

17.3. Discuss the combined factors of influence and the familiar systems method. What are the main differences between them?

NOTES

1. H.E. Frederick, "A Reliability Allocation Technique," *Proceedings of the Fourth National Symposium on Reliability and Quality Control* (1958): 314–17.
2. J.S. Chipchak, "A Practical Method of Maintainability Allocation," *IEEE Transactions on Aerospace and Electronic Systems,* vol. 7 (1971):585–89.
3. H.S. Balaban, H.R. Jeffers and D.O. Baechler, "The Allocation of System Reliability," ARINC Research Corporation, Publication No. 152-2-274 (November 30, 1961).
4. W.H. Von Alven, *Reliability Engineering* (Englewood Cliffs, N.J.: Prentice-Hall, 1964), pp. 189–192.
5. K.C. Kapur and L.R. Lamberson, *Reliability in Engineering Design* (New York: John Wiley & Sons, 1977), pp. 407.
6. *Handbook of Reliability Engineering,* NAVWEPS 00-65-502, Directorate of the Chief of the Bureau of Naval Weapons (Washington, D.C.: June 1964), pp. 2.19–2.35.
7. *Quality Assurance,* AMCP 702-3, U.S. Army Material Command (Springfield, VA: National Technical Information Service, October 1968), pp. 4.8–4.11.
8. *Reliability of Military Electronic Equipment,* AGREE report, Advisory Group on Reliability of Electronic Equipment (Washington, D.C.: Office of the Assistant Secretary of Defense, 1957), pp. 52–57.
9. C. Singh and R. Billington, System Reliability Modeling and Evaluation (London: Hutchinson, 1977), pp. 4.
10. *Reliability Engineering Training Course Manual* Douglas Report SM–48915 (Santa Monica, CA: Missile and Space System Division, Douglas Aircraft Company, July 1965), pp. 43–45.
11. J.S. Chipchak, "A Practical Method of Maintainability Allocation," *IEEE Transactions on Aerospace and Electronic Systems,* vol. AES–7 (1971): 585–89.

12. J.E. Arsenault, J.A. Roberts, eds., *Reliability and Maintainbility of Electronic Systems* (Potomax, MD: Computer Science Press, 1980), pp. 396–402.

18

Reliability and Maintainability Data Collection and Analysis

In order to perform reliability or maintainability analysis, the availability of failure data is vital. Therefore, the required failure data has to be collected before it can be analyzed. This process requires careful planning well in advance. Because failure data collection normally has a high price tag, we have to be sure of what, when, why, and where to collect.

Once enough failure data has been accumulated, the next step is to perform failure data analysis and to estimate desired parameters. These parameters provide useful input when making decisions to develop a new system, unit, or component and when developing maintenance policies, life cycle cost models, and so on.

RELIABILITY DATA COLLECTION

Types of Data

There are four basic types of data:

1. *Type I:* This type of data is known as performance data. It is subdivided into attribute data, operating time or cycle data, and variables data. Information regarding product performance (i.e., whether it performs

according to specified conditions) is yielded by attribute data. The second type, operating time or cycle data, contains information regarding mean time between failure (MTBF) or mean time to failure (MTTF). Variables data consists of such data whose value is in some functional test either less than the lower limit or above the upper limit.

2. *Type II:* This type of data, known as configuration data, contains information regarding the configuration. For example, in some cases a fully developed system may not contain specified components or it may consist of incorrect components; this could be a factor for issuance of a failure report.
3. *Type III:* This data is concerned with collecting cost information and summarizing problems. This type is known as management data.
4. *Type IV:* Known as discrepancy data, this type of data results from functional test reports or field reports. This type of data provides useful information.[1]

Data Sources

In the system life cycle there are eight data sources.[2] These sources are shown in Figure 18.1 and are described in detail below.

♦ **SYSTEM DEVELOPMENT DATA** This data is collected during the development phase of the system. Although this could be very productive, to collect data at this stage is rather a cumbersome and time-consuming task. The difficulty arises because often during the breadboard development phase some failures occur, which may not be actual failures but the result of human errors; short-circuiting the components, wrong connections, and so on are examples. Therefore, collecting data during system development requires daily contact with the facility and with the people generating such data.

♦ **ACCEPTANCE TESTING** During the acceptance testing phase of a product, the necessary data may be retrieved. Since the acceptance testing data are usually documented in quality control and manufacturing reports, the data are generally retrieved from these reports with little effort. In acceptance testing rejections are due to product testing errors, poor workmanship, application of wrong parts, wiring errors, soldering, replacement of defective parts, and so on. A common problem experienced here is identifying and separating the rejection data.

♦ **PAST EXPERIENCE DATA** This type of data can be obtained from similar or identical systems or products. This data is very useful because any system is 90% or more evolutionary in design.[2] In other words, it has only 10% or less innovative design. Users of similar products are a good source for previous experience data.

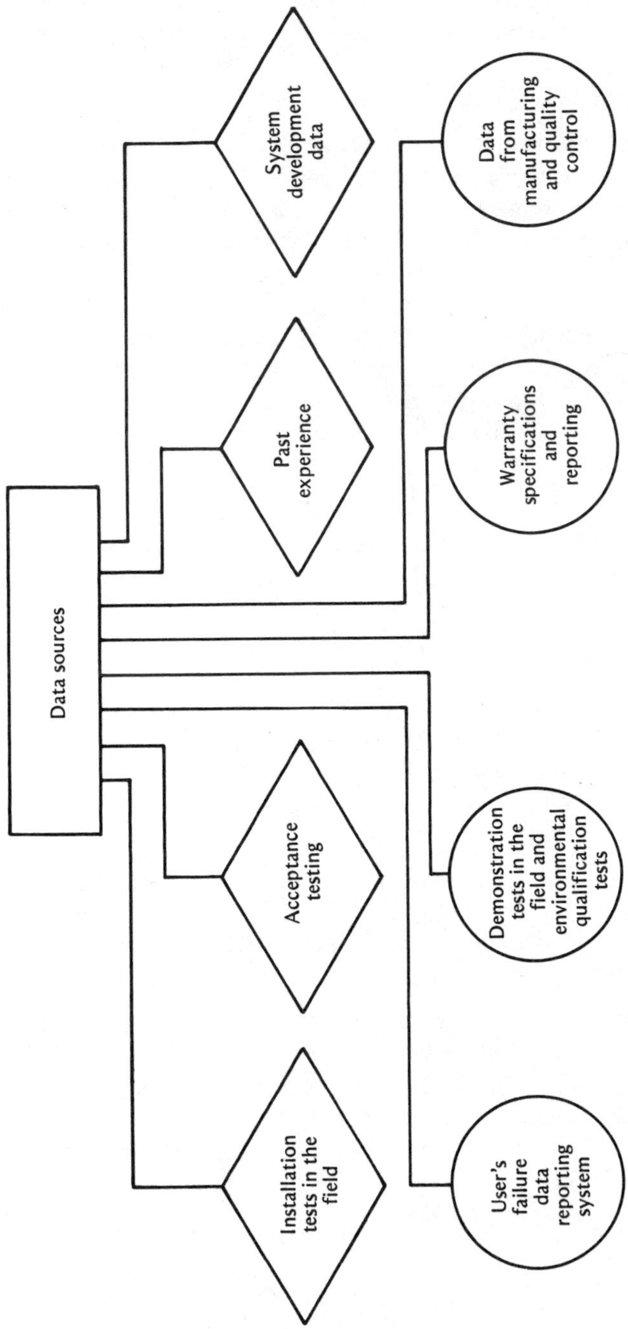

Figure 18.1 Data sources

♦ **DATA FROM QUALITY CONTROL AND MANUFACTURING SOURCES** The quality control and manufacturing groups generate a large quantity of inspection data. Access to this type of data is quite easy, however, the data are highly contaminated.[2]

♦ **DATA FROM FIELD INSTALLATION TESTS** Once the equipment is fully operational, then it is fielded. During this period the product exhibits its real performance and performance deficiencies. Therefore, data obtained from field engineers will provide a true picture of the equipment or of product performance because these engineers have no reason to hide the deficiencies of equipment under study.

A general tendency of field engineers is dislike of paper work. Therefore, the reliability engineer has to design the data collection forms and procedures in such a way that field engineers will spend minimum time to complete them. In order to make sure that field engineers accept data collection as a part of their responsibilities, their field engineering manual should contain the data collection forms and procedures.

♦ **FIELD DEMONSTRATION TESTS AND ENVIRONMENTAL TESTS DATA** In the life cycle of a product this may be the most carefully documented phase (demonstration and environmental tests) because these tests are usually involved in contract acceptance. Therefore, any failure occurring during this phase is thoroughly examined before the product is officially released. Arrangements have to be made so that this data is available immediately to the concerned reliability engineer. Furthermore, the reliability engineer has to keep a continuous check on when such tests are conducted so that the prepared reports data and test log data are compatible.

♦ **WARRANTY SPECIFICATIONS AND REPORTING** Many times an engineering product is subject to certain warranty clauses. Usually the hardware warranty from the day of sale varies between 90 days and two years. Therefore, the reliability engineer can extract data from the claim reports fielded by the customers because of warranty on the product.

♦ **CUSTOMER'S FAILURE DATA BANKS** Many engineering system users have their own failure data banks. This is a very good source for obtaining most of the failure data anyone needs. However, one may experience difficulty receiving needed data on time and on a regular basis. Failure data obtained from the customer's source may have the following deficiencies: no serial number of the failed unit, the elapsed-time meter readings are not reported, and it is difficult to identify within equipment the exact location where work was performed.[2]

Failure Data Collection Form

The main objective of any data collection form is to ensure that the necessary information is collected with minimum effort. However, there is no single form which is used to collect failure data by various organizations. Generally, the failure data collection form is designed according to the needs of a company. Nevertheless, below are the important points which may be considered when designing a form:

Form number

Date: of form completion, failure occurrence, failure correction, failure detection, etc.

Hardware location

Level of failure (system, subsystem, etc.)

Configuration information of failed unit

Damage to components within vicinity of the failed unit

Description and symptoms of failure

Failed item's serial number

Manufacturer's name

Item's operation hours from the last failure

Replaced part's serial number and the name of the manufacturer of the part

Repair time and repair cost

Number of repairmen and their names

Signatures

Brief description of system, subsystem, or component

Deficiencies in Existing Electric Power Plant Failure Data Banks

In order to present existing typical deficiencies in failure data sources, the deficiencies of an electric power plant failure data source are listed as an example.

1. Inconsistency in term definitions
2. Time-consuming data feedback
3. Nonstandardized data reporting

4. Validity of data questionable (sometimes)
5. Lack of accuracy in many component repair times
6. Unavailability of item failure rates as a function of environment and of operational conditions.
7. No classification of item data by the manufacturer
8. Difficult to pinpoint the causes of failure
9. Lack of item description
10. Restrictions on data[3]

FAILURE DATA ANALYSIS

This section presents techniques to estimate the parameters of various statistical distributions.

Hazard Plotting Technique

This is a graphical method used to estimate statistical distribution parameters. The technique can handle incomplete and complete failure data.[4] Complete data occur when the failure times of all components or units in a sample are known. In contrast, incomplete failure data occur when a sample contains running times of unfailed components or units and failure times of failed units.

The basic theory associated with hazard plotting is

$$z(y) = \frac{f(y)}{1 - F(y)} \tag{18.1}$$

where

y is time

$z(y)$ is the distribution hazard rate

$f(y)$ is the probability density function

$F(y)$ is the cumulative distribution function

The cumulative hazard, $z_c(y)$, is defined as follows:

$$z_c(y) = \int_0^y z(x) \cdot dx \tag{18.2}$$

Equations (18.1) and (18.2) are utilized to develop straight line cumulative hazard equations for the Weibull, Rayleigh, and exponential distributions.

♦ **WEIBULL DISTRIBUTION** The Weibull probability density and cumulative functions, respectively, are defined as follows:

$$f(y) = a\,b\,y^{b-1} \cdot e^{-a\,y^b} \tag{18.3}$$

where

- a is the scale parameter
- b is the shape parameter
- y is time

And

$$F(y) = 1 - e^{-a\,y^b} \tag{18.4}$$

By utilizing equations (18.3) and (18.4) in equation (18.1), the resulting hazard rate equation is:

$$z(y) = a\,b\,y^{b-1} \tag{18.5}$$

Substituting equation (18.5) in equation (18.2) and integrating yields:

$$z_c(y) = \int_0^y a\,b\,x^{b-1}\,dx$$
$$= a y^b \tag{18.6}$$

Taking the natural logarithms of equation (18.6) leads to

$$\ell n\, z_c = \ell n\, a + b\, \ell n\, y \tag{18.7}$$

The $\ell n\, z_c$ against $\ell n\, y$ plots as a straight line with slope b. In other words, the slope of equation (18.7) is equal to b. The vertical axis intercept of the straight line is equal to $\ell n\, a$. This leads to

$$\ell n\, a = \alpha \tag{18.8}$$

where α is given by the point where the straight line intercepts the vertical axis.

The result of utilizing equation (18.8) is

$$a = e^{\alpha} \tag{18.9}$$

Thus, a can be estimated from equation (18.9).

♦ **RAYLEIGH DISTRIBUTION** At $b = 2$, equation (18.7) reduces to the one for the Rayleigh distribution as given below:

$$\ell n\, z_c = \ell n\, a + 2\, \ell n\, y \tag{18.10}$$

The $\ell n\, z_c$ against $\ell n\, y$ plots as a straight line with slope equal to 2. The point where the straight line intercepts the vertical axis is equal to $\ell n\, a$. Thus, the value of a can be estimated from equation (18.11)

$$a = e^{\gamma} \tag{18.11}$$

where γ is the value at the point where the straight line and vertical axis intercept.

♦ **EXPONENTIAL DISTRIBUTION** Setting $b = 1$ in equation (18.7) reduces to

$$z_c = a y \tag{18.12}$$

The above equation is the equation of the straight line that passes through the origin. The slope of the line is equal to a. In other words, the slope of the straight line can be used to estimate the value of parameter a.

Nelson presents several numerical examples on the application of the hazard plotting technique.[4] His examples are concerned with incomplete failure data analysis.

Least-Squares Technique

This is a commonly known technique to engineers. The method is concerned with fitting a linear line to failure data or other data. Because of past experience and judgment, the straight line may be fitted graphically to the historical data. Once the line is fitted to the data, then its parameters may be estimated graphically or otherwise. The equation of the straight line is defined by

$$y = \theta + k t \tag{18.13}$$

where

- y is the dependent variable
- t is time and is known as the independent variable.
- θ and k are the straight line parameters.

We should note here that the values of θ and k can be estimated graphically or analytically. Once a straight line is fitted graphically to the historical data, then the slope of the line provides the value of k, and where the line intersects the y-axis that value is the estimate for θ.

The analytical procedure to estimate k and θ is more complex than the graphical approach. In the analytical approach we assume that there are m data points. In addition, y_j, corresponding to t_j, denotes the jth data point. Thus, we may write that the jth data point's estimated value is given by:

$$\hat{y}_j = \theta + k t_j \tag{18.14}$$

Subtracting equation (18.14) from equation (18.13) yields the jth data point's error:

$$E_j = y_j - \hat{y}_j = y_j - \theta - k\,t_j \tag{18.15}$$

For m data points, squaring both sides of equation (18.15) and then summing yields the total of the squares of the m deviations (errors):

$$T_s = \sum_{j=1}^{m} E_j^2 = \sum_{j=1}^{m} (y_j - \theta - k\,t_j)^2 \tag{18.16}$$

In order to find the minimum value of equation (18.16), differentiate that equation with respect to θ and k, respectively, and then set the derivatives equal to zero as follows:

$$\frac{\partial T_s}{\partial \theta} = \sum_{j=1}^{m} \{2(y_j - \theta - k\,t_j)(-1)\}$$

$$= -2 \sum_{j=1}^{m} y_j + 2\theta m + 2k \sum_{j=1}^{m} t_j = 0 \tag{18.17}$$

$$\frac{\partial T_s}{\partial k} = \sum_{j=1}^{m} 2(y_j - \theta - k\,t_j)(-t_j)$$

$$= -2 \sum_{j=1}^{m} y_j t_j + 2\theta \sum_{j=1}^{m} t_j + 2k \sum_{j=1}^{m} t_j^2 = 0 \tag{18.18}$$

Solving equations (18.17) and (18.18) yields the expressions to estimate θ and k as follows:

$$k = \left(m \sum_{j=1}^{m} y_j t_j - \sum_{j=1}^{m} y_j \sum_{j=1}^{m} t_j\right) / B \tag{18.19}$$

where

$$B \equiv m \sum_{j=1}^{m} t_j^2 - \left(\sum_{j=1}^{m} t_j\right)^2 \tag{18.20}$$

$$\theta = \left(\sum_{j=1}^{m} t_j^2 \sum_{j=1}^{m} y_j - \sum_{j=1}^{m} t_j \sum_{j=1}^{m} t_j y_j\right) / B \tag{18.21}$$

Thus the straight line equation parameters can be estimated (for given m data points) by utilizing equations (18.19) and (18.21).

Example 18.1

The observations data of t and y are as follows:

t	2	5	3	4	2	3	2
y	4	10	6	7	6	8	7

Estimate the values of the straight line parameters k and θ by assuming that a straight line is to be fitted to the given data. Utilizing the given data results in:

$$\sum_{j=1}^{7} t_j = 2+5+3+4+2+3+2 = 21$$

$$\sum_{j=1}^{7} y_j = 4+10+6+7+6+8+7 = 48$$

$$\sum_{j=1}^{7} t_j^2 = 4+25+9+16+4+9+4 = 71$$

$$\sum_{j=1}^{7} t_j y_j = 8+50+18+28+12+24+14 = 154$$

$$m = 7$$

Therefore, utilizing the above results in equation (18.20) leads to:

$$B = 6(71) - (21)^2 = -15$$

Similarly, from equations (18.19) and (18.21) we get:

$$\hat{k} = \{6(154) - (48)(21)\}/(-15) = 5.6$$

$$\hat{\theta} = \{(71)(48) - (21)(154)\}/(-15) = -11.6$$

Thus the estimated values for k and θ are 5.6 and -11.6, respectively.

SUMMARY

This chapter is concerned with failure data collection and analysis. The discussion on failure data collection is divided into the following four sections: types of data, data sources, failure data collection form, and deficiencies in existing electric power plant failure data banks. The failure data analysis portion of the chapter contains the hazard plotting and the least-square techniques. The equations for the cumulative hazard of Weibull, Rayleigh, and exponential distributions are developed. The least-square technique is also demonstrated.

EXERCISES

18.1. Suppose you are given an assignment to develop a component failure data bank. What sources would you consider collecting the data from? Discuss them briefly.

18.2. Discuss at least three types of data.

18.3. The failure and censoring times of eight identical units put to test at time zero are as follows:

Unit No.	*Failure and Censoring Times (hours)*
1	100
2	500
3	1,000
4	200*
5	1,500
6	2,000
7	5,000
8	600*

Tabulate the cumulative hazard values corresponding to units failure times. The asterisk (*) denotes censoring times. (Consult Nelson.[4])

18.4. The observation data of variables x and y are as follows:

x	y
5	10
10	18
15	35
20	50
30	65
40	100
25	40
10	15

Estimate the value of parameters α and β of the straight line equation $y = \alpha + \beta x$. Assume that the straight line is to be fitted to given data.

NOTES

1. *Reliability Reporting Guide,* Reliability Division (Milwaukee, American Society for Quality Control, 1977): 6–7.

2. R.F. Hahn, "Data Collection Techniques," *Proceedings of the Annual Reliability and Maintainability Symposium* (1972): 38–42.

3. R.J. Duphily and R.L. Long, "Enhancement of Electric Power Plant Reliability Data Systems," presented at the Fourth Annual Reliability Engineering Conference for the Electric Power Industry, New York (June 1977). Available from Mr. R.J. Duphily, Holmes and Narver, Inc. 400 West Orangethorpe Avenue, Anaheim, CA 92801, USA.
4. W. Nelson, "Hazard Plotting for Incomplete Failure Data," *Journal of Quality Technology*, vol. 7 (1969): 27-51.

Index

Acceptance testing, 256
Air traffic control system, 184
Availability
  achieved, 191
  instantaneous, 180
  parallel system, 182
  mission, 181
  series system, 182
  steady-state, 181
Average outgoing quality limit, 49

Bathtub curve, 33
Binomial theorem, 10
Break-even charts, 122

Calculated-risk index, 125
Close mode failure, 25
Coefficient of variation, 102
Confidence interval, 109
Confidence limits, 108
Configuration management
  characteristics, 169
  goals, 167
  history of, 165
  techniques
    accounting and auditing, 169
    control, 169
    identification, 169
Configuration manager, 170
Contracting, 11
Contract negotiator, 158
Contractor, 160
Contracts
  firm targets, 156
  fixed price, 156
    with escalation, 156
    with incentives, 156
    with redeterminable, 156
  letter, 156
Corrective maintenance, 190
Corrective maintenance cost, 148
Cost-effectiveness approach, 146
Criticality analysis, 223
Critical path method, 121
Cumulative distribution
  function, 17

Data collection, 255
Data sources, 256, 257
Data types, 255
Dean-Sengupta index, 125
Debugging time, 113
Definitions
 active repair time, 174
 availability, 174
 corrective maintenance, 174
 differentiation, 13
 downtime, 174
 hazard rate, 27
 integration, 14
 Laplace transform, 7
 maintainability, 2
 management, 2
 mean time between failures, 3
 mean time to failure, 54-55, 92
 mean time to repair, 3
 operating time, 174
 preventive maintenance, 174
 probability, 15
 probability density, 53
 reliability, 2, 91
 repairability, 2, 64-68, 91
 steady state availability, 4
Dependent events, 16
Depreciation techniques
 declining balance, 144
 straight line, 143
 sum-of-digits, 145
 units of production, 145
Differentiation, 13
Duane's model, 112

Electric power plant, 259
Engineering
 economics, 141
 standards, 132
Environmental test, 132
Equipment
 maintenance, 187
 replacement, 150
 replacement policies, 187

Failure data
 analysis, 260
 banks, 259
 collection, 259
Failure mode
 close, 25
 mutually exclusive, 60, 84
 open, 84, 86, 87
 short, 61, 84, 86, 87
Failure modes and effects
 analysis, 223
Failure rate, 127, 186
Fault tree(s)
 characteristics, 230
 gates
  AND, 229, 231
  OR, 229, 231
 symbols, 230
Field installation tests, 258
Fluctuating weather, 66
Fluid flow valve, 69

Gantt charts, 121

Hazard plotting, 260
Hazard rate curves, 2, 3
Hazard rate models
 bathtub, 32, 34-40
 beta, 31
 complex, 32
 exponential, 30
 gamma, 30
 non-conventional, 41-42
 Weibull, 28

Independent events, 16

Laplace transforms, 9
Least-squares technique, 262
Life cycle cost, 152, 161
Life cycle phases, 152

Maintainability, 2
Maintainability allocation, 239, 248
Maintainability functions, 182
Maintainability management
  administration, 176
  analysis, 174
  coordination, 176
  design, 176
  documentation, 176
  history of, 173
Maintenance cost, 150
Maintenance parameters, 190
Manley method, 125
Manpower planning model, 134
Matrix organization, 120
Maxima, 12
Maximum likelihood estimation, 35
Mean down time, 190
Mean repair time, 184
Mean time to failure
  exponential distribution, 55
  gamma distribution, 57
  Rayleigh distribution, 56
  uniform distribution, 57
  Weibull distribution, 56
Mean value theorem, 15
Military documents, 173
Minima, 12
Mottley-Newton method, 122
Mutually exclusive events, 16

Networks
  bridge, 82
  k-out-of-n units, 39, 76, 104
  parallel, 71, 97, 182
  parallel-series, 78
  series, 37, 74, 88, 93, 182
  series-parallel, 77, 87
  standby, 40, 80
Normal weather, 67

Open mode failure, 84
Operational readiness, 177, 180
Operation cost, 146
Optimal inspection frequency, 196, 198
Optimization, 151, 12

Partial failure, 62
Parts suppliers, 133
Pascal's triangle, 10, 11
p-chart, 50
Poisson model, 206
Premature switch activation, 81
Present worth, 142
Preventive maintenance, 190
Probability density, 53
Probability distributions
  bathtub, 26
  binomial, 26
  exponential, 19, 262
  Poisson, 22, 207
  Rayleigh, 21, 261
  Weibull, 20, 261
Probability distribution's
  mean, 18
  variance, 18
Product assurance, 131
Profitability index, 123
Program evaluation review technique, 121

Quality control
  definitions
    bath lot, 48
    inspection lot, 48

Quality control
  definitions (continued)
    lot size, 48
    quality, 48
    quality control, 49
  department, 50
  techniques
    acceptance sampling, 48
    control charts, 49, 50
Queueing theory, 203
Queueing theory models
  multiple-channel, single-phase, 215
  single-channel, single-phase, 208, 220, 221

Random sampling
  advantages, 49
  disadvantages, 49
Relative worth method, 124
Reliability
  allocation, 239
  allocation techniques
    AGREE, 244
    ARINC, 239
    equal apportionment, 244
    factors of influence, 247
    failure rate, 240
    reliability, 241
    similar familiar, 247
  documents, 159
  evaluation techniques
    block-diagram, 85
    decomposition, 82
    delta-star, 82
    fault tree, 229
    joint-density-function, 107
    Markov, 94
  growth warranty, 160
  history of, 1
  manual, 138
  program, 158
Repair effort optimization, 149
Repair rate, 183, 186
Repair rate function, 183
Replacement decision models, 193
Residual errors, 113

Salvage value, 150
Series
  exponential, 11
  geometric, 12
  logarithms, 12
Short mode failure, 84
Single component Markov models
  non-repairable, 58-64
  repairable, 64-69
Sobleman method, 123
Software reliability, 113
Stormy weather, 67
Subcontractors, 155
System
  approach, 46
  availability, 180
  characteristics, 46
  classifications, 46
  effectiveness, 166, 173, 177
  engineering, 45
  models
    analog, 48
    mathematical, 47
    schematic, 48
    physical, 48

Three state device system, 85

Unavailability, 149

Value engineering
  history of, 119

job plan, 126
techniques, 127
Variance, 18, 101

Waiting lines, 203
Warranty
lost models, 162
risks, 160
Weighting factors, 251

x-chart, 50